BORN IN THE LAP OF THE DRAGON

. . . .

DWIGHT GREGG PERETZ

For Tanya — a Saturnia
neighbors

Dwight

2006

TRAFFORD
PUBLISHING™

Note for Librarians: A cataloguing record for this book is available from Library and Archives
Canada at www.collectionscanada.ca/amicus/index-e.html
ISBN 1-4120-7803-2

*Printed in Victoria, BC, Canada. Printed on paper with minimum 30% recycled fibre. Trafford's print shop
runs on "green energy" from solar, wind and other environmentally-friendly power sources.*

Offices in Canada, USA, Ireland and UK
This book was published *on-demand* in cooperation with Trafford Publishing. On-demand
publishing is a unique process and service of making a book available for retail sale to the
public taking advantage of on-demand manufacturing and Internet marketing. On-demand
publishing includes promotions, retail sales, manufacturing, order fulfilment, accounting and
collecting royalties on behalf of the author.

Book sales for North America and international:
Trafford Publishing, 6E–2333 Government St.,
Victoria, BC V8T 4P4 CANADA
phone 250 383 6864 (toll-free 1 888 232 4444)
fax 250 383 6804; email to orders@trafford.com
Book sales in Europe:
Trafford Publishing (UK) Limited, 9 Park End Street, 2nd Floor
Oxford, UK OX1 1HH UNITED KINGDOM
phone 44 (0)1865 722 113 (local rate 0845 230 9601)
facsimile 44 (0)1865 722 868; info.uk@trafford.com
Order online at:
trafford.com/05-2700

10 9 8 7 6 5 4 3

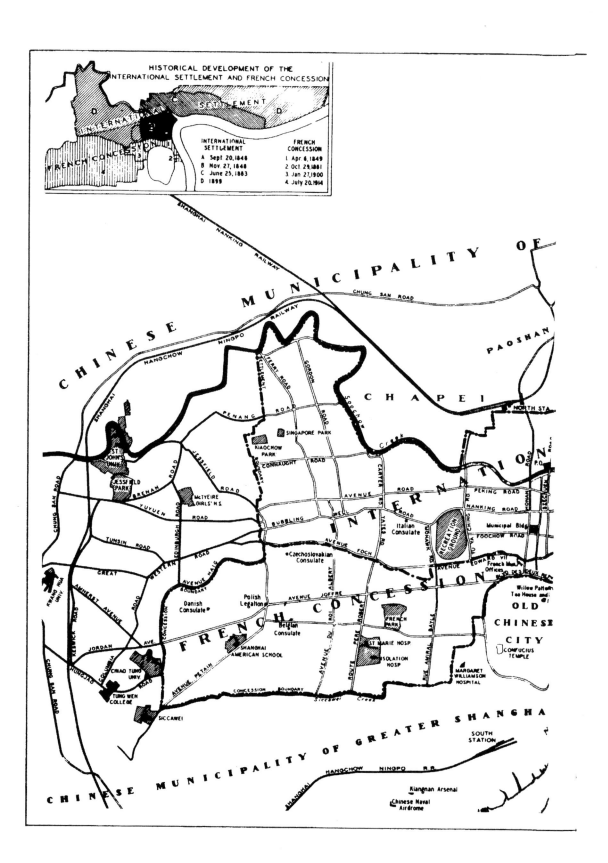

HISTORICAL DEVELOPMENT OF THE
INTERNATIONAL SETTLEMENT AND FRENCH CONCESSION

INTERNATIONAL SETTLEMENT
A Sept. 20,1846
B Nov. 27, 1848
C June 25, 1863
D 1899

FRENCH CONCESSION
1 Apr. 6,1849
2 Oct. 29,1861
3 Jan. 27,1900
4 July 20,1914

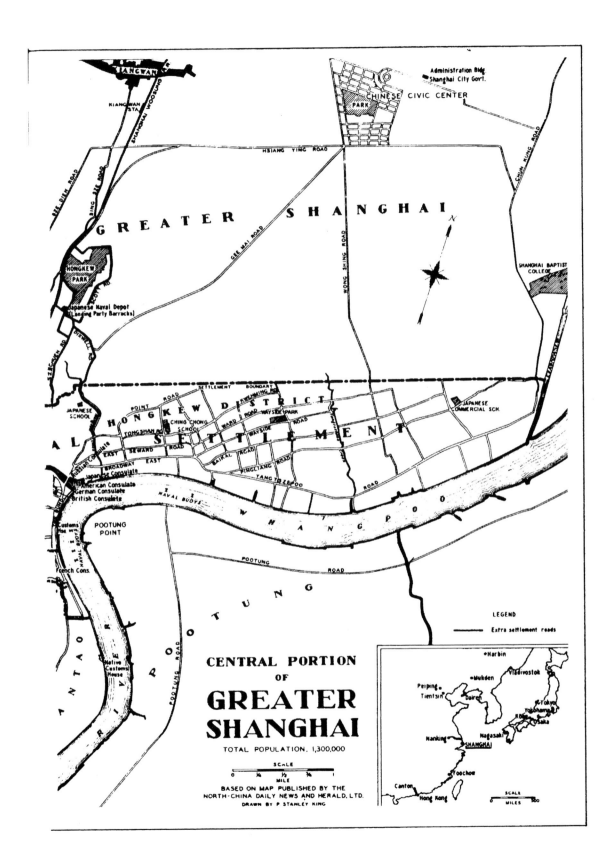

KIANGWAN

KIANGWAN STA.

Administration Bldg.
Shanghai City Govt.

CHINESE CIVIC CENTER

PARK

HSIANG YING ROAD

G R E A T E R   S H A N G H A I

HONGKEW
PARK

N

SHANGHAI BAPTIST
COLLEGE

Japanese Naval Depot
(Landing Party Barracks)

SETTLEMENT   BOUNDARY

JAPANESE
SCHOOL

POINT   ROAD

H O N G K E W   D I S T R I C T

WAYSIDE PARK

JAPANESE
COMMERCIAL SCH.

CHING CHONG
SCHOOL

TONGSHAN

WARD   ROAD

WAYSIDE

A L   S E T T L E M E N T

EAST   SEWARD   ROAD

BAIKAL   ROAD

BROADWAY   EAST

PINGLIANG ROAD

YANG TZE POO

ROAD

Russian Consulate

Japanese Consulate

American Consulate

German Consulate

British Consulate

W H A N G P O O

Customs House

NAVAL BUOYS

POOTUNG
POINT

French Cons.

P O O T U N G

POOTUNG   ROAD

LEGEND

——— Extra settlement roads

Native
Customs
House

R I V E R

W H A N G P O O

W
H
A
N
G
P
O
O

R
I
V
E
R

CENTRAL PORTION
OF
GREATER
SHANGHAI

TOTAL POPULATION, 1,300,000

SCALE
0   ¼   ½   ¾   1
MILE

BASED ON MAP PUBLISHED BY THE
NORTH-CHINA DAILY NEWS AND HERALD, LTD.
DRAWN BY P STANLEY KING

Harbin

Mukden   Vladivostok

Peiping
Tientsin   Dairen

Tokyo
Yokohama
Kobe
Osaka

Nanking   Nagasaki

SHANGHAI

Foochow

Canton   Hong Kong

SCALE
0   500
MILES

Table of Contents

Introduction:
Positioning the Narrator

Contrary to popular belief, scientists write a great deal of prose. My career as a cardiologist produced some eighty peer-reviewed papers and portions of several textbooks. Science demands precise language, fitting in well with George Orwell's maxim that "Good prose is like a window pane." In other words, the goal in science writing is to efface the personality of the author and let the facts speak for themselves without ornamentation. Ideally, the science writer should vanish from his or her work.

I never intended to write an autobiography. The original goal was a short booklet for my sons and grandchildren and my brother Godfrey's sons and grandchildren, so that they might know the story of the family's fascinating origins in a foreign country. I wanted to tell them why my Northern Irish father and American mother moved to Shanghai before either my brother or I was born. I wanted to tell them how we and other foreign nationals managed to live a lovely life in the midst of the Sino-Japanese war, with all its atrocities, if only to reveal how rude an awakening we had with Pearl Harbor and the opening of World War II in the Pacific. I wanted to tell them about being humbled, how the Allied Partners' citizens (British, American, French, Dutch, and some others) in the occupied territory were rounded up and initially placed under house confinement with curfews, then taken in as prisoners of war in various concentration camps throughout occupied China. Really what I wanted to show was how strong you can grow through adversity, that nearly any "problem" can be viewed as an opportunity.

However I was a busy cardiologist with a consulting practice and a professorship at the University of British Columbia (UBC). As if that wasn't enough, I was running numerous studies and chairing several organizations to do with cardiology and, in the earlier days, respirology, for clients as esoteric and demanding as NASA. For years I was occupied for over 12 hours a day, seven days a week.

Eventually I retired and had time on my hands, but then I found myself busily engaged in many other things that so much work had precluded. Also, keep in mind that as early as grade one I earned the nickname of "The Procrastinator". Fortunately, the Canadian Broadcasting Corporation (CBC) came calling. They wanted to interview me about 1930s and 1940s Shanghai for a series called *Sin City* that would air in the spring of 2005. I accepted.

We combed through old photographs and digitized them as part of the interview process. Looking at them projected onto a screen, I found that the memories surrounding each faded person and place started not only to sharpen, but also to expand, deepen, and interlock with memories surrounding others. Concurrently to this, we dug through a large amount of official documentation in my possession. Suddenly I realized there was a thick, quite daunting book that needed to be written. I was on the verge of a new career.

Change is intimidating. I felt a definite temptation to pull the disappearing act of the scientist, and deal with the subject in an impartial, clinical tone. Yet my initial impulse to write was based on the hope that people I care about will benefit from my experiences, since I believe that wartime's hazards and, yes, rewards, made an indelible imprint on me. If I was the subject, how could I disappear?

One form of comfort when facing a new challenge is to find models, to look to those who have gone before you. A favorite book of mine is Henry David Thoreau's *Walden*, which conveys extremely well the *feel* and *quality* of a remote time, along with an experience well outside the average reader's way of life. On page one he positions his narrator thus:

> In most books, the *I*, or first person, is omitted; in this it will be retained; that, in respect to egotism, is the main difference. We commonly do not remember that it is, after all, always the first person that is speaking. I should not talk so much about myself if there were anybody else whom I knew as well. Unfortunately, I am confined to this theme by the narrowness of my experience. Moreover, I, on my side, require of every writer, first or last, a simple and sincere account of his own life, and not merely what he has heard of other men's lives...

The inertia of my career pushes me to find an objective truth outside myself, of what happened in Shanghai in that period, yet Thoreau stresses that the very strength of the narrow viewpoint of the first person *is its narrowness*. A historian who was not there can write very well about the broad sweep of events, and this has value. Indeed, the book does include a short history, plus information on climate, the economy, and other areas of interest. More than anything else, though, I wanted to transport the reader both chronologically and geographically. The experiences of a small boy are vivid, particular, and, as the reader will learn, sometimes all-too visceral. I was there, and I can convey that distant time and place best by bearing witness to what I saw, heard, smelled, tasted, and touched.

Readers who also were there may have seen things from a different point of view and interpreted them differently, which is only natural and to be expected. I make no apologies. This all took place 60 and more years ago, but I have tried to be as accurate as possible. My memory is good and I have substantiated many facts from discussions, letters, and a large number of official documents. These documents are in my possession because my stepfather was involved with British, U.S. and French intelligence during the War, as was I to a small extent. This information became available after the war was over and new testimonials as to our part in the war were forthcoming from various governments.

It gets more subjective with the concentration camps in which the Japanese interned Allied nationals. Anyone caught with a diary or any written information was severely punished, but this has no bearing on my story. Despite my intentions regarding the small pamphlet for my loved ones, I have chosen not to detail the concentration camps. My mother and I were interned twice, but for relatively short periods of time, and so most of the "action" I saw was out in the countryside and on the streets of Shanghai. Moreover, there have been many books — almost all of which have been nearly identical — about those camps, and it would be useless to repeat all of this.

Suffice it to say that in and around Shanghai there were three major camps: Lunghwa, Chapei, and Hiaphong, as well as Pootung in the early years. There were many others around China, the nearest at Yangchow. One has to appreciate at this point that in Southeast Asia and Indonesia there were a large number of Allied military personnel, such as Canadian troops in Hong Kong, in concentration camps. These camps were governed by the Japanese military; not a very nice situation. In so-called "Occupied China" we civilians were interned by the Japanese Consular Corps, and treated considerably better than the military were treated down in Southeast Asia.

Dr. Dwight Gregg Peretz
West Vancouver
January 2006

Acknowledgements

I would like to thank my editor Roger Holden (rogerholden@gmail.com) so much for his very astute advice regarding what should and shouldn't be done in the construction of the book. Roger is a phenomenally intelligent individual with a wealth of facts and a wealth of information as to where to get those facts today, particularly on the Internet and such areas. Once he joined me as the editor of this book, his knowledge of China and its history grew very, very quickly. To Susan Ross, my secretary of many years when I was practicing medicine, and now my secretary for a few hours a week, I would like to give thanks for doing so much excellent work typing down what Roger and I had to say regarding the construction of the book. It was an absolutely excellent combination.

Thanks to a former patient of mine, Ron Millership, whose father, Idris James (Jim) Millership was born in 1901 in England, and came to Shanghai in 1925 to work for the public health department of the Shanghai Municipal Council. Idris Millership was a busy man, but managed to find the time to take many fine photos of China. When Ron found out I was writing this book, he brought over a stack photo albums containing many incredible images. I've included several of them, including probably the most dramatic series, the executions.

I would also like to thank Mr. Arthur Knight for his work in Appendix A on the British population in Shanghai and the Cathedral School for Girls and Boys in Shanghai. My thanks also to Mr. Peter Reeves for his work in Appendices B and C on Tsingtao (Qingdao) and St. Giles School in Tsingtao, respectively. I actually met neither Arthur nor Peter in Shanghai in the 30's and 40's but I know them well, as they both live very close to where I do now, 60 to 70 years later in West Vancouver, British Columbia. They both, however, give us what the situation was like apropos European versus Chinese, etc., and I thought it would be very good to include it in this book.

Arthur Knight lived in downtown Shanghai, which was a pretty usual place for many Caucasians to live, but I had virtually never had any experience there, so I asked him if he would write a page or two about what it was like, and since we're into the schooling aspect, what it was like in the Cathedral School, which of course, in British style, was the Cathedral Girls' School and the Cathedral Boys' School. Arthur left Shanghai shortly before the war, but you will note from his comments that they knew the war was coming nine or ten years before the shot was fired.

Peter Reeves had a much more extensive sojourn in a northern Chinese city, Tsingtao, where his father worked, but Peter was in a British private school, and seldom got into the then village and now town of Tsingtao (Qingdao). These are both observing, critical and very intelligent people, and we can count on what they say as being very true and down to the point. We should appreciate that Arthur Knight's middle name is "Anatole", from his mother's side of the family. Many years before this book was written we traveled together to both Finland and Russia, and visited St. Petersburg, where his mother played in the symphony.

Two Notes on the Text

1. Establishing a rule of nomenclature.

The names of most buildings, streets, and places in and around Shanghai have changed since 1949. In this book I am attempting to recreate a place and an epoch in which I lived, so I will use the names used in that place and that epoch. To be rigorous, the first appearance in the text of any building, street, or place name is accompanied by the modern name in brackets, if the name has changed. Thereafter, only the old name appears.

2. Footnotes and Endnotes

Footnotes will accommodate digressions and asides that, I hope, are interesting. They are numbered i, ii, iii, etc.

Endnotes will reference sources. They are numbered 1, 2, 3, etc.

Chapter 1

Back to Shanghai

It was the spring of 1938 and Japanese soldiers were living in our house. Luckily we weren't home. Friends sent us the news by telegram, as we were away from Shanghai on five month's home leave to San Francisco, Ireland, and New York. It turned out that the Japanese troops who patrolled the outskirts of Shanghai had decided they needed a place to bunk down a few miles west of the city rather than return to their garrison. I can only assume that they marched from gate to wrought-iron gate of the large houses owned by Western executives who preferred to live in the countryside. Finally they found a house where no one, at least no one non-Chinese, was home. Our servants, confronted by stoic Japanese faces behind glinting, skyward-pointed bayonets, quite sensibly opened the gate and cleared out.

My father received the cable in our hotel in Honolulu. We'd stopped there en route from San Francisco to spend some time on the beach. He booked us on the only ship available, a German liner called the *Gneisenau*. It was a fast ship but the trip would take three weeks, as it was a southern route via the Philippines and Hong Kong. We cut our stay short and boarded within a few days, on February 23rd.

The *Gneisenau* was like heaven to me, a magnificent ship with all of the amenities that a boy of seven could possibly want. The Germans at that time were not only building an enormous stockpile of unfortunately excellent weapons; they were also manufacturing excellent toys. The two are no doubt closely and strangely related, so this brand-new liner was virtually a cornucopia of all of the latest German trinkets, such as windup ships and submarines that self-propelled around the bathtub on a long wire through which you could steer the rudder. At the *Gneisenau's* stern flew a red flag with a swastika in its center.

1

Our cabin was on the starboard side of the ship. The last few days of the voyage we'd been on a northward course along the coast of China, stopping briefly in Amoy. Each morning the rising sun had pushed orange spots through the portholes and onto the curtains. March 15th, the day we were to arrive home I awoke before dawn, too excited to sleep, and sat up in the top bunk to watch my toys take form in the growing light on the table down below. I observed that the orange spots did not appear, so jumped down in my pajamas, got up on a chair, and pulled the curtain aside. The sun was barely visible behind us, but only when I pushed my face close to the glass. I closed the curtain, got down and shook my older brother.

"Godfrey, we've changed course!" I whispered.

"Oh come on Dwight, go back to sleep." He yawned, and my parents stirred in their bed on the other side of the cabin.

"The sun is behind us. We're going west!" I jumped back up on the chair and opened the curtain again.

"Well done Dwight," dad said in his educated Northern Irish brogue. Sitting up, my father, Robert Gregg (RG) switched on the bedside lamp and reached for his glasses. "We've turned from the East China Sea into the Yangtze."

"Maybe we can make port by lunch." Mother sat up and put on her dressing gown. We packed our trunks and went up for a very early breakfast.

It was a beautiful spring day; the passengers gathered outside. We bunched up on the port side of the wood-planked deck in order to gaze at the only visible shore of the Yangtze estuary. The deep blue of the ocean that had long slipped by the sleek German hull had turned to brown, the silted drainage of a 3,200 mile long watershed that was home to about one hundred and eighty million people.

Tall, thin, regal, my forty-four year old father had his arm around his wife. The wind from our movement blew my mother Gwendoline's dress, and messed her curly hair (though it may have been a well-affixed wig, as she owned thirteen). She was thirty-eight, a calm and graceful woman. Her hands held a big sun hat whose brim flexed with the steady pressure of warm air. RG's custom was to wear a fedora over his thinning blonde hair, along with a three-piece suit, but today was the last day of home leave, so he wore shorts and a white shirt open at the collar. Shading his eyes, he scrutinized the passing shore for signs of war.

War talk was everywhere aboard the ship. Since the Japanese had invaded China the previous summer, surrounded Shanghai, and sacked Nanking, many Western executives and their families had quite prudently moved back to their home countries. With this in mind, no doubt some passengers aboard the *Gneisenau* felt like they were going the wrong way. To make matters worse the Germans had invaded Austria in the *Anschluss*, or "reunification" a few days before. Since the shipboard announcement, the passengers had most definitely split into political factions.

Before the shore and marshy scrub in the distance, the odd filthy-sailed junk listed slowly along. Much closer to us, shallow-hulled sampans barely got out of the *Gneisenau's* way and bucked in the wake of her 18,160 tons. Lanky, dapper at fourteen years old, Godfrey leaned on the teak railing in his blue blazer and inspected the sampans' various cargos. His blonde, newly-combed hair shone in the sun as he tracked the passage of barking dogs, chickens, snakes, bags of rice and sweating oarsmen pulling it all to safety.

Typical Wenchow Junk on the Whangpoo River.

The coastline was flat and drab. I tore around the deck in my shorts, skinny legs propelling me between other families, dashing for the door and the toys inside, only to be called back by my mother. I was about to go on another circuit when a Japanese destroyer appeared, seemingly sailing out from the shore ahead. We'd spotted them all along the coast, but way off in the distance. This one passed so close I could see the officers at their posts, and several of the crew swabbing the deck in the fresh morning. Gray painted batteries of guns seemed to track the sun.

The coastline opened up into the quarter-mile wide Whangpoo (Huangpu) River, and we turned into the channel, both of its shores still churning with the destroyer's wake. Shanghai was 14 miles (23km) due south, with a few bends for our large ship to negotiate. The *Gneisenau* slowed down in the narrower channel, the air felt hotter without the breeze, and I could smell the earth from the nearer shores. Things started to look familiar. I stood beside my father, who patted my head. There wasn't a cloud in the sky.

We were headed west before a final turn south at Pootung (Pudong) Point when the grass and brush of the shore thinned. Passing below was an utterly desolate area fronted by the narrow ends of long metal sheds, a tangle of pipes and valves before a jetty, and half a dozen huge storage tanks squatting behind. Dad inspected each passing glint of metal, because he was chief engineer of Standard Oil for the Far East, and this was the company's Installation for processing products like wax of many colors, and storing oil, kerosene and gasoline. In imitation of dad, I scrutinized the passing buildings just as closely, and in their midst I spotted a small house with a garden. I got so excited I started to jump up and down.

This little oasis was where the Jacobs lived. They were a charming French couple that oversaw the Installation and entertained the Standard Oil executives and their families who visited on weekends. The Jacob's had no children and Godfrey and I were free to roam around as the "boss's children", literally allowed to do anything that we wished inside the factories. Waste wax in all colors would easily peel in large sheets off work surfaces. We would make them into "snowballs" about the size of a softball, and they became quite hard when they cooled. We would then have a fantastic time throwing them at each other and at the Chinese children and workers who got caught up in it too, starting a melee and making a terrible mess around all the high-tech instrumentation. The workers all thought this was great fun and I believe they looked forward to the both of us coming around once every two or three months. They always covered up very well for us when dad arrived.

There had been a huge garden party there a couple of summers before. It was a hot day and all of the staff's children and their friends were there. We had a marvelous time playing and running all over the place. Mrs. Jacobs was a fabulous cook, baking bread and making all kinds of pasta for the party. Then she brought out the first blueberry pie I'd ever sunk my teeth into. Much to my stomach's dislike, I ate seven pieces.

"So Dwight, what do you want to be when you grow up?" my father asked, perhaps misinterpreting my enthusiasm. "An engineer perhaps?"

He put his hand on my shoulder while I thought about for a second. Then my mind skipped back to the new toys in my trunk.

"I think I would like to be a German U-boat captain."

Dad nearly choked. He had been an engineering officer in the Royal Navy, luring and hunting German submarines aboard Q-Boats all through World War One. Luckily for me, just as he opened his mouth to reply, the sandbagged positions of the Fourth Division U.S. Marines came in to sight. The marines had dug in at the perimeter of the Installation the previous August to protect this huge American interest from both the Japanese and the Chinese. There was no sign of movement from their positions as they faded in the distance.

The shore became boring again. We both turned and leaned against the railing. Germans talked to Germans in tight little groups. My mother was talking to the Irvings, friends she'd made on the voyage, and Godfrey had walked over to the starboard side of the ship as we passed the outskirts of the Hongkew (Hongkou) district of the city. This was where the bitter house-to-house fighting had gone on in the battle for Shanghai the previous summer and fall, so it held a particular fascination for my brother. Dad and I walked through the cool shadow under the ship's bridge to join him on that side. Mother spotted us as we passed, and smiled.

The city became more and more built-up behind the rusting freighters tied to wharves. There were sheds and smokestacks. The ship listed slightly to starboard as we made our way round the bend of Pootung point. Moored in front of Japan's consulate, a Japanese warship with three tall funnels pumped its bilge into the river.

"What sort of ship is that?" My father quizzed Godfrey, who was shielding his eyes against the mid-day light that glittered on the chop.

"Cruiser."

"Which one?"

"Flagship. The *Idzumo*, I think."

Not far beyond the sharp grey bow of the *Idzumo*, the mouth of Soochow (Suzhou) creek interrupted the shore. The Garden (Waibaidu) Bridge cast a shadow over a tangle of sampans floating on the water beneath it. Japanese troops guarded the bridge on the side of the *Idzumo* and the Japanese consulate. Across the bridge the Seaforth Highlanders, the 4th Division U.S. Marines, and the Shanghai Volunteer Corps (SVC) took turns guarding the entrance to the International Settlement. It looked like the SVC was on duty that morning. Chinese were lined up on the Japanese side, waiting to cross over.

Dad rubbed his jaw and watched the Japanese soldiers strutting around with their rifles, scrutinizing papers and packages. RG was a cool customer. He was also the boss, so wasn't in the habit of showing what was going on in his head, but he must have been strategizing pretty heavily as to how to face down the Japanese soldiers living in our house.

"Aren't the trees in the park green!" exclaimed my mother, rejoining us and squeezing my shoulders. She was putting on a very brave face. I looked up at her, and she was beautiful. "Oh, and they repainted the gazebo: look!" The bell-shaped roof of the gazebo, now a bright red, seemed to float between the passing trees. These grew within the infamous Public Garden, at whose gate a sign had supposedly once declared: "Chinese and Dogs Not Permitted."

All around us, newcomers to the city betrayed their general sense of unease and fear by chattering away about anything and nothing in particular. We passed the boundary of the park and green leaves gave way to the impressive stone façades of banks. The road that had passed between sandbags, crossed over the Garden Bridge, and ran behind the Public Garden, here became "The Bund" (Zhongshan Road), Shanghai's great waterfront boulevard and prime real estate in all of Asia.

Twenty blocks of the tallest buildings outside North America were lined up along the Bund to meet us. Next door to the British Consulate General was the Nippon Yusen Kaisha, then the Banque de l'Indochine, and further along past four or five insurance buildings, the Yokohama Specie Bank Building and the Bank of China. At the feet of the grand façades, dark green double-decker buses with beige tops passed back and forth along the wide boulevard, as well as streetcars and a tangle of rickshaws. The street seemed to be a river itself, comprised of people hurrying about their business in this economic miracle of three million souls.

The Bund. Photograph taken about 1930.

As we slowed against the rolling murk of the outgoing tide, the windows of the banking towers took their turns reflecting the ship's black hull, passing it along. Below its green pyramid of a roof, the higher windows of the Cathay (Peace) Hotel reflected the single golden stack of the Gniesenau. Our ship's black bow had long since darkened the rippled windows of the smaller Palace (Peace, South Wing) Hotel next door, and now its stern slowly passed by, the swastika flag lazily flapping above the ship's reduced wake.

Following tracks and an overhead wire off the Bund, a streetcar disappeared between the two hotels, having turned inland down Nanking (East Nanjing Lu) Road. Mother's hands squeezed my shoulders again. The air was hotter here than downstream. I looked down the streets between buildings and, though we'd been away for a good portion of my life, I knew that this was my home.

Slowly the Chartered Bank, the *North China Daily News* building, the Central Bank of China, and the Bank of Communications all drifted past. Finally the *Gniesenau* ploughed to a stop, mid-channel in a snarl of red and white-sailed junks and ferryboats. Looming over us was the imposing stone edifice of the Customs House, and, next to it, the unbelievable palace of the Hong Kong & Shanghai Bank. The Customs house was surmounted by a clock tower. With its enormous clock, locally called the "Big Ching", the building looked like it belonged in Liverpool. The hands were nearly together at the top of the clock's face.

The deck rattled with the release and playing out of anchor chains. Godfrey and father turned to us. That instant a tremendous boom issued from Pootung point, passed over us, over the crowds on the Bund, then echoed back from the granite pilasters, marble cornices, and windows of the banks and hotels. It was the gun that fired every day at noon, and you could pick out the newcomers from the crowd on deck because they flinched. My father smiled.

A small launch pulled alongside the *Gniesenau,* and sailors yelled back and forth in an odd mixture of German and Chinese while they worked the ropes to secure it. We shuffled with the crowd across the gangplank. I gazed up at the clock face of the Big Ching, and it reminded me of a lesson the ship's navigator had given me on latitude and longitude.

"Dad, what are the coordinates of Shanghai?"

"Latitude 31 degrees, 14 minutes North, and Longitude 121 degrees 29 minutes East," he said, taking my mother's hand and helping her down from the gangplank onto the launch's deck. I was always asking questions like that, not just because he always had answers, but also because he had patience with such things. All settled in the launch, the crew untied and we motored toward the Customs House.

We cleared customs with the remarkable speed only a free port such as Shanghai, Trieste, Lourenço Marques, or Goa could afford; in these places a passport was optional. I ran ahead of my family and the porters, and pushed through the revolving doors onto the street. The air was like a hot, wet wall. Coolies shouted, trams rattled, engines revved, and horns honked.

Dressed in the dark blue suit, cap, and white gloves of a New York City chauffeur that one sees in the movies today, "Driver" was obsessing over our big black Packard with a feather duster. His function in the household was the only name by which my parents ever addressed him, so Driver was his name. Our car and Driver's services had been on loan to friends while we were away, so here at least was part of our household untouched. He positively beamed when he spotted us, and opened the back door while yelling directions in Chinese to the porters, who were setting the steamer trunks down behind the rear luggage rack.

Mother, father, and I got in the back, while Godfrey as usual chose to ride up front in the open air. Driver had all the windows open, but it was still boiling inside. I folded down a jump seat and faced backward toward my parents. The car bounced a little as the porters loaded the trunks. Soon they were stacked so high I couldn't see out the back window.

There was a glass windscreen behind my back that separated us from Driver, requiring the passenger to give orders through a microphone. I loved speaking through this apparatus, but father suddenly looked very serious, so I didn't dare ask. When all the jostling of the car was finished, Driver took the right-hand seat up front, behind the gigantic, almost horizontal steering wheel. Father took up the microphone and spoke.

"Driver, take us up Nanking Road to Cathay Mansions."

Honking the horn, Driver pulled out into the tangle of rickshaws, cars, and buses to make a miraculous U-turn. My mother seemed as preoccupied as my father, so I turned around in my seat and looked out between Godfrey and Driver over the long shiny hood. My father's limousine, like the vehicles of many non-military executives in various offices, had small national flags mounted on pins that extended from the front mudguards of the car. This would be like we see today with the vehicles of diplomats and heads of state in capitals such as Washington, DC or elsewhere. As my father's employer was American, the Stars and Stripes hung on the left pin. And as RG was Northern Irish, the Union Jack hung on the right pin.

We followed the Bund for a few blocks, so slowly that neither flag moved much. The shouts of rickshaw coolies, whose sweaty faces passed by our open windows, followed by the indifferent, hat-shaded faces of their passengers, drowned out the sound of the car's idling engine. It was as if a river of humanity carried the huge car along, and us in it.

Finally we turned left between the Palace and Cathay hotels, following the overhead wires and tracks of the streetcars. Stone façades loomed on either side, like a canyon. It was into this aperture that Chinese flyers had accidentally dropped a bomb in a botched attack against Japanese warships on the river. That was the previous August 14th, the second day of the battle for Shanghai. In the concussion and flying glass, about 700 people had died. Driver worked the gears and the flags started to fly with the roar of the engine.

We drove on the left side of the road as is done in England. Streetcars passed back and forth in the middle, and cars going the other way passed on the far right. All sorts of shops flew past the open windows. Red signs with gold characters loomed over various wares and browsers on the crowded sidewalks. Nanking Road was one of the major thoroughfares across Shanghai from the Bund to the far west of the city. Further south and parallel to Nanking road, Avenue Edward VII (East Yanan Lu) was the southernmost boundary of the International Settlement, which was pretty much the British and American area. Also running east to west, Avenue Joffre (Huaihai Lu) was the main street of "French Town", the French Concession, south of Avenue Edward VII.

Porcelain Shop on Nanking road. Typical Chinese shop in downtown Shanghai.

Only a couple of blocks from the river we passed the American Bookstore, which was on the right hand side of Nanking Road, and the Chocolate Shop, which was on the left.

This was a very American operation, where you would buy ice cream cones, sundaes, and that type of thing. My mouth watered, but glancing back at my parents I decided to hold my tongue until later. Besides, the second Chocolate Shop was only about three miles (5km) down the road and maybe they would have cheered up by then.

Then we passed the Wing On Company, which in Canada would be like the Hudson's Bay Company or in the United States like Sears Roebuck, a large department store selling clothing and other kinds of articles that were available. We all shopped there. Sun Company and Sun Sun, two other department stores, were close by. Near to them was what I think most westerners would have considered the best Chinese food restaurant (Cantonese) in Shanghai: Sun Ya (Sin Yi). Three stories high, superb food, and we would eat there probably once a month, which was often, considering how long a drive it was from where we lived in Hollyheath Estate (5 or 6 miles, which in metric is 8 or 10 km).

The road started a long curve to the left and we approached the golf course and a large area called the Public Recreation Group (Renmin Park) situated on the inside of the curve. I loved the park. There was a horse racing track and all manner of sporting areas for the general public, although they were virtually all Caucasians who went there. On the right hand side was a large movie theatre and hotel, very first class. I'd just been to San Francisco and New York on home leave, so now I knew this complex would not look odd situated in those places. Next door to the hotel stood what must have been the largest, most magnificent YMCA in the world. It was like an expensive hotel in and of itself. Following this was the Union Jack Club, which would take on an ominous character when the war started.

The road continued around the park in a more minor way, but veered right in the main, which is where we went. Driver slowed the car a bit as we soon approached a juncture, in the middle of which was a concrete-enclosed well whose water bubbled, likely from swamp gas. At this point Nanking Road became Bubbling Well Road (West Nanjing Lu). It just continued straight on and you wouldn't know you had gone from Nanking Road to Bubbling Well Road if you didn't live there.

Driver slowed down through the gears and we turned left, southward, on Moulmein Road, which became Rue Cardinal Mercier once we passed over the border into the French

Concession. We then passed the Lyceum Theatre and pulled in front of Cathay Mansions, an opulent brick high-rise of about thirteen stories. Driver was careful to park under the portico. Across the street stood the Cercle Sportif Francais (Jin Jiang Club, "Jin Jiang" meaning "Chinese who have been expatriates; those who have lived abroad"), an architecturally beautiful club that was quite forward-thinking, offering membership to women, though capped at 40 at a time.

"Dwight, stay in the car." My father said as Driver opened the door and he got out. My mother took RG's hand, stepped out, and they went inside. Porters came out of the apartment hotel and there was again much bouncing around of the car as they muscled away the trunks. I took up the microphone to speak, but Driver was around the back of the car to supervise the unloading, and Godfrey was with him. It wasn't any fun to broadcast if there wasn't an audience, so I put down the microphone and waited.

I suppose my parents were checking in, but it took a long time, so there must have been a bit of a conference as to whether to take us along. Sitting still in the car I found the city was coming back to me just as rapidly as when we had been driving through it. I watched the people walking past, breathed the warm, humid air, and peered out at the storefronts. Godo's was near to the French Club. It was a Japanese store, pretty unusual for that area, and it sold delicious foods of all varieties, a fairly small restaurant or take-out type of affair. Close by Godo's was Russian, a restaurant owned by the father of Godfrey's friend Pavlo, a kid who went with my brother up to Tsingtao for summer camp every year. Pavlo's father was said to have been a general or something like that in Russian Army before the Bolsheviks took over. At any rate, mom and dad eventually came out from the hotel and got back in the car.

"Driver, double back and take us out," my father said into the mike. Another miraculous U-turn and the flags took to flapping again as we headed north on Rue Cardinal Mercier, then Moulmein, turning left back onto Bubbling Well Road for a long westward stretch until, finally, we passed the border of the International Settlement and Bubbling Well Road became Great Western Road (Huaihai Lu).

The city started to thin out, buildings gave way to more and more greenery. I got very excited and in fact stood up because the garrison of the Seaforth Highlanders was rapidly coming up on the right. This had always been a great event for me because the

Union Jack flew on the right side of the car and there was a guard posted out front of the garrison at all times. There he was. You could hardly see what he was guarding, in that the armory and other buildings were probably 200 or 300 feet behind where he stood on Great Western Road. He saw the flag flapping on the big car and immediately snapped to full attention, his rifle presented before him. I laughed. My father told me to sit down, but I could tell by the look on his face that this projection of British power (which far surpassed any other Western military presence) pleased him too. I watched the guard recede rapidly behind us, still standing at attention. When he finally vanished from sight, I sat down.

Great Western Road turned into Columbia Road (Fanyu Lu) as we passed Columbia Circle, where the American club was located. Then a quick right on Hungjao Road (Hongqiao Lu), but Driver eased off on the gas rather than accelerate, because we were coming up to the tracks of the Shanghai Hangchow Ningpo Railway. This railway encircled the city and effectively marked out the perimeter of the free settlement (French Concession and International Settlement), beyond which was China. All roads out of the city had to cross the tracks. Since the retreat of the Chinese in the previous summer's shooting war, these crossings had become checkpoints controlled by the Japanese army.

Driver slowed as we approached Hungjao road's Japanese military checkpoint next to the railroad station (Xujiahui), and the crowds of peasant farmers entering and exiting the city became dense around the car. The checkpoint was a small hut manned by three Japanese soldiers with rifles, bayonets fixed. One bored soldier yawned in the midday heat. We stopped completely and the engine idled, as there was a cart ahead of us, presumably being searched. The wind that had been roaring through the window was replaced by waves of stifling heat. Coming from the other side, farmers with carts filled with chickens and rice rolled past. A coolie carried a heavy load past my open window, rhythmically chanting "hey-haw, hey-haw!" to ease his burden. Over his shoulder he balanced a six-foot long bamboo pole, bent by a heavily laden basket suspended from each end. Chickens hung by their feet from the bamboo pole, squawking and fighting upside-down. Sweat poured from his forehead and he smelled pretty strongly. He didn't look into the car, but stared straight ahead toward his goal.

Rice field with worker utilizing typical conveyance of goods.

Driver edged us forward, and the Japanese soldier that had just stepped back from searching the cart pretty clearly registered the flags. My father murmured "um-hmm", expecting we'd be waved on. Instead the soldier put out the flat of his hand and we stopped. Then Driver put the car in park and reached for the door handle. Dad lurched forward in his seat and clicked on the mike: "Driver, what are you doing?" but Driver was already stepping out. Godfrey and father frowned at each other, then we all watched the spectacle of Driver bowing deeply to the Japanese soldier, who smirked and didn't bow back. Driver got back into the car, not making eye contact with dad, who was clearly fuming. The soldier waved us on and we eased over the tracks with a double bump, but driver couldn't speed up because the cart ahead was weaving back and forth too much to pass.

Cries rose from a pond that filled the low area between the road embankment and the railway embankment. Godfrey rapped on the glass and pointed. There were three Chinese standing chest-deep in the water; two men and a woman chained down, flies and mosquitoes and other terrible insects swarming and biting their heads and bare shoulders. My mother gasped and, in spite of my father, I stood up again, because here was something I had never seen before. The Japanese soldiers had thrown rice onto the pond, and it had swelled to the point that it covered the surface and pushed up against the prisoners' skin, which became maddeningly itchy. We would later learn that this was punishment for stealing, not obeying orders, and other objectionable affairs, with immersion generally lasting for a day or less. My father calmly told me to sit back down, and stared ahead, deep in thought.

After a liberal application of the horn, Driver finally managed to get us past the weaving cart, though it wasn't long until we approached the intersection at Chungshan (Zhongshan) and Hungjao Roads, only about a half a mile beyond the tracks. He turned the car to the left into Hollyheath Estate, a 200-acre area in which our house was located, along with 19 others, all in modern Western style. Each house had a good piece of land, and a network of streets connected all of them. Driver slowed the car as we passed the long hedge that marked out our property, and stopped at the wrought-iron gate. It was open, and there weren't any soldiers in sight, though there was debris such as ammunition crates all over the lawn, and the garage door was open. My father reached for the microphone.

"Just pull right in the driveway, and honk the horn so they know we're here," father said calmly, and Driver did what he was told.

With the engine off it was very still in our yard. Driver got out and opened the door for my father.

"Wait here and keep quiet," my father said, and got out. As he walked across the lawn toward the house, the front door opened, and right away you could tell that the man who stepped out was in charge. The Japanese colonel glanced at the car then scrutinized the tall, stern-looking man walking rapidly toward him. My father stopped and bowed slightly, as did the colonel, both men following the decorum of the top social level.

My father, a very straightforward and somewhat aggressive individual, said to the Japanese colonel: "Well, we're back, what is going to happen?"

Colonel Yamamoto led him inside, and we sat in the car, while it grew hot under the summer sun. Nonchalant, Driver pulled out his feather duster and set to work. Godfrey looked back at us, eyebrow raised, and shook his head, then turned and watched Driver scrape dead bugs from the grill with the handle-end of the duster. Its brown feathers were the same color as the Japanese uniforms. Two soldiers came out of the house and watched us, though they came no closer than the front steps. Mother made me sit next to her and squeezed my hand very tightly.

Finally my father and the colonel came out the front door, conversing freely. The two more junior men stepped aside then followed down the front steps. After a few more words my father left the colonel and his men standing on the lawn, then came over to the car to get us. He was laughing.

"You've got to come and see this," father said as Driver opened the door. We got out, Godfrey jumped out of the front, and father led us past the colonel, who was in deep conference with his men.

As we crossed the threshold of the house I tried to place an odd smell, and understand why there was ankle-deep muck rather than parquet floors, but couldn't figure it out until we stepped through into the living room. Standing next to the grand piano, a horse swung its head around, looked at us, and whinnied. I don't remember whether my mother was laughing or crying as we walked out of the house.

She went to the car to wipe her tears. Father introduced Godfrey and me to the colonel, who was personable and quickly became Yamamoto-san. (In Japan people will add "-san" to the end of many men's and women's names. This is not necessary but it's generally done and it doesn't indicate any particular socioeconomic status or anything else.) I looked at the colonel's sidearm while he presumably ordered his men to go inside and begin the cleanup immediately. After they set off, he promised my father that the house would be habitable within a few weeks. Mother came back with dry eyes and the Baby Brownie camera. She had us pose with Yamamoto-san for the photograph that is the cover of this book, then we got back in the car. The Colonel smiled and waved as Driver backed us out.

Chapter 2

A Recent History of China and the West

My first recollections are from when I was about five years old and in the German Hospital on Hungjao Road for a hernia repair. The hospital was excellent and near our house. Doctor Gardner, an American surgeon, was my doctor and I can quite plainly remember the crib and the ward. It's funny what one remembers about things, but an impressive thing to me over the next several years was that this hospital had deep red walls on the outside on all four sides. Three or four years later I would often ride my bicycle past and admire a hospital with deep red walls.

One wonders about the improbability of an American/British youngster landing up in a German Hospital in China to be treated by an American surgeon. This certainly impresses me now, not only in that my parents were people who held no grudge with race, color, creed or nationality, but also how odd the whole situation really was. Shanghai was truly a multicultural city.

Christmas party, 1932. Godfrey wears a high white hat and my Amah (nurse) holds me.
Note the many nationalities, especially Chinese, participating in a Christian celebration.
Note also the western kids dressed as Chinese.

Whenever I tell people that my parents moved to China in the 1920's, I'm always asked if they were missionaries. The concept is well established in people's minds that all white people who went to China were missionaries, but in the last two centuries nothing could be further from the truth. The inertia of perception is understandable: missionaries have been in China since at least 1582, when Matteo Ricci entered the scene and made a very significant contribution to the introduction of China to the West and the West to China.

Almost all of the cities that existed when I was growing up in China were very well established when Ricci was there in the 1500's, including Shanghai, but not the Shanghai of *Western* creation. Only one hundred years before we sailed into port and the *Gneisenau* dropped anchor, no skyscrapers fronted the Whangpoo River, there was no Bund, and therefore no maze of traffic-choked streets behind the Bund. There was nothing beside the bend in the river but an empty marshland that drained through several creeks, though the creeks themselves were busy with sampans. The old walled city of Shanghai, which in Chinese means "beside the sea", sat south of this marshland, near to the river's edge and beside a fishing village called Nantao.

By the late 18th century, a very limited trade had opened due to Ricci's introduction, and Western merchants were beginning to moor their ships and take quarters in the old city of Shanghai. As there were no roads to speak of, and of course no railway, waterways were the only way to distribute goods to and gather commodities from the heart of China. The Yangtze River was the superhighway, running 3,200 miles (5,149 km) from the southwest to the northeast of the country, studded with the oldest and most established cities, and home to tens of millions of people. The Whangpoo swirled into the Yangtze only 40 miles (64 km) from where the great river itself finally emptied into the East China Sea, and the old city of Shanghai was only 14 miles (23 km) up the smaller river, a perfect anchorage and place for storing and accounting the goods that flowed back and forth.

The flow of goods was initially, overwhelmingly, out of China. The Western nations wanted tea and silk from China, but the Chinese didn't want much of anything the Western nations had. Knowing that opium would create its own market, British merchants very slyly started bringing it in, bribing customs agents and using Chinese intermediaries to form networks of addicts up every river and creek. The emperor understandably took exception to this, though more for economic reasons than moral scruples as the resulting imbalance in trade was emptying the country of silver reserves. An opium suppression commission confiscated drugs and placed foreign merchants in Canton under house arrest.[1] The British sailed their gunboats upstream to Nanking in response, and this show of force resulted in the Treaty of Nanking, and an end to the "opium wars".

In the treaty, the emperor granted concessions to the British in the form of land near various important trade locations, Shanghai being one. Canton (Guangzhou), Amoy (Xiamen), Foochow (Fuzhou), and Ningpo (Ningbo) were the others. Also part of the treaty was the secession of Hong Kong, payment of a large indemnity, and low tariffs on foreign goods. Tsingtao, Tientsin (Tianjin), Pei Tai Ho (Beidaihe), and other areas were also eventually divided up, generally amongst the British, American, French, Germans, and Dutch.

In the case of Shanghai, the emperor granted the marshland fronting the river north of the city's walls to the British for 100 years. The French shortly thereafter requested a concession as well, and in fact got a better, drier piece of land between the British parcel and the walls of Shanghai itself. Within these concessions, the traders had the right to govern themselves under their home country's laws. Another aspect of the treaty — one that would prove to be crucial — was the right of self-defense against all comers, including the Chinese. British and French gunboats, and ships with rifles in their holds, dropped anchor before a towpath that would become the Bund. Soon their hulls reflected an incessant pounding back to the shore, where pilings on which to build were being driven deep into the mud.

Peking eventually granted concessions to twelve more nations, including the large American Concession, an area following the bend of the Whangpoo north and east of Soochow creek and the British settlement, granted in June of 1863. Thirteen of the fourteen nations amalgamated their treaties in December of that same year to form the "International Settlement", which encompassed all of the area north of the French concession. Only the French abstained, and their treaty area remained the French Concession, eventually coming to be known as "French Town". The British ran the customs and the police force, whereas the French ran the post office. Then there was the law. There is a dissertation by Counselor John Seddon, whose father was a judge in the court in Shanghai, as to the ins and outs of practicing law in a country where they of course had their own laws, but in treaty ports such as Shanghai, various nationalities who were caught at some inappropriate type of behavior would be tried in a court of their own country in Shanghai. In this way, a productive equilibrium set in amongst the powers.

Outside the treaty ports, however, China was not in such a balanced state. Great dynasties had ruled the country through a civil service, which to some extent held sway over many "warlords". The warlords commanded private armies who in turn exerted force over their local regions. The last of the dynasties was the Manchu family, founded in 1644. The family came from North China, from what became known as

Manchuria. Under the dynasty, officially the country could be administered in a half way fashion because the administrators, dating back for millennia, were awarded their jobs by very rigorous examinations that took years of preparation and this was followed by very difficult examinations which only a small percentage of candidates passed. The officials — the civil servants if you will — were the crème de la crème of Chinese intelligencia. They could communicate with each other, but not all that well with the various local warlords and their troops, who pretended to listen but often did the opposite of what they were told. So, in this vast country of China, with so many dialects, many of which are entirely separate languages, not understandable one to the other, it was very difficult for the Manchus to control the hinterland, especially the southern half of the country.

Around 1851 the Taiping rebellion had begun, based on promises to common people to alleviate their suffering under the Manchu. By 1860 the rebellion had moved in absolutely massive numbers from the South, its conscripts murdering an estimated 20 million people along the way. Seemingly unstoppable, they attacked Shanghai, but found the foreigners with their rifles and gunboats to be stern adversaries. There was a second and a third battle in 1862, with the same outcome of defeat for the Taipings. Word got around that Shanghai was a safe haven from the turmoil of the interior, and the Chinese started to move to the city in large numbers. This was the beginning of the general rule that "China's losses were always Shanghai's gains."[2]

In fact, the world's losses were often Shanghai's gains. For instance, the American Civil War of 1861 to 1865 interrupted the supply of cotton from the southern states to European manufacturers. Cotton grew very well near the mouth of the Yangtze, so this became a big export, especially by the Japanese. Opium, however, was the early basis for Shanghai's prosperity, and was essentially legalized in 1860 with the Treaty of Tientsin, signed by the emperor to end the second Opium War. Article XXVIII of the treaty exempted foreign goods from China's domestic transit taxes, and this really opened things up to those who had vision.

A January 1935 article in Fortune magazine stated that "...toward the end of the nineteenth century...the Standard Oil Co. out-grew its American market for kerosene. Learning that 400,000,000 Chinese were burning sesame oil in their lamps, Mr. Rockefeller set forth to tap that enormous market in the nineties." Standard Oil took a classic kerosene driver lamp with a wick and a glass reflector; a type used all over North America and elsewhere, and called it the "Mei Foo". In a stroke of brilliance, they *gave* these away all over China. The lamps were valued at just over a dollar so it cost the company some money, but the Mei Foo could not burn sesame oil, so each lamp that Standard Oil gave away enlarged their long-term market for kerosene.

There was a major bit of luck associated with the naming of the lamp. The first symbol, Mei, means "beautiful" but it can also be interpreted as "American", and the second ideogram, Foo, can have several interpretations, but generally means "to float," and Socony Vacuum's ocean-going tankers certainly floated into Shanghai Harbor, making it a very realistic term. There is, by coincidence, a third interpretation of the word: "confidence", a singularly good combination. Chinese words oftentimes have these different meanings depending upon the context in which they are found. This type of combination of words would mean to the average uneducated Chinese that the Americans, no matter how you cut the cake regarding political likes or dislikes, were very respected people who could float this marvelous elixir that could be put into their lamps and the wick lit would burn all night, giving the household light that was virtually unavailable before.

It went over wonderfully. To give you an idea, between 1900 and 1914, the Chinese imports of kerosene from the Standard Oil Company almost tripled. In the first third of the 20th century, kerosene was the leading American export to China, with the Socony Vacuum dominating the market. "With its head-quarters in Shanghai, his [Rockefeller's] company expanded until its hong (brand) name, Mei foo, became a passport to the most distant villages of the interior."[3]

With the revolution of 1911 and formation of the Republic of China, with Dr. Sun Yat-Sen as the first president, the tenuous bureaucracy that had half-worked under the Manchu dynasty fell apart. There was rarely enough money to pay the soldiers, so the warlords' private armies quickly devolved into marauding bandits. They stole from everybody and anybody. Trains, buses, and cars were favorite targets since people who could afford to ride in these vehicles must be "wealthy", by their standards. Unfortunately, if they found nothing to reward them for their efforts they were known to behead travelers (a favorite Chinese method of execution), or simply shoot them in the back of the head.[4]

A typical execution. Notice the "soldiers" on the left hand side,
totally ignorant of these young men being executed ten feet from them.

To the best of my knowledge, these "armies" never executed Europeans or North Americans. Westerners did carry money, jewelry, and other valuables on their person, but they didn't, like many Chinese, try to hide these things. They simply handed them over and there were no reprisals.[i] It's also important to note, and this is just an impression of mine, that Chinese generally felt that white men were superior in those days and would strongly hesitate to execute or even injure them. But if you were Chinese and tried to cross a warlord's land, God help you. This caused more movement to the city. Yet again, China lost and Shanghai gained.

At this time, across the world in County Down, Northern Ireland, my father Robert Gregg was studying engineering at the University of Belfast. He was a wanderer, an adventurer, and worked in shipyards during the summer breaks, dreaming of where they might one day

---

i   When I was very young (too young to remember clearly) we accompanied dad on a business trip to Soochow, just 50 miles west of Shanghai. About halfway there, uniformed men stopped our bus, we were all taken out at gunpoint, and the soldiers took literally everything from us—dad and one of the other Standard Oil men's money, and even our clothes and shoes. They then tied us all together to a tree just in our underwear. One Chinese man on the train had no money and the bandits thought he was hiding it. He nearly lost his life, whereas the soldiers wouldn't have dared harm us.

sail. In fact he worked on the construction of the *Titanic* (though he had nothing to do with the allotment of lifeboats, or bulkhead heights!). Finally RG graduated, signed up as an officer in the Royal Navy, and hunted and destroyed U-boats in World War I. (About which I was to learn in detail a short time after stating my life's ambition aboard the *Gneisenau*.) Season after season, year after year he sailed the dark waters of the north Atlantic. In fact three years after the war had ended he was still on active duty.

This all changed when his ship moored in San Francisco harbor in 1921 and he met my mother, who lived in the city with her parents, having moved down from New Westminster, British Columbia, Canada with two of her sisters, Jean and Phyllis. Dad was quiet and stoic, but I'm sure he had a lot of glamour surrounding him, having traveled so far and experienced so much. He had that look in his eyes that comes from staring great distances for a very long time, and he was looking east, all the way to China. He convinced mother to come with him.

After mother and RG were married in San Francisco he had to ship out one more time as an engineer officer on a dreadnaught, as battleships were then called, and sailed her to Hong Kong in order to be decommissioned. Mother took a boat directly to Shanghai (via Honolulu, as all boats did then) to await him coming up from Hong Kong after decommissioning. They managed to meet up in Hawaii and honeymooned at the newly opened Royal Hawaiian Hotel on Waikiki Beach before parting ways once more.

Mother went on to Shanghai, and lived in a boarding house to await dad's arrival. Every morning she read the *North-China Daily News*, in which Western businesses advertised for executives. In it, Standard Oil placed an ad for a petroleum engineer. Mother spotted the ad and of course thought that dad obviously would fit the bill. Not only did RG have an engineering degree; he had been engineering officer on ships using very complicated oil pumps. She answered the advertisement and assured the company that dad would be in Shanghai within a few days for the interview. That's how my father got into the executive suite of Standard Oil, and he never looked back.

The city was a very exciting place in the twenties. The International Settlement and the French Concession now dwarfed the old city, whose walls had been taken down in the revolution. The old city had in fact been engulfed, a sort of Chinatown in China. The new city had become the "Paris of the Orient", home to vice, opium, wine, women, and song. It was such a free-for-all that an inordinate amount of policing was required to keep order; so glamorous that even the police had style.

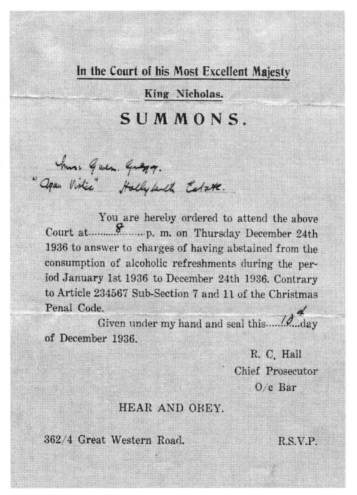

In the Court of his Most Excellent Majesty

King Nicholas.

SUMMONS.

Mrs. Gwen Gregg.
"Aqua Vistie" Hollybush Estate.

You are hereby ordered to attend the above Court at........8........p. m. on Thursday December 24th 1936 to answer to charges of having abstained from the consumption of alcoholic refreshments during the period January 1st 1936 to December 24th 1936. Contrary to Article 234567 Sub-Section 7 and 11 of the Christmas Penal Code.

Given under my hand and seal this......10th.....day of December 1936.

R. C. Hall
Chief Prosecutor
O/c Bar

HEAR AND OBEY.

362/4 Great Western Road. R.S.V.P.

Party invitation from Bob Hall, the Chief of Police, a good indication of the level of frivolity in Shanghai, what people most certainly couldn't do back home.

The main group of police was Chinese, dressed in dark blue uniforms (short khaki pants in summer) with a striped band around the wrist indicating they were on duty and carrying a gun. This was the typical uniform of British police all over the "empire".

Chinese policeman in British uniform directing traffic in the International Settlement.

In addition there were the very colorful Sikh police, usually on horseback with very beautiful turbans in red and yellow, reminiscent of the Royal Canadian Mounted Police, used for ceremonial purposes as well as routine policing. The French Concession had its ordinary police force similar to the Settlement, but in addition had an elite group of Annamites from French Indo China (Vietnam).

Aside from the police, there was also the Shanghai Volunteer Corps (SVC), which was a paramilitary group of young men organized into platoons and companies just like the army. When he was old enough my brother Godfrey joined the American corps. Personnel were dressed in the official army military uniforms of their country (usually out-of-date, often World War I vintage), with issued armaments including rifles and pistols. They also had armored personnel carriers and even some light tanks. When things got rowdy the SVC would be called out to protect certain areas of the city, when various factions would try to enter. More such attempts were ahead.

With the death of Dr. Sun Yat-sen in March of 1925, General Chiang Kai-shek took over as head of the Kuomintang, or Nationalist Party. He subjected the country to yet another murderous mass march from the south in 1926, pushing a large and turbulent wake of labor uprisings and dissent in general. Anyone who opposed the general was spared the bullet in the back of the head from a Warlord's soldier, but given something worse. That is, the Kuomintang's firing squads were very poor shots, so soldiers would draw swords and behead 200 prisoners at a time.

They were headed for Shanghai, so Britain, America, France, Spain, Italy, and Japan all brought in troops to help the SVC defend the Settlement and Concession. Chiang Kai-shek and his army took the Old Chinese City in March of 1927, and they stayed a few weeks, trying to determine their chances against the assembled international force. Finally they retreated and established a capital upriver at Nanking. Like the Taipings and the warlords, the Nationalists had driven people and capital to the former marshland beside the Whangpoo. Suddenly there were 3 million Chinese in Shanghai, compared to only about 20,000 westerners plus 25,000 refugees from the Russian revolution.

There was a major problem with the new government in Nanking that echoed the failings of the Manchu dynasty. That is, its members were elite and highly educated (oddly, those closest to Chiang Kai-shek were alumni of American Ivy League schools), but there were fundamental problems with communications. The Nationalist government Chiang Kai-shek formed was a closely-knit group of his in-laws. Madame Chiang was one of the Soong sisters, highly educated in the United States at Wellesley, while the Generalissimo could not speak English and in fact only spoke his area dialect. The head of the Bank of China was the famous T.V. Soong, Madame Chiang's brother, a Harvard graduate of 1915 and later to become the Prime Minister of China. Soong organized a Harvard Club of China, which "included a larger proportion of the high officials of Chiang Kai-shek's government in Chungking [where the government moved in 1937] than a Harvard Club would have in John F. Kennedy's Washington."[5] It's hard to imagine that sitting around the inner cabinet everyone could talk to each other EXCEPT the generalissimo, and he couldn't even talk to everyone else because of dialect differences.

Unfortunately, this inept government was about to face a new enemy. By 1930 there were more than 30,000 Japanese in Shanghai, as opposed to slightly less than 10,000 British, and less than 5,000 Americans. Most Japanese lived in Hongkew, which had originally been the American concession. They owned more cotton mills than anyone else, and had invested enormously in factories and infrastructure. Japan had become a serious player in Shanghai and, therefore, in China. Their ambitions were enlarged, had in fact become imperialistic.

On September 18th, 1931 they drummed up an incident, an explosion on a Japanese-owned railway line in the resource-rich province of Manchuria. Using this as a pretence they occupied the entire province by December. Chiang Kai-shek, wanting to preserve his forces for possible combat with the communists, offered no resistance, and stood by while the Japanese created the puppet state of Manchoukuo and installed the boy Puyi as its emperor. Puyi was the youngest son of the last Empress of China. This made it more acceptable to the Chinese who after all had owned Manchuria prior to that time as a province.

In protest, Chinese citizens of Shanghai very effectively boycotted Japanese businesses. After a crowd of Chinese attacked some Japanese monks (again a contrived situation), the Japanese demanded an end to the boycott. Without awaiting a response, their army massed in Hongkew and attacked the railway yards of the North Station in Chapei, which the Chinese Nineteenth Route Army defended. Both sides quickly dug in and reached a stalemate. The Japanese started carpet-bombing the whole area — this was the world's first systematic, large-scale civilian bombing — and ten thousand people died. Chapei, an overwhelmingly Chinese area, was completely flattened; yet directly south across Soochow creek the International Settlement remained almost completely unscathed.

Refugees flooded the International Settlement. Hungry children and their mothers crowded on the sidewalks and streets between the office towers. High up in the towers, Western executives worked away at their desks, seeing to the affairs of Standard Oil, Texaco, Shell, BA Tobacco, Jardine Matheson, Hong Kong & Shanghai Bank, and other major firms. Glancing up every now and then from their work, those with northern-facing offices watched enormous plumes of smoke rising from the black rubble of Chapei. Dad had long since become Standard Oil's chief engineer for the Far East. The job entailed traveling all over China and Southeast Asia, so he had had many dealings with Japanese clients. What he saw out his office window both shocked and disgusted him.

RG (back row, indicated by arrow) and other Standard Oil Executives on business trip to Japan circa 1934. Note the Geishas the Japanese contingent brought along, as opposed to their wives.

To be fair, a lot of Japanese executives watched from their offices with equal horror and disbelief. This went on for five weeks until a truce on May 5th, 1932 stipulated that the Chinese army had to leave the city, as did the Japanese, excepting those who belonged to the garrison in Hongkew. The Japanese had shocked the world, and earned enmity from the other powers in Shanghai.

Things were changing, but there was to be a short reprieve, one more boom. Around the time the Nationalists had formed their government, Sir Victor Sassoon moved his money and companies from the family base of Bombay, incorporated his companies in Hong Kong, and bought up much of the land along the Bund. Sir Victor's detractors in Shanghai said he made the move simply to avoid paying British taxes, but they didn't say it too loudly, as his millions were a boon to the city. His purchases included the major holdings of Silas Hardoon upon Hardoon's death in 1931. Broadway Mansions, Embankment House, and Cathay Mansions (where we were staying until our house was ready) were all his developments. By the mid-thirties, Sassoon's Cathay Hotel had joined the Customs House and the Hong Kong & Shanghai Bank building in dominating the skyline of the Bund. His investments in the city buoyed the economy, and, with a quick rebuilding of Chapei, Shanghai actually grew through the depression.

The city was growing so rapidly that the Chinese government granted extraterritorial rights to a large number of homes (probably three or four hundred) outside the International Settlement, just like the concessions of the foreign nations of Shanghai. The fenced-in property of each house, plus an outside buffer of six to eight feet, was not considered to be China. Completed in late 1932, our house was one of these. Our family moved out of the Gresham Apartments on Avenue Joffre in the French Concession, and in to a concession of our own.

By 1937, Japan's imperial ambitions regarding Southeast Asia had increased, and their army was still in Manchuria. Protests by Chinese in urban areas such as Shanghai, plus direct pressure brought to bear on Chiang Kai-shek, shifted the Nationalist Government's focus from their internal enemy of the communists to the Japanese. Seeing this United Front forming, the Japanese drummed up another reason for war before the Chinese became too unified. The opportunity came while the Japanese army maneuvered near Peking on July 7th. One of their soldiers disappeared, and they claimed the Chinese had abducted him. Even though the Chinese found the soldier in a brothel and returned him unharmed, the Japanese cried foul and used this as an excuse to roll in massive numbers to the south. They took both Peking and Tientsin within a few weeks.

Thinking back to 1932, Chiang Kai-shek decided to draw the Japanese into a battle for Shanghai that might, through extreme destruction, boost Western sympathy for China. My mother and I were already in California, having left in December of 1936 for an extended visit (I didn't yet have to attend school), but Godfrey and dad were still in Shanghai. Under the generalissimo's orders, the Chinese army massed outside the International Settlement in early August. By a stroke of luck, dad and my brother were actually due to depart for home leave. As to what to do with the house, RG perhaps thought back to 1932 as well, how the Japanese had respected the extraterritoriality of the International Settlement. He left the staff in charge of the house, all under protection of extraterritoriality, and Driver took him and my brother down to the jetty with their trunks. Heading out to sea, their ship practically passed the flagship *Idzumo,* which was leading the Japanese navy up the Whangpu, ready to shell the Chinese troops. The first shots were fired on August 13th.

On August 14th two Chinese airplanes attempted to sink the *Idzumo*, which had moored in front of the Japanese Consulate. One accidentally dropped its bombs on Nanking Road at the Bund, which was clogged with refugees from Chapei. 729 people died and 861 were wounded. The other dropped its bombs at the crowded intersection of Avenue Edward VII and Thibet road. 1,011 people died, and 570 were wounded. A large battle ensued in Chapei, resulting in a second flattening of the area, and heavy casualties on both sides until November 5th, when several divisions of Japanese soldiers landed at Hangchow Bay and advanced on the rear of the Chinese. Defeated, the Chinese had to strategically retreat toward Nanking.

Things were different than in 1932. Regardless of who dropped them, bombs had fallen on the International Settlement. The British ambassador's car had been machine-gunned during the battle of Shanghai. After the battle, on December 3rd, Japanese General Matsui Iwane paraded 6,000 of his troops through the International Settlement. A strong diplomatic protest by the other treaty nations made no difference whatsoever. Iwane left town and headed up the big river — as the Rape of Nanking in all its horror was to commence only ten days later — but he left soldiers behind to surround Shanghai and repel Chinese guerrilla attacks. It was these soldiers who knocked on the door and found we weren't home.

Chapter 3

The Japanese Colonel Keeps His Word

The morning light flooded through the thin white curtains of my bedroom in Cathay Mansions. It was our seventh day back in Shanghai. I dozed while a horn honked below on Rue Cardinal Mercier, and an airplane droned over, heading inland.

I was starting to wake up when the latch clicked and my door swung gently open. There was an unmistakable sound of tiny shoes clip clopping across the hardwood floor toward my closet. I sat up in bed and my heart overflowed with love when I saw who it was.

"Amah!" I cried. Amah was the name for a child's nurse people in the Far East and India generally used instead of Nanny.

She glanced over and addressed me in Shanghainese: "Hao bu hao erh Young Master." This meant "how are you this morning, good or bad, Young Master number two?" My brother, being older, was simply "Young Master."

"Wo hao (I'm well), Amah."

"Young Master's clothes dirty," Amah said, rapidly flicking through the hangars, which she had to stretch to reach.

Her dress was flat black, her usual choice of attire — aside from an occasional dark blue cotton jacket with trousers — and her hair was pulled back in a severe black bun, as always. She was at most 5 feet tall with feet bound since birth, an old Chinese tradition in those days, but stopped in 1940, with the toes rolled under the sole, not more than five inches long and two inches wide. She couldn't run and this was the general idea: the wife couldn't run very far from her husband. There is another theory that Chinese males at that time found small feet to be sexually attractive: strange! Although probably no different than the very high or spike heels that Western women wear that must be very uncomfortable. The bound feet were outlawed decades ago when the last of the Manchus were dethroned and China became a republic. The men's queues (a long braided ponytail from a tuft of hair on the back of an otherwise bald head) were outlawed at the same time. I haven't seen a queue since I was very little, but there are still some bound feet to be seen on rare occasions in very elderly women.

I jumped out of bed and ran and hugged her. She kept working for a second, but then stopped and hugged me back. It was as difficult to stop her from working as to stop a freight train from rolling.

"Missy and young master number one waiting for you at breakfast," she said. I didn't answer, just kept hugging her.

"Ni shawta, bu shawta." She gently pushed me away. This was also Shanghainese, meaning "you understand, you don't understand," a sort of binary form of question that, without being a question, asked: "Do you understand?"

"Wo shawta (I understand)," I replied, and hurried down the hall to the washroom. This was actually the day we were due to return, had we not gotten the telegraph about the house. I have no idea how she found out we were in Cathay Mansions, but there was a very efficient word-of-mouth communications network out in the countryside, where she had been, called "the bamboo telegraph".

When I turned on the light, my heart sank when I saw what hung on the wall opposite the toilet. My mother had purchased a new Mandarin language chart, just like the one hanging in the bathroom at the house, if the soldiers hadn't torn it down. There were many charts and this one, like all of them, had twenty characters. Interestingly, the characters are identical in all the Chinese dialects but the words are pronounced very differently. For instance Mandarin (official Chinese now) is as different from Cantonese, the major language in south China, as French is from English. Mandarin has four inflections, which makes it hard enough, but Cantonese has seven inflections, each with an entirely different meaning!

Godfrey and I learned these characters when we went to the washroom: no Sears Roebuck catalogues for us. We also picked up Chinese in the vernacular from the children of our servants at the house, who were now apparently dispersed to their homes throughout the area. The children were my friends and since they didn't speak a word of English I naturally acquired Chinese.

Chinese is an easy language to learn, particularly if you are immersed in it since there is almost no grammar as we know it. There are a large number of conventions that educated people have to adhere to but the difficulty for English speaking people in languages, as I see it, is that most of us don't know any grammar, and to learn a language like German or French, or Japanese for that matter, requires an intense grasp of grammar. Not so in Chinese, where you learn many words and then say the tenses: I go, I will go, tomorrow, 5 days from now, next year. Just say it with a string of words. We learned about 500 characters (ideograms), which is about as many as most reasonably educated Chinese would know at that time. I learned another character while heeding the call of nature, washed up, got dressed, and made my way down the long hall to the dining room.

My brother, in tennis whites, and mother, in a summer dress, were waiting for me at the table, which was absolutely piled with food. Normally father would be there too, in his three-piece gray pinstripe suit, but he had left early for work. RG had had some pretty high-level meetings with Rockefeller in New York[ii], and had been away for months, so it had been a heavy week for him. The windows were thrown open and sheer curtains blew around.

The instant I took my place I realized Cook (as with Driver, I never learned his true name) must have heard from Amah that we were back, and come to us. The spread, with its abundance, bore his signature.

"Is Cook back?"

"Yes, he came back with Amah," mother replied. And as if timed to confirm her words, there was a clanging of pots and pans in the kitchen. At this time in Shanghai you didn't have to be wealthy to have several servants. The pay was five dollars a month and a picul (about 40 pounds) of rice a quarter. The worldwide depression of the 30's was virtually unknown in Shanghai[6], and dad was paid in U.S. funds, which went a very long way because the U.S. dollar was worth far more than the Chinese yuan ("yuan" meaning, literally, "round"). The

---

ii We had an apartment right downtown on Fifth Avenue for about two weeks while dad worked in head office. Godfrey and I wandered all over Times Square (imagine doing that today) and loved to go into the "crack-a-joke" shops with masks and fire crackers for sale. One evening dad had a number of VIP Standard Oil executives over for drinks, a formal cocktail party. John D. Rockefeller was also at the party. We decided to stuff the cigars with small, match sized, fire crackers set to explode when the cigar was about half smoked. Well, it worked, and what a commotion! Godfrey and I hightailed it for the self-serve elevators to escape the wrath of all. We loved to play with the self-serve elevators. Elevators were rare in Shanghai, and always operated by Chinese men, so the buttons in New York elevators were a real treat.

Nationalists introduced the "fapi" in 1935 as a replacement to the yuan, which had often been called the "Mex", because it was based upon Mexican silver price in the world, whereas the U.S. dollar in those days was based on gold in Fort Knox. Actual Mexican silver pesos were used as currency in the 20's and 30's. I don't smoke, but to this day I have several ashtrays of solid sterling silver with Mexican silver dollars as the base.

On our breakfast table was the usual weekday fare: any kind of eggs ordered the night before, bacon, toast fitted into a silver toast holder just like the one at the house[iii], cocoa for us, and tea for the grownups. But there were also the weekend things. Saturdays and Sundays began with pretty spectacular breakfasts like you still see in England, Ireland and Scotland. Kippered herring, sausages, game birds, potato pancakes, ordinary pancakes — always with homemade syrup made with Mabeline or Log Cabin Syrup when it was available — eggs and scones. It was amazingly good, but looking back you wonder how you survived.

"Today *is* Monday, isn't it?" I asked, putting the napkin on my lap.

"Yeah," Godfrey said, stabbing some bacon with a fork, "but I think Cook is glad we're back, so he went a little overboard."

I grabbed a couple of pancakes, a few sausages and, I think, some breast of quail. We ate in silence. Perhaps we were still all talked out, having spent so much time together on the trip. Mother was sort of looking past me, perhaps wondering what was going on with the house. Godfrey was dipping a thick slice of bread in the bacon fat, and I mean saturating it with the fat, all the while spinning his tennis racket on the floor next to the table.

The door buzzer sounded. It was Driver, back from taking dad down to his office at 207 Canton Road (Fuzhou Lu), just off the Bund. Godfrey put down his cutlery and wiped his mouth.

"Where are you going?" I asked.

"Out to Columbia Circle." He pushed his chair out. "Going to see if I can line up a game."

Mother said: "Why don't you come home for lunch and take Dwight to the French Club?"

---

iii Which my wife uses now to hold letters and bills on her desk. I never did understand the toast holder, a very British phenomenon, since the pieces of toast, held vertically and separate from one another, grow cold very quickly.

"Oh, Godfrey, could we?" I asked. It had been a week of intense boredom for me. It seemed like all my friends, those that hadn't moved back to their home countries last summer when the shooting started, were still on home leave. Even when they did come back, I'd been away for over a year of my mere seven-years existence...

"Sure. We can take a swim in the afternoon." He kissed her on the cheek, messed my hair, and squeaked down the hall in his tennis shoes, swinging his racket back and forth before going out the door.

Mother finished eating before me, and put on a pair of thin white gloves that had been set beside her plate. Cook appeared from the kitchen and handed her a freshly ironed edition of the *North China Daily News*. The ironing prevented newsprint from blackening fingers, but she wore the gloves anyway. Had my father been home, they would have shared the paper, a morning ritual.

While mother read the paper I pushed away from the table and went back to the bathroom with the intention of filling the tub and playing with my toy ship from the liner. Amah was already in there with a pile of clothing bigger than her, and a 3 ft. by 2 ft. wood-framed iron scrubber that was made to sit in the bathtub. It didn't matter — I was bored with the toy ship.

The phone rang when I was wandering back into the living room. Mother answered, all blasé and bored, but the tone of her voice changed right away when the other party spoke. It was the Japanese Consulate General passing on a message from Colonel Yamamoto that he and his troops had cleaned up and were moving out as they spoke. They were most humble and apologetic.

As soon as Driver returned from Columbia Circle, mother went out to Hollyheath Estate to inspect the house. I paced around the apartment for a couple of hours while, down the hall, Amah scrubbed away. It was an odd music she made with that board. Finally, flush with victory, every set, Godfrey came back a couple of hours later and we went across the street to the Cercle Sportif Francais.

Over a very late dinner that evening, mother reported that the horseshoes had completely destroyed the parquet floor. Also, one of the horses had kicked a hole in the wall of the living room. These and other repairs needed to be done, so we would have to stay in Cathay Mansions through Easter. Mother was quite cheerful for a woman whose house was uninhabitable. Then again, she was a highly organized woman, with incredible attention to detail, and perhaps this project was something to really sink her teeth into.

"Well, at least they did their best to clean up," she commented over desert. The house was Spanish-looking and mother and dad had christened it "Aqua Vista", because there was a well at the bottom of the garden. In typical British tradition, there was a brass plate beside the front door bearing the house name. It turned out that the Japanese had really put some effort into polishing the brass nameplate. Indeed, it shone like never before.

Later that evening, dad was sitting in an armchair and enjoying a glass of scotch after a very long day at the office. The telephone rang, and he got up and answered. It was the watchman that mother had hired to keep an eye on things when the contractors had finished for the day. The watchman said there was a man at the gate claiming to be our Number One Boy.

"Go and let him in and put him on the phone," RG said, and waited.

Number One Boy, actually about 35 years old, was at the top of the servant hierarchy, master of our household's accounts. He kept the books, approved all the buying of food and other necessities around the house and was the ruler of the staff, which pretty much correlated with the average foreign executive's household. Below the Number One Boy was a Number Two Boy (also a grown man), who generally kept up the house, vacuuming, dusting and arranging things.

In a class by himself was the cook. Cook was the boss of the kitchen, very good at culinary art. He had to answer to Number One Boy regarding purchases, but *no one* entered his kitchen without permission, not even my parents. Years earlier mother had once walked into his kitchen to see what he was cooking, and that was bad enough, but then she made a big mistake.

"Cook, that looks fine, but you might want to try frying the onions a bit first."

Deadly silence, Cook's shoulders tensed and his eyes moved from his work to her. His face turned red.

"Get out of my kitchen!" Cook screamed, grabbing an enormous meat cleaver. She ran into the dining room and he chased her several times around the dining room table, swiping the huge blade back and forth. Mother managed to get away with a good cross-table bluff maneuver and ran upstairs screaming and crying. Her skull had very nearly been parted, yet neither she nor dad had the heart to fire Cook because he was actually an incredibly talented chef. In fact, other households in Shanghai desired his services and were constantly alluding to the fact half-jokingly at our parties. Cook stayed on; the simple solution was that mother never went into the kitchen again. Nevertheless, she did form interesting ideas and opinions regarding the food we ate in Shanghai. Refer to Appendix E for the text of a speech mother gave years later in Vancouver on the customs of eating in China.

After Cook, Driver was next in line, then the two gardeners, full-time, and a coolie, the lowest rank of paid staff who did the heaviest work. He moved things either by hand or in a hay-haw fashion: a 3 or 4 inch thick 6 foot long bamboo pole balanced over the shoulder with a fair-sized bucket balanced at each end. These loads were usually very heavy and he would chant "hey-haw, hey-haw" throughout the whole journey. Sometimes coolies would walk for many miles with loads of grain, bricks, rocks, potatoes or what not.

There was also an essentially unpaid staff such as the "learny cook", a student who was learning from the master chef and paid a paltry sum with no allotment of rice. As you can probably imagine, the house was a real beehive of activity. Most members of staff had homes away from our house but oftentimes stayed for many days at a time, and several stayed permanently, so there were quarters for them at the north side of the house where they and their families lived. The many children of the staff ran all over the place and, as I've mentioned, they were my friends.

Father waited on the telephone line until an absolute torrent of apologies came from the other end. Number One Boy, being as empowered as he was, must have felt full responsibility for losing the house. Dad quickly assured him that surrendering the property, rather than opposing a bunch of armed men, had been the wise thing to do.

"But what happened to the rest of the staff?" RG asked, taking a sip of scotch.

Number One Boy explained that everyone had gone home, that no one had been harmed.

"And the dogs?" We had five German shepherds, which, along with high, spiked fences was a pretty standard security setup for the house of a na-ku-ning (foreigner) out in the Chinese countryside. The smallest was called Puni. She, Cora, and two others ran up and down wires stretched along the four fences. Each was limited to patrolling one fence. Blitz was the fifth, the biggest, and most dangerous. He roamed freely around the garden at night.

RG with Cora and Blitz.

Number One Boy said that the Japanese had in fact given them a bit of time to leave. It was morning and the dogs had already been kenneled. Number One Boy coordinated everyone and they quickly packed, then he led the staff to the kennels. Number One Boy put a heavy leash on Blitz, and wrapped it around his hand. Number Two Boy took Cora and Puni. Coolie and the gardener each took a dog as well. On the way out through the gate it had been tense, as Blitz growled and barked at the Japanese soldiers. But the soldiers calmly waited at the gate, some on horses, some on foot. After the staff got past the soldiers, who moved right in, they managed to place the dogs with neighbors before fanning out to their homes.

RG complimented Number One Boy for having had a cool head, and asked that he stay on at the house. Once he had retrieved the dogs, he could dismiss the watchman. And, perhaps during the day whilst the contractors were working and mother was there, he could endeavor to retrieve the rest of the staff. Dad thanked Number One Boy again, and hung up.

Another week passed. Easter was April 17th that year, and I hunted for eggs through the apartment. Mother and Amah were wily, but I found them soon enough. Through that week I gained an odd obsession, based in the logic of a child. The thing is, I didn't care whether or not soldiers had used my room, but I was worried that they might have stolen my toys. Before she'd had a chance to really look over the house in detail, mother had speculated that things might have been stolen. My father disagreed, as honor and discipline were pretty central to the Japanese army, notwithstanding the Rape of Nanking. I nevertheless applied her uncertainty to my sizeable toy collection. The prospect was appalling.

Godfrey of course had been collecting toys for years before I arrived so by the time I was five there were many teddy bears, games, cats and dogs (stuffed) and I felt very lucky. By 1938 Godfrey had obviously grown out of all of these and was into BB guns and .22 rifles, and even shotguns.

By this time I had model trains, a major pastime of just about all the boys I knew. We had all the best from the States, Standard gauge and Lionel O gauge sets with an amazing amount of sophisticated anti-collision electronics for that time. The engines and cars sat side by side, with stacks of track sections, both curved and straight next to the rolling stock.

I had kites too. Kite flying was another very popular pastime for both the Chinese and the na-ku-ning in the late spring and fall. The Chinese are past masters at this sport.

And aviation of course was all the rage — maybe we didn't realize then how new it was. I had model airplanes: both those very popular ones made of silk with a rubber band that you wound up the propeller with, and those with a gas motor (which fewer of us had). Bill Allan[iv], the brother of my brother's future wife Peggy, was insane about model planes and had them all over the ceiling of his bedroom on Rue Admiral Corbet in the French

iv Bill was a great guy, always had a kind word for everyone. Although I never knew him in Shanghai (I knew his sister well since she and Godfrey were thick as thieves and I was the little brat), I got to know him over many years after the war on the west coast, as he lived in Seattle, only about 140 miles (225 km) from Vancouver, 500 miles (805 km) from San Francisco.

Concession. He later became chief pilot of United Airlines, and still had a passion for model airplanes.

Then of course there were the model boats, which were as popular as the planes. We all would go out to Jessfield (Zhongshan) Park in the northwest corner of Shanghai. It was a large park covering about a quarter of a square mile, with a lake in the middle, a zoo and, close by, St. John's University (East China Institute of Politics and Law), which had many faculties including a medical school. The university's grounds were about another quarter square mile. In the summer, many Chinese and white families had picnics in the park. Sunny days with a bit of the wind, the lake was host to a Cowes Regatta in miniature, with small model sailboats, some with very sophisticated electronic controls, tacking back and forth into the wind. On calm days, silk planes glided quietly overhead, and the gas-powered ones buzzed in circles, sometimes crashing into the grass propeller first, with a sudden silence.

It was spring and I dreamt of the summer to come, filled with toys and friends. Every evening mother reported the details of the house repairs to dad. It seemed to take forever, but finally the day came, and we all piled back in the car for our second arrival at the house.

The whole drive there I was just itching to get out of the car. Again there was the jam of traffic at the railway tracks. Again Driver had to get out and bow, apparently a new policy ever since the Japanese took over. We got through and passed by the torture pond at the Japanese outpost. It was vacant at the moment, but two Japanese soldiers stood at its edge, rifle butts against the ground, smoking, and watching our car pass. It was early in the day, so there was no haze of heat yet, only a fresh, clear vista over the green countryside. We turned into Hollyheath Estate. High hedges and gates passed on both sides until we came to ours. Number One Boy, who had been waiting for us, swung the gates wide open, and driver nosed the car though. Big engine idling, we rolled forward, maddeningly slow. The gravel of the driveway lazily crunched under the tires until we finally rolled to a stop, and Driver turned off the ignition.

The house looked immaculate, and both gardeners were at work digging the flowerbeds. While Number One Boy closed the gates behind us, Number Two Boy and Coolie materialized and set to work at the back of the car, untying the trunks. Driver opened the door and we all got out, Amah and I last, as we had the jump seats. He closed the door and joined the men around back to see to the luggage.

Number One Boy greeted us. Dad was "Master", mother was "Missy", and Godfrey and I were both "Young Master". Dad complimented him on having assembled the staff. Number One Boy beamed with pleasure. Then, briefing RG, he led us toward the open front door. I brought up the rear, but Amah stayed close.

Inside, Cook hailed us from the opening up of the far end of the front hall. He had gone to the market early that morning and was stocking the pantry. Cook wore his obligatory collarless white smock with rope buttons, and had a bunch of carrots in his hand, gathered from the back garden.

Now, I had purposefully hung back behind my brother and parents. Amah had reached down to take my hand, but I didn't take it. I slowed right down as everyone headed down the hall. Very sneaky, but my shoes squeaked on the new floor as I turned. Oh well, too late! I thumped up the stairs, tore into my room, and screeched to a halt at the doors to the big toy cupboard. Well, let me tell you, the situation was tense. I held my breath, and opened the doors.

It appeared that everything was still there. The kites were up top, airplanes on the next shelf down. Below them, the railway tracks were stacked, both curved and straight sections, next to the rolling stock and the control box. The boats languished on their keels on the shelf second from bottom, and below them, next to a box of stuffed toys was my box of lead soldiers. Everything was in order. Now, this was bliss because, having being away for so long, my toys were almost like new things to me.

There was a general commotion and tramping up the stairs as Amah lead Coolie and Number Two Boy carrying Godfrey's trunk up to his room. Then they went back down. I was reaching for one of the silk planes when a thought occurred to me: were all the lead soldiers there in the box? Maybe a soldier had stolen my soldiers. Maybe, being Japanese, whoever bunked down in my room had broken the rifles off my Chinese soldiers.

This was a strategic issue that could make or break my summer before school began. Everyone had large numbers of lead soldiers. Some of my friends had thousands of them, and soon we would start to make fortifications in the garden or in the surrounding countryside, one man's army against another. Soldiers, horses, tanks, artillery with great strategies acted out and companies and regiments and whole battalions being moved around and usually after several days one army or the other would win. There were miniscule ranges of hills near Hollyheath, only a few feet high, perfect in scale for our soldiers.

My forces totaled about five hundred, so the box was very heavy. I struggled to pull it out and, huffing and puffing, opened the top. It was quite impossible to tell the situation as they were all massed together. Perhaps it was time for a parade and review. I reached in and pulled a few out, but just then there was more heavy lifting on the staircase, and behind my back, Amah directed the placement of my steamer trunk beside my bed. The latches clicked on the trunk.

I continued to place my soldiers in rank and file while she unpacked. There was a clip-clopping sound back and forth between the steamer trunk and the closet as the tiny shoes on her bound feet struck the shiny parquet floor. I saw her appear and disappear in my peripheral vision, shirts, ties, and trousers in hand. She pulled a wind-up replica of the *Gneisenau* out of the trunk, walked over and handed it to me. I jumped up and put it on the shelf next to my other boats.

"Number 2 Son, go outside play," she said, before I could kneel back down to the important work at hand, and that actually seemed like a pretty good idea. Coolie was standing in the door, waiting for something to do. I put the few soldiers I'd unpacked back into the box and waved him over. Then I led him down the stairs and he carried the box.

Downstairs in the living room things were just as they had always been. There was the wicker and upholstered furniture, the grand piano with its lid open (which I liked to drop), and in the corner, the grandfather clock ticking away like nothing whatsoever had happened. Mother was in the pantry, speaking with Cook. Father was standing in the comfortable sun conservatory off the dining room, hands in his pockets, looking out into the yard. Godfrey stood next to him with the same pose. I joined them.

"Godfrey," he said. "Why don't you go and exercise the dogs?"

"Sure dad. You want to come, Dwight?"

"No, I have to check on my soldiers."

"Okay, you do that." Godfrey went through the doors that gave onto the veranda, I followed close behind, and Coolie followed me, heavy box clinking with his steps. Dad called after me.

"Looks like the Japs cut down all the milk trees."

I giggled. About a year earlier, when I was about six, dad arrived home from the office and found me watering the lawn with a mixture of a can of "tinned milk" as the English called canned milk, diluted in a watering can with water. He asked what I was doing and I told him I was planting the seeds for a milk tree, much to his amusement.

The veranda — and therefore the ground floor of the house — was three or four feet higher than the lawn. There was no railing and normally I liked to jump onto the grass, but this time I used the stairs because coolie seemed to be following me with great exactitude, and I didn't want all the soldiers to burst through the bottom of the box. This height differential was by design, in order to accommodate the Monsoon rains, which came for six or eight weeks a year, generally during the late summer or early fall months. The rains came down like none of us would possibly believe. Sheets and sheets of water, and there was nowhere for it to drain. We didn't have basements because the water plain was only 4 inches (10cm) beneath the surface[v]. On the ground floor of a normal house you would suddenly have to wade through 4 inches to a foot (10 to 30cm) of water.

---

v How they came years later to build 60, 70, 80 and even 88-storey high-rises and a subterranean train, which probably is the best in the world to take you around the city some 65 to 130 feet (20 to 40 meters) below the road, is beyond my conception. I just don't understand how that could have happened.

A Chinese raincoat.

The flooding was really quite disastrous. All over Shanghai, which was flat as a pancake, you couldn't travel by car or even walk; you traveled by rowboat. This went on for several weeks a year. Fortunately they were virtually contiguous, the weeks, but nonetheless, it was a very disturbing situation. Everybody tried to get their houses barricaded with sandbags and that type of maneuver before the monsoons came, since they were quite predictable year by year. For now it was spring, sunny, and I had my army to inspect.

Our House "Aqua Vista" from the front yard, looking north.

Coolie followed me as I marched out and over the two-acre lawn to a gazebo that we had at the end of the garden, close to where our chickens, ducks and other assorted animals were. When the chicks were born and it was cold outside we would take a tray out there from the kitchen, bring 30 or 40 of them inside, and slide the tray into the electric oven on a very low setting during the night. There was also a pen for golden pheasants, which dad bred and then released in the fall during hunting season, with a number of the neighbors taking part in the hunt. The same went for the ducks which we bred in the "back 40", where we also had a few sheep. The golden pheasants were magnificent creatures: golden, yellow and deep red feathers with a plume on their forehead.

Those that were shot in the hunts on Sundays were hung up to rot, literally, in the true English tradition, until the bodies fell off the legs. This would happen about three or four days later, then they were gutted outside in the elements, even when it was remarkably warm. They were green, moldy, and delicious roasted after the mould had been washed off. The public health people would certainly not allow that type of thing now. I learned from it however and love to cook and even to this day leave roasts out at room temperature for 24-36 hours before cooking. This makes them much more tender.

The gazebo was on the other side of the vegetable garden. We boys played there often, and mother would have tea parties there on hot summer days. The damp land at the end of the yard had lots of big green frogs that we loved to catch and take to the gazebo to frighten my mother and her lady friends. This is where I told Coolie to leave the box, which he did.

After he'd left, I turned the box over and dumped the soldiers out on the deck. Then I stretched out on my belly to set them up. Somewhere to my left I could hear a dog barking. I pushed with my hands on the planking, and glanced over my shoulder toward the house. Godfrey had Cora by the collar, and then he let her go and chased after her.

Back to ranking and filing of soldiers. They looked fine. All seemed to have armaments. I placed an English soldier, kneeling and aiming his rifle, separate from the rest. My face was touching the planking and I squinted, so the soldier looked almost real. The well was in my line of sight behind the soldier, and Cora ran there. She really started to bark, jumped up and put her forepaws on the well, then whimpered. I looked at her and the soldier blurred. Godfrey ran up and looked down the well, and turned quickly away, hand over his mouth. He was white as a sheet. I jumped up and ran down the steps of the gazebo toward him. He strode forward to intercept me. Cora was going nuts, and now you could hear the dogs all the way from the kennel by the house, especially Blitz's deep bark.

"What is it?" I asked.

"Nothing. Come on." He was very pale.

"I want to look." I tried to pull away, but Godfrey had me by the wrist.

"No, we've got to get dad." He dragged me toward the house.

Father actually stepped out of the house, alerted by the dogs, and met us in the middle of the lawn. Number One Boy was close behind him.

"What is it?" he asked Godfrey.

"In the well."

"Let's go look. Dwight, you stay here."

I made a move to follow, but Number One Boy grabbed me. I could only watch dad and Godfrey walk down the lawn toward the well. Later I found out that Yamamoto's men hadn't been so scrupulous after all. There was a decomposing Chinese soldier in the well, and a bunch of rifles and other armaments rusting under the well water, stuffed down there with him.

Chapter 4

Life (and Death) in the Chinese Countryside

Even in the midst of the Sino-Japanese war, rural life in China continued on pretty much the way it always had. The Japanese had taken the area from the East Coast of China into China, which most people called "Occupied China" for about 200 miles inland. From then on to the west border of China it was Chinese and we all called it "Free China". These terms were fairly academic though, as the Japanese lacked the manpower necessary to exert widespread and continuous influence over Occupied China. For instance, with Shanghai they did little more than control the movement of people and goods in and out of the city. Hence the guardhouse where Hungjao road crossed the tracks, and the torture pond for smugglers and other transgressors.

There was one sort of cargo that wasn't searched at all thoroughly: "nightsoil". Hollyheath Estate was in rural China but at the same time within 15 minutes' drive of one of the most populous cities in the world. (American and Canadian equivalents would be, for instance, Alameda to San Francisco, and West Vancouver to Vancouver.) Vast fields of grass, vegetables, rice, and crops of all sorts surrounded a dense concentration of three million people. As we've already seen, Shanghai grew very quickly, often in a slipshod sort of way to accommodate refugees from crises in the interior of China. Due to the speed and nature of growth, plus the special plumbing challenges of the swampy land the city was built on, there was no comprehensive sewage system. Human waste had to be carted away, and the crops surrounding the city needed fertilizing. This led to a large "nightsoil" industry.

At night the nightsoil people would visit the hovels and small houses of which most of the Chinese areas of the city were comprised. There were no bathrooms in virtually any of the places where lower socioeconomic Chinese lived. They had almost nothing to live on, and so there were often 8 to 12 or 14 living in a room. Indoors they would have a covered bucket, and outdoors, in the alley beneath tangles of clotheslines, there would be a sort of outhouse. The nightsoil man scooped out the pit beneath the outhouse, and dumped the buckets left beside front doors into a 5-foot wide and 5-foot deep (1.5 m by 1.5m) barrel on wheels. When the barrel was full, he would then cart it to a cattle drawn wagon, or a sampan if they were near a creek.

It wasn't just the hovels that lacked comprehensive plumbing. Dora Sanders Carney, mother of Canadian senator Pat Carney and a dear family friend, recalls her first night in Shanghai in 1933, spent in the comparatively posh but aged Astor Hotel:

At about two in the morning, I was awakened by the stealthy opening of my door. By the dim light which came through the windows, I saw a small shadow slip in and glide to the bathroom. There was a stifled clank of buckets, one withdrawn, one replaced, and then the bedroom door closed again.

I heard wheels rumble on the carpet of the hall — stop — rumble on again — stop — rumble...

Soon there were small wagons clanking softly on the cobbled street, the louder sounds of tanks being loaded into barges on Soochow Creek. To the subdued chanting of coolies poling their laden craft upstream I went to sleep again.[7]

Under the stars the nightsoil collector would drive his wagon, or pole his barge, deep into the countryside. Then he would transfer the load to a smaller, but equally effective conveyance, a bamboo pole with two smaller barrels, one at each end. As dawn lightened the sky, he carried his load out to the fields where, at intervals, there were large pots buried in the ground. He would dump the barrels into the pot where the mixture of fecal matter and urine would ferment, waiting for the tenders of the fields to come each day or two and spoon out a ladle full of human manure onto individual rice, cabbage, lettuce, or other plants.

The idea of adding a spoonful of human waste to rice might conjure an odd picture, as it's a pretty common misconception that rice grows entirely in water. That is simply not the case, as water coverage is only part of a laborious, backbreaking process.

First, rice seedlings must be cultivated. The farmer broadcasts (or scatters) rice over a fairly small area in heavy quantities. He keeps the area very moist, but not flooded, at all times. In 30 to 40 days the seedlings will grow to about 6 inches (15 cm) tall.

Next, the farmer and the others planting in his field take square-foot, or so, sections of the earth in which the seedlings are rooted — like cutting pieces of sod — and move them to the edge of a field under 4 or 6 inches (10 to 15cm) of water, coverage running an acre or two, more or less. The farmer, his wife, and his children then walk down row upon row of the field, up past their ankles in water all day long, pushing these 2-seedling to 6-seedling clumps into the wet soil, each the span of a hand apart from the last. It means constant standing up and bending over thousands of times a day to do the planting, walking down long rows of mounds of soil under a water covering. This is absolutely backbreaking work.

When the rice begins to ripen the farmer breaks the dikes and the water drains off, so the ground is dryish by harvest time, the plants (a form of grass, really) being about three feet tall by then. There were often two and occasionally three crops a year, and the work continues. Rice was and is the number one crop in Asia, so the amount of periodic water coverage is necessarily large. Unfortunately, the water gives rise to another crop, mosquitoes, the vector of transmission for malaria.

"Malaria is one of the most serious infectious disease problems in the world despite the impressive results of the World Health Organization's sponsored malaria eradication program, begun in 1956."[8] It accounts for more deaths worldwide even today than any other illness. The causative organism of this medical problem, which is very prominent throughout the Far East, Africa and even North and South America, is a protozoan organism (not a bacteria) of the genus Plasmodium. I didn't know this before, but there are four species known to infect human beings: Plasmodium Vivax, Ovale, Malariae, and Falciparum.

The female Anopheles is the only mosquito vector. She bites someone who is already host to the organism, sucks up their blood, and through a series of stages within her these infected blood cells become the transmitter of malaria to someone else. It takes about two weeks and then if that same mosquito sticks her proboscis into another human that person may well get malaria.

Essentially, the four species all manifest themselves in a very similar way. I first got malaria when I was nine. It is a formidable disease, occurring a week or ten days after being bitten. You feel sick then undergo the paroxysms of a half hour of intense coldness and violent rigors — the bed would actually shake for 20 or 30 minutes — followed by a hot, profuse sweating stage of temperatures up to 107°F (41.7°C). The attacks become less severe as the days go by. Other manifestations are enlargement of the spleen, anemia, and a chronic relapsing course. The parasites land up in the liver and are released from time to time, hence the recurrence of malaria, sometimes year after year.

The treatment had for many years been quinine, an agent that is extracted from the bark of the cinchona tree. There is a long and very interesting history of quinine and the cinchona tree. This tree grew in the Andes Mountains in South America and the Indians there realized by 1500 A.D. that quinine was a medication useful in treating several different diseases. However, the trees began to die during the mid-1800's, but, most fortuitously, many others were planted in India, Indonesia, and especially Java. As a result, most of the quinine was (and is) only available from trees from those areas, which of course the Japanese were to take complete control of in the Second World War. Therefore, quinine became unavailable to anyone but the Japanese, a formidable tactical advantage. The U.S. military quickly pushed the western pharmaceutical groups to developed man-made drugs, which they did, with atabrine, chloroquine and primaquine. They were not only replacements but also advancements; quinine could never kill the parasites in the liver where they are stored, whereas these new drugs could, if taken for weeks after returning from an endemic area. War demands ingenuity, and in its unfortunate presence, drives human advancement. Isolated as we were in Shanghai through those four years, neither quinine nor the new drugs were available to us, but ingenuity was, most prominently through my stepfather. This will be described in due course.

As with any disease, prevention is far better than cure. Summers, early in the evening, the high-pitched whine of the mosquitoes began. Amah would take down the mosquito netting that hung over my bed, and with great care tuck it between the box spring and mattress. The mesh was small and thick enough to stop mosquitoes and a menagerie of larger creatures such as flies, bees, and similar insects like wasps. But the mesh didn't seem to stop the larger creatures.

There were monstrous centipedes all over China, from dimensions both the width and length of your index finger to twice that size. They were really quite formidable and several of these creatures would climb into your bed at night. It was too hot to sleep in anything by your undershorts. For the young guys (below 35 or 40) *the* brands were Jockey and BVD's. It seems amazing in retrospect that these had been imported from the United States and

Great Britain, rather than the other way around, which is what we have become used to. They were white (was there any other color in those days?) and this was very satisfactory because any other color would attract the centipedes. And they were tight, which was also satisfactory. When you went to bed, just as carefully as you checked the seal of netting to mattress, you would verify the integrity of seal between your undershorts and your skin, in order to protect your valuables from being stung.

When you awoke in the morning you could oftentimes see centipede marks all across your body, little steps with black dots. I am not sure what kind of centipede produced those because I am certain that there were many other centipedes that crossed you, and you never even knew they did that because they left no marks at all. Winters were a reprieve from all this. They were actually very chilly (very rarely, snow even fell[vi]) and killed off this microcosmos, so you would swap the mosquito net for cozy flannel pajamas. However summertime was really the norm, as it extended for at least half of the year.

In the morning you'd sit up, pull the mosquito net from under the mattress, and have a really good look around before you put your feet down. The search was most vigorous around your slippers to make sure that there wasn't a scorpion or some other vile, stinging, and poisonous insect nearby. Before you put the slippers on you would always knock them out, then look inside just to be sure that there were none of these varmints (or vermin) in there.

Once you had your feet safely on the ground it was great fun walking out in the countryside around Shanghai, though you had to continue throughout the day in being cautious as to where you stepped. When you were walking outside during the summertime you certainly avoided bamboo mangroves because the bamboo snakes could be there and they were serious problems if you were caught in their fangs. We never had any such problems but we took a number of precautions to avoid them.

The terrain was very flat surrounding Shanghai until the Zso-Zse (Sheshan) hills, about 10 miles (16 km) out past the Hungjao (Hongqiao) airfield. In fact, if you are on a Chinese

---

vi It was in fact a snowy day in February, the Year of the Sheep, and Chinese New Year's Day when I was born. Chinese New Year changes every year compared to the Gregorian calendar. Snow, birth, New Year are all portents of good joss (luck) and the combination unbelievably powerful joss. I am indeed thankful that this Chinese philosophy has stood the test of time. I've had ten guardian angels on my shoulders! Sometimes they flap and flutter around but they have stood me in very good stead for more than 70 years under what would have to be considered unusual circumstances through several eras of my life.

domestic flight (the new airport in Pudong handles international traffic), and approaching from the west, the plane will fly right over these hills. They are not particularly high, only a few hundred feet, and are comprised of granite. There has been much quarrying in the area for stone in building homes, bridges and other structures.

There is a book I still have called *Shanghai Country Walks*, which has sketches and dialogues of many walks in the area. One of the longest was from the railroad (not far from our house) right out to the Zso-Zse hills. A popular walk was from Siccawei Creek (which runs into the Whangpoo River skirting the south border of the city) up north about 5 miles (8 km) to Jessfield Park. Walking was a very popular pastime on weekends. There were radios of course, and several station such as XMHA, but no TV to tie one to a chair all day. It was always great fun at 7 or 9 years of age strolling through the fields with friends just doing nothing. God knows almost never again in my life could I "just do nothing".

What particularly fascinated us were the graves. The Chinese bury their dead above ground in caskets surrounded by clay tiles, and covered with a tiled roof, like a small house. These were all over the place, many of which had been there for 50 or more years. Sadly they were often disrupted in the late 30's with people kicking the sides in. Clearly we boys knew we were not allowed to, and didn't even want to, touch or desecrate such a personal, small, mausoleum. Nevertheless we would occasionally happen upon broken ones with bones strewn around, either from the winds, some of which were very strong, the monsoon rains, galloping horsemen, or bandits trying to rob the grave. I would have to assume that some had also been destroyed by the Sino-Japanese conflict.

Chinese funeral procession. Note the predominance of white.
White is the color of death in China, red the color of marriage.

As to galloping horsemen, the Shanghai Paper Hunt Club was an organization that all the "who's who" belonged to. A lead horseman would place a paper trial well ahead of time and the Club would then follow the trail on horseback with hunting dogs. It was quite something to see these many horses and dogs, riders all dressed for the hunt, thundering across the countryside, much to the disgust of many of the Chinese farmers, even though the horsemen tried not to trample too many fields.

Farmer in typical clothing stands beside his field just outside Shanghai.

The farmer probably shook his head in wonder at such decadent use of large, strong animals: there were no combines or motor-driven harvesters for him, just the brute force of his water buffalo. Together they worked the fields all day. The water buffalo pulled the plough and turned the water wheel to move water up 2 or 3 feet (60cm to 1m) from one field to another for irrigation purposes. Snorting, shaking off the flies, the poor dumb beast would simply walk around in a 10 or 12 foot (3 to 3.5m) wide circle all day long, rotating a wheel that was integrated with another wheel (set at 90 degrees relatively), which pulled up bucket after bucket of water from a passing stream or a lower field.

Water buffalo lifting water from low level to higher level. More water for rice to grow.

We would watch the farmers working in the fields and talk to them. Sometimes, much to my parents' dislike, Godfrey and I actually walked through the water-laden fields with the kids, helping them. Now, I've already mentioned malaria as one disease offshoot of all the water in the fields and the resultant mosquito vector. My parents' concern was that there were snails in the water and they carried Schistosoma Japonicum, a parasite that causes Schistosomiasis. It is a nasty little beast that penetrates through the skin, finds it's way into the bloodstream, and then into the liver. It causes a very serious illness from which people die, and was very common in the Far East when I lived there. Modern drainage systems, actually developed by a single individual, a young man in Sichuan province, changed much of that. Systematic field drainage resulted in snail destruction.

Chinese peasants pedaling water slightly uphill from one rice field to the next.

Snails are a major vector of serious illnesses in the Far East and, incidentally, in much of the rest of the temperate and tropical world. Other such serious snail-vectored illnesses which one is exposed to in this environment are the Giant Intestinal Fluke (fasciolopsiasis), a much rarer disease than Schistosomiasis, and the Chinese liver fluke (clonorchis sinensis), a very common disease in the Far East. This latter disease is contracted by eating inadequately cooked fish, which have the parasite under the skin, having gone through a phase in the snail.

The oriental lung fluke (Paragonimus westermani) also vectors through the snail, and further incubates in crayfish and crabs. Inadequate cooking of these foods allows the disease to pass to the human. It is a horrible parasitic infection where one coughs up the half-inch parasites or swallows them to be passe out the bowel.

Intestinal worms, tapeworms, pinworms, and many others were also very common, easily cured now but very difficult in those days. These, as well as infectious hepatitis, typhoid fever and cholera, all very, very common, came from consuming contaminated water or food. This was very easy to do. For instance the seller would often pump watermelons as full as possible with water out of the local roadside pool or stream to make it weigh more, since you bought it by the pound. Therefore everything had to be thoroughly cooked and you would only eat raw things that had a skin, like apples, oranges, and bananas. If you wanted to eat fruit or vegetables raw, then they would be put in the sink with water and a teaspoon of potassium permanganate, deep purple crystals that kill bacteria by oxidation on contact. They were then washed off, dried and eaten. I've used this same technique in modern times in Mexico, China and Nepal with great success, never as a child or adult having contracted any of these horrible parasitic gastrointestinal problems.

Prior to home leave, we often purchased fruits and vegetables on the weekends when we traveled to small villages around Shanghai. There were many in the area, some within walking distance, and all very nice and picturesque. Almost no one in these villages spoke anything but Chinese and in fact the dialect was (and is) often so localized that it was difficult to easily recognize what they were saying. We would go into teahouses for some green tea and a talk with the locals. These little homelike eating-places were a vast contrast from similar Japanese establishments. The Chinese were much more friendly and accommodating and would be more than happy to speak to you but everything was dirty. In Japan those places were very clean, spotless in fact, but unfriendly.

In the villages, as in the cities, shopkeepers would get up early and set a rattan chair or stool in a shady spot in front of their shop. There they would sit all day long with their family. Except for the odd, annoying, entrepreneurial type, they would never push you to buy. Out in the boiling sun, dogs and cats ran all over the place and were well tolerated.

Children would run around naked in the summer till they were three or four. In the winter they would wear clothes, but diapers were completely unknown. They had a slit in their pants from front to rear and until three or four or more years of age they would just squat down when they had to go. They learned that this was done outside on the sidewalk area (there were no real sidewalks outside the big city), or out in the fields. It was a very convenient and effective method, if somewhat contaminating. Adults used the covered buckets, again collected by the nightsoil man.

Rural Chinese children.

Sunny days the women washed clothes in the local stream that would run through most villages. There was much gossip, and much pounding of clothes on nearby rocks. A great deal of soap drifted downstream, contaminating the already contaminated water, before the women laid out the clothes to dry, or sometimes put them out on clotheslines.

The men in small villages (and big cities) would go out early in the morning with their birds in cages, mynah birds and many other smallish birds, colorful like parrots. There were usually two to a cage and the cage was covered with a surrounding cloth cover, which was removed when it wasn't too bright or too cold. The men would sit down and talk with others on benches outside for hours and watch their birds, much like Europeans would sit in a coffee house. They were usually delicate people with delicate creatures, but sometimes the birds were real fighters and aggressive to each other in the cage.

Birds were the vastly predominant pets to be paraded around in China, nearly always by men.

A favorite "sport" among Chinese that you can still see in the villages and cities is cricket fighting. Crickets are very strong for their size and will literally kill another cricket if taught to do so. Breeding of good fighters was as involved as the breeding of thoroughbred racehorses and although they didn't cost as much they were still very expensive and the bets were high on the winner.

The crickets are kept in 6 to 8 inch (15 to 20cm) round and 2 1/2 inch (6cm) high walled pottery dishes with flat covers. The covers are removed on the two dishes and, after everyone is assembled to watch and the bets are on, one of the crickets is generally moved into the other dish, or both are put in a third dish. The crickets then start to maneuver, avoiding each other around the edge, like boxers in the ring. The more aggressive may move forward in the attack stance but still unsure if he can kill the other one. (I don't know if females or males or both are used.) A little coaxing is needed and the owner has a 10 or 12-inch (25 to 30cm) long stem of a flax-like weed that the last 1/2-inch (1.3cm) is stripped off leaving a fuzzy end like a very slim paintbrush. He tickles the few hairs that stick out the back end of the cricket and this appears to make him mad, excited, and belligerent. The attack is on and the other master is trying to tickle his cricket to go after the other one, no holds barred.

Eventually one creature kills the other, bets are paid off and the winner goes home, often with a somewhat mangled cricket but nonetheless the winner. This is a very fine art and a big money maker among the professionals. Everyone had crickets and we all fought them, but not like the professionals.

Cockfights were the most vicious. They were very popular but not nearly as frequently seen because cocks were expensive, few people had them, and it was usually a well-rehearsed, theatrical-like production. Again, big bucks passed hands and the audience, (and the arena) was much larger. These beautiful birds all plumed in deep reds and golden feathers (even black ones) would fight to the finish, destroy each other. This was usually an all-afternoon affair, the day's entertainment.

If all this seems bloodthirsty, you have to remember that in the villages there were no radios, TV sets, or even entertainment halls. We are talking about the days when there was no electricity outside the city, and, except for cars and flashlights, batteries were unknown. Vacuum tube radio sets were readily available, but useless, though some peasants had crystal sets for wireless reception. Aside from the military machine of the Japanese army, which had really just battled through in order to take the large cities, the 20th century hadn't yet inundated the area outside Shanghai. Country life (and death) went on much as it always had.

Chapter 5

My Father and the Good Doctor

There was a point each summer when the weather got unbearably hot and people who could afford to headed north. You could only get to points north of Shanghai by ship, as highways weren't yet developed, and anyway there was the wide Yangtze delta to cross. Most kids went north to summer camp in places like Tsingtao (see appendix B for a description of the place) where the weather was cooler. That's where Godfrey went that summer of 1938, as he had almost every year of his life, for baseball, tug of wars, campfires, and all the usual activities of North American camps.

Godfrey at bat in Tsingtao.

Shortly after Godfrey left, Mother and I sailed north to Unzen, a coastal resort in Japan that provided cool ocean air and shade under the trees, not to mention hot springs.

Mother and I, with some of her friends, at Unzen Kanko Hotel.

It is indicative of the political situation at the time that my mother and I, taken to be Americans, were followed once by the Japanese secret service while out shopping for something as innocent as strawberries. Also indicative of the political situation was the fact that dad didn't accompany mother and me to Unzen. Things were beginning to fall apart for Standard Oil's operations in China due to Japanese aggression, and dad and his engineers were working ridiculously long hours trying to plug up the gaps.

It wasn't widely reported in the press, but when the Japanese bombed and sank the American gunboat *Panay* on December 12, 1937, they also destroyed twelve vessels belonging to Standard Oil. Both the gunboat and the Socony (Standard Oil) oil tankers had the day before evacuated dignitaries and employees of the company from the horrors of the "Rape of Nanking". The convoy sailed to avoid shrapnel and anchored twenty-seven miles (43 km) upstream from Nanking, about 221 miles (356 km) from the sea.[9] They thought they were safe there, however, Japanese airmen mistook the convoy for another, which was reportedly moving Chinese troops. Regardless of cause, the bombs were dropped on the ships and many died, including one Standard Oil captain named Carlson. Among the twelve ships, Standard Oil lost three of their largest river tankers: the *Mei Ping*, the *Mei Hsia*[vii], and the *Mei An*, each about 200 feet long, and carrying "…diverse cargo, including two grades of gasoline, lubricating oil, diesel oil, kerosene, and fuel oil…"[10] It was tragic and also very costly.

The oil company's claim for twelve vessels and sampans, amongst other damages, totaled $1,594,426. Japan paid right away (though not the full amount), but they claimed salvage rights, so the company lost most of its fleet. Things were tougher in that area and for the firm after that, trying to find alternate routes of distribution. Naval historian David H. Grover writes:

> Standard-Vacuum [Socony-Vacuum Oil Company] tried to operate with what was left of its fleet, but Japanese intimidation and dominance made those operations unpredictable at best. In 1938, for example, the *Mei Yun* was denied permission to go from the upper river to Shanghai for repairs; that same year, the *Mei Heng* was machine gunned by Japanese planes at Changsha, and the launch *Mei Foo V* was boarded by Japanese troops."

As chief engineer, RG must have been absolutely inundated by requests and reports from his engineers and their foremen. He also had to travel a great deal. Looking back with the advantage of hindsight, I think RG knew he was engaged in a sort of war. He was, in fact, deeply involved in the first real conflict between Japan and the economic interests of the United States.

I became involved in a war of my own when I returned to Shanghai late in the summer, though it was fought with lead soldiers rather than aircraft, bombs, and ships. The general of the leaden-army that opposed mine was my best friend Richie Hale, who lived down the street from me. His house was on the side of the estate away from the roads and open to the fields, so I would go over there, carrying reinforcements of lead soldiers.

Like most of the twenty families in our development, they were American. Richie's

---

vii Captained by A.B. Jorgensen, uncle of Lorry Jorgensen, Godfrey's best friend and future cabin mate across the Pacific to San Francisco for university. A.B. Jorgensen in fact piloted the ship out of Shanghai harbor when the boys left in 1941 on their incredible journey, described in chapter 7.

father, William A. Hale, was the president of the Underwriters Bank (out of New York) for the Far East. American households in and around Shanghai were less formal than their British counterparts, with less staff. Though Godfrey and I more and more considered ourselves Americans, our house was under the sway of my Northern Irish father and my English-born mother. Therefore it always surprised me that at the Hale's house you could just walk through the open gate and practically open the front door and go inside without being met then announced by a number one boy.

Sometimes Richie would answer the door, sometimes his mother Bess, or his sister Margaret, who was four or five years my senior, or the eldest, Ted, who was the same age as Godfrey, though they were never close friends. Then Richie and I would go through his back gate over to these tiny hills that were only waist-high, out into the open countryside. On these hills, the battles of our lead soldiers had been epic.

It was the middle of the afternoon, very near the end of the summer and the start of school. Richie and I wandered through the fields. We were doing nothing in particular, just avoiding the fact of the huge change about to occur in our lives. We were walking along a sort of track between two fields, reddish dirt kicking up from our shoes, disputing, testing each other's ideas with all the solemnity and abstraction of Socrates and Plato strolling down a street in Athens.

"So you're telling me that a Siberian tiger couldn't whip a polar bear in a fight?" Richie said.

"The polar bear is twice as heavy."

"But the tiger is faster."

"Look brainless, it doesn't even matter because they would never bump into each other, so the fight wouldn't ever happen."

"No, you're brainless — Siberia is really cold. Of course they've got polar bears in Siberia."

"It's still not cold enough."

"Oh yeah? This one time my mom bought a whole bunch of silk and we went to this seamstress downtown — "

" — What does that have to do with anything?" I cut him off.

"Let me finish! They were White Russians. The seamstress had all these pins in her mouth and I was thinking she might swallow some but she didn't, just kept sticking them into the silk, while mom just stood there looking in the mirror. It got really boring so I went into their kitchen. Her husband was sitting there reading the paper and I noticed he was missing his ear."

"Was there just a hole?"

"Yeah, just a hole and a bit of extra skin, and an earlobe."

"Gosh! Did you ask him what happened?"

"This is what I'm getting to. I asked him what happened to his ear and he said that the Bolsheviks took it."

"Did they cut it off?"

"That's what I asked him, but he said that when he was a kid they had to take the train across Siberia to get away from the Bolsheviks, and he had been awake for days and finally he fell asleep, but must have leaned against the window and it was so cold outside that his ear froze, then it turned black by the time they got to Harbin and it died."

"Baloney!"

"It's true."

"Gee whiz, I wonder if it hurt." A silence ensued. The missing ear had displaced the battle between the bear and the tiger in our thoughts as we walked home, two blonde-haired, blue-eyed boys under the Chinese sun. We were a few feet apart, and I was slightly ahead. It was the hottest part of the day, completely without wind. Towering sunflowers that grew here and there stood very straight and alert. "Hey," I said, staring ahead at the brown haze over the city, "when we get home, we should get some ice cream."

"Good idea Digger! I'm going to have vanilla. No, wait, maybe chocol — " Rich's voice suddenly ended, just vanished.

"Richie?" I spun around, and he was gone. A dragonfly buzzed past. Suddenly his head burst from the coppery, coil-colored ground, millions of maggots all over it, white like his eyes.

"Fuuuhhhhh!" He screamed, then threw up and started spitting. It took my brain a second to understand what had happened. The ground was that coil-color in a rough circle and he was in its centre. He'd fallen into an overflowing nightsoil cistern that had crusted over in the sun. I rushed to his aid, admittedly with some reluctance. Gosh, the stench was unbearable now the crust had been broken!

I grabbed his hands. It was a slippery grip, but I managed to pull him out of the cistern. It was like pulling a big fish over the transom of a boat. He flopped around on the ground, slipped in the overflow, trying to get up. Finally he stood before me, completely coated. We stared at each other for an instant. He looked like some sort of creature.

"Come on!" I cried. We broke out into a sprint. It was about a mile back to Hollyheath. I don't know if we broke four minutes, but I'm sure it was close. He was blubbering away in shock. Finally we ran through the gate and he was stripping off his clothes as we crossed the lawn. Ted was sitting on their back verandah reading.

"Holy mackerel! What happened?" he said, standing and putting down his book.

"I fell, I fell, I fell — "

"Richie fell in a nightsoil pot!"

"Don't go in the house. Hang on a second." Ted ran around the side, and came back dragging the garden hose. Rich was already down to his shorts, so his brother pulled the trigger. I jumped back, but still got some of the deflected spray. My shirt was covered, and my arms and hands too, so I pulled it off and wiped my hands, then when his little brother was dealt with, Ted sprayed me too. What a way to cap off the summer. And Richie didn't get sick at all.

Some days later another of that type of catastrophe occurred in the Hale household. Again, I was in their home and Ted, the eldest brother was disturbed by something tickling or even maybe biting him on his right leg, so he dropped his trousers and there was the biggest centipede one would ever want to see hanging from his undershorts. We got rid of that pretty quickly. Many years later, when the Hales lived on the East Coast of the United States, I had an opportunity to write to Teddy and I told him that I was starting to write a book or at least thinking about it and did he remember the story about the centipede hanging on his underpants and he said, "My gosh, I sure do" - and he said every year it seemed to get longer and longer!

But there was going to be an even better capper to the summer of 1938. Mother had worked hard for months getting the house in order, and decided to hold a large garden party on Labor Day, a very fancy affair. She invited all the 'important' people in town: doctors, lawyers, business chiefs, the judiciary, and many others, along with their children. There were going to be 300-odd people, a lot of mouths to feed, and a lot of details to attend to. In other words, this was going to be mother's kind of project.

The staff rose before dawn, and mother did too. By the time the sun was up, Coolie was in the pens at the end of the yard pulling chickens, ducks, and pheasants from their cages one by one and flapping like crazy. It was always quiet out in the country that time of day, except for the occasional passing of a train on the Shanghai Hangchow Ningpo Railway. Therefore the frantic squawks and clucks and quacks — each suddenly silenced by the dull thump of the hatchet against a block of wood — could be heard all the way up at the house. These sounds woke me, or maybe it was Cora barking at the sound, and I remember looking down from my window at the inexplicable sight of mother overseeing the gardeners digging three big holes in the middle of the lawn. While I learned some more Chinese characters from the charts in the bathroom, there was the sound of a heavy truck idling in the driveway then the grinding of gears as it pulled out the gate.

I went downstairs and there was a storm of activity in the kitchen. The butcher's truck had just arrived with half a cow, half a pig, and half a lamb, and Cook was running them through with spits. He still had managed to put together breakfast, though. Godfrey and dad were waiting for me outside on the terrace, where the meal, opulent and heavy on the cholesterol as usual, was already laid. We waited for mother to join us, but she kept darting back and forth, giving instructions to any member of staff (excepting Cook) who didn't look like they knew exactly what to do.

"Come on Gwen, breakfast is getting cold," RG said.

"I can't, the catering staff just called and they'll be here any minute." Mother sounded very tense.

"I'm sure Number One Boy can handle it." Dad looked very, very tired.

"No he can't. He can't make this perfect, which is what I intend. Besides, I'm not hungry anyway." And with this the front doorbell rang with the arrival of the additional staff hired to cater the event.

Dad shook his head and started to eat. Godfrey scooped mother's plate onto his. We ate our breakfast and watched while mother personally supervised the whole operation of setting up of dozens of round tables on the back lawn, all surrounding those mysterious holes that the gardener had dug. She not only required great precision as to where the tables were placed, but as to where the cutlery was placed on the table. It was a beautiful morning, already very warm when the extra servants arrived, on loan from neighbor's houses. They gathered around Cook for a briefing.

And then the mystery of the holes was solved. Already sweating, Coolie pushed a wheelbarrow with a shovel in it up from the back of the yard, and dumped a large load of charcoal briquettes into the central of the three holes. Then he shoveled the pile of dirt beside the hole into the wheelbarrow, carefully placing the sod on top, repeating this process for each pit. I ran down as soon as dad would let me leave the table to watch Coolie light the kindling, then catch the briquettes from the wood. I helped him set up the tripod, then we helped Cook carry out the spits so he could get the pig, the cow, and the lamb cooking very early.

Cook and I prepare for garden party in the yard of "Aqua Vista". Note the long pants and sleeves on both westerner and easterner on a hot summer's day, though the white color mitigated the heat somewhat.

The air filled with smoke and cooking smells and guests started showing up. Many of the doctors, lawyers, judiciary and Indian chiefs in general were there, the people who ran the city. They stood around talking shop and downing various drinks: gin and tonic, wines, or anything else that they might wish. It was a ball and everyone was having a marvelous time. We children mainly ran around, playing tag and other games. There were lots of women in hats and their husbands in shorts and blazers. A band played and this is how the afternoon passed.

Unfortunately, by an oversight the potato salad was left in the sun the entire time. Also, in spite of the fly net that covered the potato salad and just about everything else, flies probably came in contact with it.

After dinner, when Coolie was lighting the lanterns, the potato salad started to take its toll. In the dusk light it was difficult to see that guests were turning pale, but they started getting up and leaving without saying goodbye. There was the odd bout of vomiting in the front drive and before long, with the roaring off of Packards and Buicks, the guests were gone and the backyard was empty. The servants started to clear the tables and gather the chairs, the odd one thrown on its back by a guest in his or her haste to leave. My mother was inconsolable, until she started to feel the effects herself. Dad and Godfrey came down with it too, but I was spared. Oh sure, I felt slightly unwell, but that was only because, having avoided supper entirely, I had eaten several slices of pie accompanied by far too much ice cream.

The next day a large number of people in the executive area of the businesses and professions in Shanghai (including the American and British law courts) called in sick. Everyone who had eaten the potato salad was very ill at home, either in bed or running to the bathroom. Let me tell you, the city generally stopped functioning for a few days!

School of course started the next day, though many schools in Shanghai had to do without their principals. We westerners went to our various schools and the Chinese children to theirs, which were the result of a magnificent five thousand year old educational system. It started off with extremely intelligent Chinese, oftentimes from well-to-do families, of which there were very few in China until very recently. These intellectuals were sent to a major educational institute in Peking (Beijing) to learn all the political, intellectual, and economic aspects, and then in more recent times to learn sophisticated other languages to accommodate Chinese to ambassadorial, consular and political aspects that the Chinese were involved with world-wide. It's very interesting to note, I have learned it for the first time very recently, that in 1421 AD the Chinese "discovered the world".[viii]

Both Chinese boys and Chinese girls went to school, particularly in the cities such as Shanghai, Nanking, Chungking, Canton, etc., and there were fairly formal all-girl schools and all-boy schools. But of course as one went down to smaller and smaller villages, a lot of Chinese were never educated. They learned how to speak very much at home, very much as we in North America learn to speak in our home area, and I am sure this also applies to Europe, as well as the rest of the world. I can't guess what percentage of the population were even remotely educated in anything but the most rudimentary words in their dialect used in their village. It is said that if you knew 500 to 800 characters (ideograms) that you had the usual amount of education for an intelligent individual in your area. Then of course there was the problem of the interpretation of what you said with the various inflections in generally North China Mandarin and South China Cantonese (seven inflections) as I've already stated.

Schooling for westerners in China was specific to nationality, the basic idea that you would educate your children in preparation for university back home. The British sent their children to several different institutions, including the Anglican boy's and girl's Cathedral Schools, the Western District Public School, and the Thomas Hanbury Schools. French children went to College St. Jeanne D' Arc, the College Municipal, the Francis Xavier College for Boys, and the French Convent Schools, such as St. Joseph's. The Germans sent their children to Kaiser Wilhelm School, and the Americans to Shanghai American School (SAS). There were other, smaller institutions too, such as the Ellis Kadoorie Schools for Indians, and the Jewish School. This sort of process happened in all the treaty ports[ix], though Shanghai of course had more selection.

---

viii Here I refer to a magnificent book called: 1421 – The Year China Discovered the World. It delineates what I am sure very few people had heard of until quite recently, that the Chinese managed to travel amazing distances during a short period of time around 1400. It's author, Mr. Menzies, was a high ranking officer in the British Navy Submarine Corps for many years and he writes from a very knowledgeable source.

ix Refer to Appendix C for an excellent description of a private school in Tsingtao by my friend Peter Reeves, who is an alumnus of St. Giles.

But where was home for Godfrey and myself? Being sons of a Northern Irishman and a mother born in England who had lived for a long time in San Francisco and considered herself an American, we were clearly of ambiguous nationality. Up until home leave, my brother had been a student at College St. Jeanne D' Arc, and as a result spoke French fluently. At first glance this might appear to be a compromise between SAS and Cathedral. The truth was that RG simply thought it was the best school, and this was amazingly evolved of him. I say this because the college was Catholic and dad was from a family in Northern Ireland so Protestant that his father was an Orangeman, as was RG. I doubt dad ever marched for this group, but he loved to walk, albeit alone. Once he was out walking near our house and ran into some Marist brothers from College St. Jeanne D' Arc on their way to the Catholic cathedral atop the Zso-Zse hills. RG enjoyed talking to the brothers so much that he invited them back to the house for tea. This developed into quite a ritual and one or more brothers would oftentimes drop by on weekends on their way walking out to the ills. If somebody was home, we would have tea outside.

Dad let the question of nationality simply come down to how we boys felt about ourselves. Well, the Hales were typical of our neighbors at Hollyheath Estate, so Godfrey and I both had mostly American friends. And of course we had just spent a great deal of time in and around New York and San Francisco on home leave. Therefore we decided to be Americans and my mother, quite pleased, signed us up for SAS.

Shanghai American School was on Avenue Pétain in the French Concession, of course, with a street name like that. It occupied a large area with playing fields for American Football, soccer, tennis, track, and all the usual things you would find in a large, first-class private school in the United States or Canada. It occupied buildings of red brick with white pillars, cornices, etc., all watched over by the traditional private school clock tower. In fact, it reminded me of buildings I had seen in New York and the New England area while on home leave.

The Shanghai American School from Avenue Pétain. Administration building, with some classroom areas.

The classrooms were spacious and there was a large library (from which I still hold a couple of overdue books). All the usual laboratories were very well equipped. It was both a day school and a boarding school: there were barracks (excuse me, dormitories) for the children of missionary parents who lived all over China and chose to send their kids to school in Shanghai. This was in fact why SAS was founded, to prepare the children of American missionaries for universities in the states and elsewhere.

The school had evolved, however, to the point where there were a significant number of Chinese students, probably two per class, along with many other nationalities not numerous enough in the city, or not wealthy enough, to start their own schools.[x] For instance, there

---

x A January 1935 article in Fortune magazine lists thirty countries as comprising the ruling western class of 19,241 Shanghailanders. The four largest groups were the British (9,331), American (3,614), French (1,776), and Germans (1,592). The remaining 15% of Shanghailanders fell into twenty-six much smaller groups, such as two Cubans, nine Canadians (our friends in Canada, the Carneys* lived in Shanghai then too, accounting for half of them), all the way up to 385 Danish. Fortune also lists 2,113 Portuguese and 313 "...Polish (largely Russians in

was a Russian boy named Basil Chiliken in my brother's class both at College St. Jeanne D' Arc and SAS. Basil's father was editor of the local Red Russian communist newspaper, and a very brave man considering this was a city home to 25,000 angry, exiled White Russians. Maybe they let him live simply because his paper had no impact, with a total circulation of about ten! At any rate, the parents imported any notions of incompatibility; we children accepted each other and got along very well.

My grade one teacher was Miss Nesbit, whom I remember remarkably clearly. In fact, the second and third grade teachers Miss Shields and Miss Lingenfelter I remember equally clearly. All very nice people but none of them thought that I would get very far. You see they could not get me to work, even at that age and as early as at that time I was awarded the nickname of "The Procrastinator". Dad's unbelievable work ethic was yet to show itself in me.

Autumn came and the leaves turned color and fell. Our family settled into a depressing routine of individual isolation, each day the same. After driving dad to the Socony-Vacuum office on Szechuen Road very early in the morning, Driver would come back to the house and pick us boys up to take us to SAS. After dropping us off, Driver would go back to the house and pick up mother, drive her to lunch at the American Women's Club, or occasionally some other organization, then to a friend's home where they might play bridge all afternoon. After returning her back home, Driver would fetch us at school, take us to the French Club

disguise) in their "polyglot odds and ends" category, totaling about 6,000 and including people from areas such as the Philippines, Syria, Turkey, India and Afghanistan. 30,000 Japanese, the largest group of foreign nationals, is included in neither category and therefore not to be reckoned with. This in itself is quite telling of the time's blissful ignorance of what lay ahead. They also exclude the 25,000 White Russian exiles "…(whom as a group Shanghai does not classify as white men)." The reader who finds the wording offensive should know this is the language of the time. Fortune magazine was at the time an institution that heartily approved of fascism and all the great things Mussolini was doing in Italy.

* Senator Pat Carney and her twin brother Jim Carney were born in the Country Hospital, which was essentially the American hospital, as were my brother and I.

RG, as with almost all men in those days, was a chain smoker. He literally lit one cigarette with the other, all day long. He never got up at night or anything like that, but all day it was smoking. Once he was puffing away on his cigarette in the bathroom getting ready to go to work and then started to look around to see where his cigarette was. He was smoking it. It was only that he got to the bathroom door window that he saw in the reflection that the cigarette was in his mouth!

for swimming, tennis, or some other lessons then home for dinner with mother. Dad would finish work very late and spend about an hour at his club, having a drink, smoking a cigar or a cigarette, and discussing the political situation with the other chiefs. Then Driver would bring him home. The rule was still in effect that Driver had to get out of the car and show his deference to the Japanese checkpoint guards, so by this late point in the day the poor man had bowed many, many times.

The only real break in this dreary rhythm was when mother hosted formal dinner parties. In spite of the garden party debacle they were well attended. Perhaps the other families felt a little isolated too: our numbers were shrinking and these parties were shows of solidarity. War was generally considered to be well on its way, as evinced by growing migration out of Shanghai and back to home countries or, closer to 1941, to the perceived safety of the British fortresses in Singapore or Hong Kong. We had only returned from home leave because my loyal and duty-oriented father had strict orders from Standard Oil to keep things running smoothly. All I knew was that these were the only weeknights where I would ever see my dad — perhaps as another show of solidarity.

I remember one time, quite late, after the guests had left the table, my brother and I emptied all the liqueur and brandy that was left in glasses into one glass and drank it. WOW. Next we discovered this lovely green liquid crème de menthe in the pantry and got into it from time to time. I thought it was wonderful tasting and I'm sure Godfrey knew better. In any case, next party no crème de menthe to be found! Number One Boy blames Number Two Boy who blames Cook for having imbibed. Finally Amah tells Missy the truth about the Young Masters and the peppermint liqueur. Godfrey and I definitely heard about that one.

And so the fall went and I felt sad and I didn't know why. School was going extraordinarily well, in spite of my initial moniker. Perhaps that was the source of my sadness. There I was, learning extraordinary things at school every day, and wanting to tell my dad about them. But he just wasn't ever at home. Who else could I tell? Godfrey wasn't around either, as he was spending a great deal of time with his new friends from SAS and had discovered both motorcycles and girls. I would try to explain the secrets of the universe to Amah while she combed my hair ready for dinner, but she would just mutter and shuffle off with my shirt, dirtied from the day at school.

I would finally go downstairs to mother in order to tell her what I had learned. We two alone again, just like our eight months in California before dad and Godfrey could join us, only this time without her parents and close relations nearby. I think she was very lonely; the same forces that were dismantling Shanghai had somehow dismantled our family. Well, we didn't know it then, but a young Viennese physician named Arthur Peretz had recently arrived in town. His arrival would signal change in our family.

Arthur Peretz's passport.

Arthur Peretz was born in Romania in 1909, but I suspect he never actually liked to admit that. As far as he was concerned he was Viennese, because he had moved there at a very early age and was schooled entirely in Vienna. He graduated in Medicine from the University of Vienna in March of 1936, and then specialized there in internal medicine, which in those days took just a year to complete. Arthur's major specialty was nephrology: kidney diseases (*nephros* is Greek for kidney).

The young doctor in training was a true renaissance man. He was an academic, a lover of knowledge and quiet contemplation, yet had a large fencing scar cut diagonally across his left cheek, gained in a fraternity duel of which he never spoke. He spoke five languages fluently: German, English, Italian, Spanish, and French. He was gregarious. The fraternity to which he belonged was absolutely splendiferous in its trappings, likely never to be seen on this earth again. He was also helpful. In spite of his heavy course load, Arthur always found time to translate his lecture notes from German into English and French, which he would distribute to American, British, and French medical students for a fee. Arthur soon counted these thankful sons and daughters of Ambassadors, Consuls, and business leaders as some of his closest friends.

He graduated with his specialization in Nephrology in the summer of 1937 to very high expectations. Then he did something really quite fishy. Rather than settling down in Vienna and becoming a preeminent internist (as he later did in China and Canada), he jumped on a train down to Genoa and signed on as a ship's doctor aboard a cruise ship. Why he did this I'll never understand. Arthur was trained as a very high-end specialist, and the sort of person who needed to be constantly challenged; exactly what the position of ship's doctor could not offer. Even in more serious cases, the shipboard doctor's role is merely to stabilize the patient until he or she can be sent ashore to a hospital. To be sure, Arthur was a wanderer. I still have his passport and it is absolutely cluttered with visas from extensive travels through Europe during his younger years and his university years. Paris, Italy, Switzerland, Turkey; all over the place. Whatever his reasons were, Arthur went to sea.

The ship had a lingering, habitual passenger, the Crown Prince (who was waiting to become king) of a Southeast Asian country (which must by necessity remain nameless), plus his entourage. He and Arthur, both young men, neither really able to relate to the crew yet constantly aboard, became friends. In my study I have a painting that the Crown Prince gave to Arthur.

One morning as the ship steamed on the deep rolling blue just north of Tunis, the Crown Prince came to Arthur's office in terrible pain. The young doctor quickly diagnosed a kidney stone in the ureter, the very small tube that connects the kidney over about a 6 inch (15 cm) distance into the bladder. A hard kidney stone traveling down that tube is an extremely painful movement, but if you dilate up the tube with some medication, the kidney stone will pass down much more quickly. Arthur gave the Crown Prince an injection of atropine, which is a dilator of certain tubes in the body and a pretty standard treatment for kidney stones, both then and now. It worked like a charm.

The Crown Prince of course was very impressed by this, and asked the doctor if he would like to come and be his personal physician at Court. This was a very seductive offer to Arthur, promising more extensive wandering and adventure, so it seems he may have accepted. Luckily for him they had several more weeks together on board ship before it was time to return east with the entourage. With the passing of the kidney stone, and through a winter of fencing on the boat deck, shooting skeet off the stern, and drinking scotch at the bar, Arthur diagnosed a disconcerting thing in the Crown Prince: absolutely perfect, robust health. The Crown Prince had the constitution of an ox.

Arthur may have been an adventurer, but his utmost desire was to be a well-trained specialist physician. The Crown Prince, from a medical point of view, would be uninteresting and unrewarding; it would be a waste of Arthur's talent, though he probably wouldn't have worded it this way. As winter became spring and the ship approached Venice, from which the entourage would depart for the east, Arthur pondered how to back out of what was no doubt considered an honor.

Unfortunately, an overly adequate excuse came about on March 12th, 1938, with the *Anschluss*, Nazi Germany's invasion of Austria. Arthur knew right away that he had to go home and be with his family. As soon as the ship made port, he took leave of the very understanding Crown Prince, and got on the first train from Venice to Vienna. Surrounded by trunks and his entourage, I'm sure that the Crown Prince shook his head at the good doctor's bravery. Arthur was a scientist, not at all religious (In all my years with Arthur as my stepfather I never heard him discuss anything about Judaism or really get into any discussions regarding religion), but he was of Jewish descent and the Nazis must have known this.

This is a book about China so I'm not going to get into a long history of Austria after the Nazis took over. Suffice it to say life became very difficult for Jewish people. There was widespread vandalism of businesses (culminating on November 9th with *Kristallnacht*), systematic seizure of property, and summary arrests. People looking for visas in order to emigrate besieged the Vienna consulates of various non-Axis nations, however most countries closed their doors. One notable exception was the Chinese consul-general, Ho Fengshan, by widespread account an extremely cultured, kind, and gentle man.

Fluent in both English and German, Ho Fengshan had arrived in Vienna with his family in 1937, having been appointed secretary to the Chinese Embassy. He likely was to become ambassador. However, in May of 1938 the Chinese Nationalist government reduced the embassy to a consulate, since they already had an embassy in Berlin. Formerly they had needed two embassies for two distinct countries, Germany and Austria, but why have two embassies for one country, a "unified Germany"? This was a form of recognition of the validity of the Anschluss by the Chinese government, to say unification was valid. Until the Americans entered World War II there was a close relationship between the Nazis and the Kuomintang:

> Generalissimo Chiang Kai-shek, the [Nationalist Chinese] president of the time, was close to the German government. He used German military advisers and weapons and had sent his younger son, Wei-guo, to be trained by the Nazis. Wei-guo became a second-lieutenant in the German 98th Jaeger Regiment and took part in the Austrian Anschluss before returning to China.[12]

Ho Fengshan was appointed consul-general, head of the reduced operation. At great risk to himself and his family, both in terms of grievous damage to his career as a diplomat for the regime of Chiang Kai-shek (he disobeyed direct orders from Ambassador Chen Jie in Berlin to stop issuing visas), as well as possibly violent reprisal from the Nazis, Ho Fengshan gave visas to anyone who asked. This was critical because, though you didn't need a visa to enter Shanghai or any of the other free ports in those days, you needed a visa to *somewhere* in order to exit Austria. Most people to whom consul-general Ho granted visas intended merely to exit the country on the Chinese stamp in their passport then emigrate to other areas, including Palestine. This of course enraged the Nazis, who confiscated the building in which the consulate was housed, claiming it was owned by a Jew. Then the Chinese government cut his funding. Undaunted, Ho Fengshan kept up the good work, renting a new office and paying for the expenses of the consulate out of his own pocket. In this way the good consul saved innumerable lives and is a great, unsung hero of the war.

Arthur certainly took the precaution of the Chinese exit visa, as page 21 of his passport bears Ho Fengshan's stamp, dated June 14th 1938. I call it a precaution, because Arthur stayed in Vienna a while longer: he only initiated his exit from Austria in late July and his exit stamp is dated August 30th 1938. I don't know what happened to the rest of his family, as he never talked about it. Perhaps they returned to Romania, but this is only speculation. All I know is that Arthur's brother Poldi (Leopold) was in Shanghai during the war, and I visited this brother in Europe some years later.[xi]

Not only did Arthur linger before finally choosing to leave, but his passage to Shanghai was different than that of other holders of Chinese visas, in that it showed several opportunities for choice and free will. I'll explain. The Nazis exerted severe restrictions as to how much money Jewish refugees could leave the country with. It was a pittance, enough for passage and little else. I quote Stella Dong at length on this, as a norm against which to compare Arthur's passage:

Almost all of them [Jewish refugees] came through Genoa, on the Italian Lloyd Triestino liners, which brought them to the Chinese port after a monthlong voyage that took them through such ports as Port Said, Aden, Bombay, Ceylon, Singapore,

---

xi We met for dinner in Vienna in January of 1971 when I was on a stopover en route to East Africa. My wife Sue and I, and our long time and very good friends from Vancouver, Elizabeth and Joe Jarvis, were going to spend some time at Treetops, William Holden's safari preserve in Kenya. (A small aside; just after we arrived at the preserve, unbeknownst to us, Bill Holden and his wife flew into the private landing strip late that afternoon. After they landed, we six dined together then viewed a new documentary about Ostriches the actor had just made. By breakfast our new and very famous acquaintances were gone.) This was just before Idi Amin took over Uganda. At any rate, Poldi was under the impression that Arthur had died weeks before. I told him that this wasn't so, that Arthur was alive and well and had seen us off from Vancouver the day before. Poldi took some convincing before he would believe me. Odd!

Manila, and Hong Kong, but did not allow them to disembark until they reached Shanghai. When they set foot on the Hongkew passenger jetty, some of the men in heavy woolen suits, the only clothes they had, few were prepared to begin life in an Oriental metropolis. Most were seriously short of funds, as the Nazis had allowed them to leave for Shanghai only on the condition that they carry out no more than twenty reichsmarks in cash and one suitcase. Moreover they were required to buy their own transportation, and the Italian liners on which they traveled charged more than double the usual rates. As a result, the newcomers arrived in desperate financial straits.[13]

When Arthur finally chose to leave Austria, he took a train to VENICE (rather than Genoa) where he boarded a ship and set sail for the Far East on September 1st. He was in no way a prisoner aboard ship, as his passport shows that he disembarked from the ship in Colombo in Sri Lanka on September 14th. He also disembarked in Singapore, where, as his passport shows, he got a visa to enter the U.S.A. that was good for a year from September 19th 1938.

US visa in Arthur's passport.

Yet even with this coveted visa, virtually unobtainable from isolationist America of the 1930s, he continued on to Shanghai rather than going to the United States. Why?

It could be argued that Arthur didn't have the funds to travel to the United States. Yet he went to the trouble to apply for the visa. Furthermore, had his funds been so limited, he would have taken the more onerous route through Genoa rather than Venice. Also, upon arrival in Shanghai, whereas his compatriots settled into the slums of Hongkew, Arthur moved directly into a nice apartment in the French Concession at 1710 Avenue Joffre. Therefore, on top of the legal ability to travel to the United States, I would argue he had the funds to do so. Why on earth didn't he go? I have for a long while suspected that Arthur had work to do in Shanghai beyond just medicine.

Dr. Alfred Schwarz
Wien VI.,
Gumpendorferstr.72

MEDICAL CERTIFICATE

Place: Vienna

Date: ...30.11... 1938.

I hereby certify that I have examined ...*Mr. Arthur Peretz*...
and find *him*.. not to be mentally or physically defective in any way, that ..*he*.. is not afflicted with tuberculosis in any form or with an infectious, loathsome or contagious disease, that ..*he*.... is not suffering from favus, lepresy, framboesia or yaws, trachoma, syphilis or scabies.

....
Medical adviser to the
British Consulate.

Mentally defective includes:
Idiots
Imbeciles
Feebleminded persons
Insane persons
Epileptics
Persons having previously had attacks of insanity
Persons of constitutional psychopathic inferiority
Persons suffering from chronic alcoholism.

I also certify that *Mr. Arthur Peretz*
has never been in a mental hospital nor in prison.

Vienna, ...30.11..... 1938.

Letter stating Arthur isn't insane, or suffering from various other quaintly named disorders.

There are two ways of interpreting why Arthur obtained a certificate from Dr. Schwarz, Medical Advisor to the British Consulate in Vienna. The most obvious would be that he wanted to emigrate to Britain and this was to back up his application for entry, which apparently wasn't sought, as an entry visa to Great Britain does not appear in Arthur's passport. Two things contradict this. First, the examination was dated June 20th, which was a week after visiting consul-general Ho. If Arthur had been in a great hurry to leave, he would simply have exited like all the others on the Chinese visa, then gone where he wanted to. (Recall he did not go to the States, though he could have.) As to the second contradiction, Arthur's name is handwritten on the blank lines of the Medical Certificate as "Mr. Arthur Peretz" as opposed to "Dr. Med. Arthur Peretz." In Austria many people going through various university faculties get the designation "doctor", so the Med. Designation would have been important. Surely Arthur, under usual circumstances, would have put his best foot forward and made damn sure the British knew he was a physician, and not only that, a talented internist, and therefore a highly desirable potential citizen. Of course, this is not a direct argument, but it raises doubt.

We know that Arthur was in contact with the British, yet not seriously applying for a visa. As I've stated, he had British and American friends in university whose parents tended to be in the diplomatic services. These consuls and ambassadors would no doubt have met Arthur when their sons and daughters invited him over for dinner. They would have learned that he could not only speak five languages, but could in fact switch between them mid-sentence; a sort of parlor trick that he would do over dessert. This would have been noted. It would also have been noted that Arthur was incredibly charming and socially at ease. And with his sudden departure to be a ship's doctor, it would likely have been noted that he was adventurous.

When Arthur returned from the winter of cruising the Mediterranean, there would most certainly have been a dinner party welcoming him back. Even though his medical school compatriots may have left for England and the States, some of their parents would be there and still be smitten with Arthur. Let's imagine one.

The conversation over dinner would most certainly have contained three elements that could combine into an idea. First, there would be a certain amount of gossip regarding consul-general Ho handing out the Chinese visas. Second, of course the conversation would also dip into anecdotes of atrocities witnessed on the streets of Vienna. Third, when the subject became too dark, the young guest of honor would most certainly have been asked about his winter at sea, and Arthur would have recounted the luxurious excesses of his new friend the Crown Prince. In other words, something new would have been noted about Arthur; that he had developed a rather important connection in the Far East.

An idea could have formed over dinner. Both the British and the Americans were concerned as to the fate of their enterprises in the Far East. As my father RG could at that time attest to, the Japanese were slowly but systematically exerting force in order to control western interests. What would Arthur care? Well, although the Tripartite pact of 1940 was yet to come into existence, Japan had already signed the anti-Komintern (anti-communist) agreement of 1936 with Germany, as well as the November 6th, 1936 protocol that brought Italy into the agreement. The Japanese were clearly allies of Nazi Germany, and therefore were the good doctor's enemy. Perhaps the diplomat father of a former fellow student made an executive decision, and asked Arthur to join him in his den for a cigar and a little talk.

Arthur could never tell me the truth, as the standard 50-year moratorium on such matters outlived him, but I've often suspected that Arthur was recruited by the OSS (Office of the Strategic Services) — a blanket organization for both American and British intelligence — before he left Austria. I gather it was with their support that he went to Shanghai.

Interestingly, when he finally disembarked onto the Bund, Arthur had to gain the support of the Nazis in order to put the plan into action. That is, the Chinese naturally wanted proof from Arthur's country of origin that he was qualified to practice medicine. With the Anschluss he was now a citizen of Germany — his passport is covered in Swastikas — so a trip to the German consulate was necessary. Amazingly, with the following document, Arthur was granted certification to work as a doctor in Shanghai.

Deutſches Reich

Certificate

This is to certify that the German Citizen
        Dr. med. Arthur Peretz
born May 28th 1909 at Itzkany, Siebenbuergen (Romania)
is in the possession of a Diploma, issued by the
University of Vienna on March 18th 1933, according to
which he was entitled to practice Medicine in Austria,
which is now a part of Germany.
Shanghai, 24th October 1938.
                        Consulate General for Germany.

fee 11 ℳ - 22 $

*German consul grudgingly acknowledges Arthur's qualifications,
albeit their originating in a nonexistent country.*

What are the possible reasons for such complicity from a representative of the German government? Perhaps the consul who signed wasn't a member of the Nazi party, and, like consul Ho in Vienna, did not follow his government's line. Doubtful. Notice the wording of the document, the grudging tone. More likely Germany granted affirmation so as to not annoy the Shanghai Municipal Council by interfering with Jews finding employment, and therefore not being idle, and therefore not being both a drag on the economy of the city, and not becoming a malcontented danger.

So, certified by the Nazis, Arthur set up a posh practice just off the Bund and within walking distance of the Shanghai General Hospital. This was a posh address, rented with, I gather, funds provided by British and American agencies. He also had an office in the hospital, one with a bird's-eye view of the harbor, which was choked with Japanese warships.

Shanghai had gained both a doctor and a spy. However, until things heated up politically, medicine prevailed. One of Arthur's first patients was an important executive by the name of Robert Gregg. It was definitely serious, because dad stayed home a full day, and then the next, with abdominal pains. RG was the stiff upper lip sort of a man, so there was no moaning and rolling around in bed, but when I went in to see him he clutched at his stomach and was clearly in incredible pain. Doctor Gardner, our family physician, had already been out to the house. He suspected that RG was suffering from severe kidney stones, and contacted the most prominent specialist in the field, Dr. Arthur Peretz.

I remember when Arthur arrived at the house. Mother led him up the stairs and they chatted. The odd European accent drew me out of my homework. I jumped up, cracked open the door to my room and peeked out into the hall. Walking past, Arthur stopped and turned and smiled, and I remember being fascinated by his scar. He said hello, then continued on to the bedroom where he set in motion his magic cure, likely using the same dilator drug as for the crown prince. Arthur Peretz had a new friend in Robert Gregg, and in my mother. Before long there was conversation and laughter, like magic.

What can I say really, except that once my father was back on his feet he practically sprinted back to the office and my mother continued to be alone. Both men were absolutely phenomenal people. RG was an excellent man, brilliant, hardworking, principled, and disciplined. Arthur was a most intelligent and thoughtful person, who respected everybody, from the youngest child to the oldest senile individual, as long as they were respectable people, and not criminals. My mother had fallen in love with Arthur, and she made the choice she had to make.

It is not my desire or intention to explore the mechanics of the divorce. I include only a few details as the steps that led to my having a doctor/spy for a stepfather a little less than two years later. The basic facts are that my mother moved out in May of 1939 and took an apartment downtown. For the time being I stayed at the house with RG. The divorce was finalized by September of 1939, by the time Hitler and Stalin were carving up Poland. The onset of war in Europe was when Arthur began to court my mother.

Oddly, or perhaps not so oddly, I don't really recall much of this time. Basically I buckled down at school, took solace in my work like dad did. In late spring Godfrey joined the American corps of the SVC.

Godfrey with the American SVC unit guarding the entrance to the International Settlement. Note the WWI trench boots.

In an unrelated incident Godfrey accidentally shot himself in the foot with a .22 caliber rifle. He had been sitting in his bedroom with his feet up on the windowsill, picking off birds in the tree outside, and from these details I suppose it's easy to fill in the blanks. The bullet missed all the bones and there was no permanent damage. That summer (of 1939) I went to the boy's camp up north in Tsingtao.

Ironically, RG's work had finally tapered off a bit by the fall of 1939, when the divorce went through. He had seen the engineering department through the repercussions of the *Panay* incident, but with the Japanese blockades on the Yangtze, the oil business (and most business in Shanghai) was unavoidably contracting. Suddenly I saw a lot more of dad.

RG had a passion for auctions, and he took me to one on a Saturday in October of 1939. I sat next to him as he bid on various haberdashery, finally winning a bid on some ties. Number One Boy received the delivery of a large box a few days later, and opened it. Inside there were two or three hundred dark green ties with white polka dots, all identical! I helped dad address packages and send out the ties to his many, many friends as early Christmas gifts. This became a bit of a Shanghai legend. For the next year or two, people wearing the would meet each other and say, "You must be a friend of Bob Gregg's! How do you do?" It was a very special club.

I remember my birthday supper in February of 1940. Mother had organized a party for me and my friends the coming weekend, but this evening was with dad. I blew out nine candles while Amah looked on and Godfrey and dad sang. Then Godfrey roared off on his motorcycle to the SVC guard post, and dad and I ate the cake. Getting up and pouring himself a coffee, dad asked what I had learned thus far in school. Well, I had learned a lot of things, but at that time I was most interested in the sort of rudimentary chemistry taught to nine-year olds. The next evening he brought home stands, beakers, graduated cylinders, and we started fitting out my own lab in one of the spare rooms in the servants' quarters. Tucking me in that night, dad promised a trip out to the Installation for some basic chemicals. I was too excited to sleep.

The day came and Driver took us to the Bund just as the Standard Oil launch pulled up at the Canton Jetty, just down the street from head office. The Whangpoo looked like mercury[xii], flowing slowly under a gray spring sky. We jumped aboard, and stood on the foredeck, my chest swollen with pride at being with my dad on important business.

RG on Standard Oil launch on his way to the Installation.

Once we got in our seats in the stern, the pilot gunned the diesel engine and we turned downstream, soon passing the *Idzumo*, moored in front of the Japanese consulate, its guns still pointed vaguely in the direction of the Customs House. We motored past the godowns (warehouses) and wharfs of Hongkew. Seagulls screeched and cried, dipped and dived over our wake and the wind was in my hair. Suddenly the pilot throttled back and jumped up from his seat. He peered over the windscreen into the water, started wrenching the wheel back and forth, muttering into his cigarette. Dad and I stood up to see what the pilot had seen and my stomach went up into my throat. We were idling through a cluster, a sort of reef of human corpses floating in the current. Something hard bumped against the hull, presumably a head.

---

xii Which I had seen for the first time in science class, when a kid dropped a thermometer, and its mercury leaked on the floor.

My mouth dropped open and RG looked at me with those cold blue eyes, waiting to see my reaction I suppose. I closed my mouth and swallowed hard, but mimicked his cool demeanor. I must have done a good imitation, as he clearly made the decision not to try to protect me like he had with the soldier down the well. What would have been the point? There are illusions and there are facts. It was a fact that floating corpses surrounded us, just as it was a fact that we were living in a city under siege.

Cursing in Chinese, the pilot alternately worked the throttle back and forth, left the wheel, ran forward and used the gaff to clear the way forward.

"Are they really people? They almost don't look like people," I said, pointing to one particularly corpulent corpse, drifting facedown in the cold swirl. It was green. By this point, having watched a few pass by, I found a cool, impassive and clinical place, a place I have found many times since, daily, in fact, as a doctor.

"Oh they're people alright. Chinese. It's just that they're swollen."

"With water?"

"No, with the gases that are produced by putrefaction. The bacteria in the corpses continue to live even though the person is dead, and they produce methane, hydrogen sulfide, and carbon dioxide. The stomach and chest cavity contain the most bacteria so they inflate like balloons. That's why they float."

"Are they men or women?"

"The ones that float face-down, like that one over there, they're women."

"And men float face-up?"

"Yes."

"Why?"

"Something to do with length of arms and legs, relative buoyancies and drag. But there was a Roman philosopher named Pliny the Elder who wrote the first encyclopedia. He once said that, 'The corpses of men float face upward, those of women face down, as if nature wished to respect the modesty of dead women.'"

"Oh." I watched a man's face drift by, lapped by our slow wake. He had empty eye sockets, plucked clean by birds. I wondered then if the women, being face-down, got to keep their eyes from the hungry gulls...but then I thought of all the hungry fish.

"But why are they dead?" I asked my dad.

"Well, some may have died of old age and their families couldn't afford to bury them, but I bet the Japanese killed most."

"Will we fight the Japanese? Everyone at school says we will."

"It's extremely likely."

"When?"

"Soon. Quite soon," dad said, as if reassuring me.

The launch finally cleared the reef of corpses and the pilot throttled up the engine as we headed downriver to the Installation. I stared at our turbulent wake once more. We grow up in increments. Sometimes those increments are much too big.

Chapter 6

War in Europe

My mother took custody of me at the end of July in 1940, but Godfrey stayed with dad at Hollyheath. Not at all dramatic, because I knew I was to come back to stay on weekends from Friday evening until Monday morning when Driver would take me directly to SAS. One very warm morning both of them helped Driver load my trunk and Amah's suitcase into the car. I looked up at the house for a while then got in the back, knowing I had left behind clothes, a lot of toys, and my lab.

"Wei," said Amah from inside the car. "Come."

Driver took us past the torture pond (with two future inhabitants wading in at bayonet-point), over the tracks, and up Great Western Road toward the International Settlement. We drove past the garrison of the Seaforth Highlanders and I took solace in the fact that this was going to be a regular route. Every Friday evening when Driver took me back home, the fluttering Union Jack on the right hood pin would induce a salute. Little did I know that the entire British force would march out of the garrison and ship out to Europe only a few weeks later. With the capitulation of France and Holland, the notion that the conflict in Europe was a "phony war" was long gone. Things had gotten much worse over there and men were needed. Besides, the British had analyzed the situation and decided that Shanghai was not a position they could hold against the Japanese, so why lose the men? On the Allied side, this would leave only the SVC and a contingent of 750 U.S. 4th Division Marines.

Mother had been living in a French Concession apartment near the racetrack, but there wasn't enough room there for Amah and me as well. As a solution she had moved in with friends, the Scott family: Scotty, his wife Mary, and their daughter Alva, for the six weeks until she was to marry Arthur. The Scotts owned the International Funeral Parlor. They lived in a large house with a lot of lawn around it, and then the actual mortuary was about half a city block away and one could not be seen from the other. The address was 207 Kiaochow Road (Jiaozhou Lu), and it was the major Caucasian funeral parlor in Shanghai, and probably in all of China. An odd place to wait for a wedding.

It was a time of great boredom for me. The other kids were up at camp, and besides, I didn't know anyone around that area. One morning I wandered across the grass towards the mortuary. Probably just morbid curiosity. I heard hammering and other noises of carpentry from an outbuilding, and walked through the door. Inside there were Chinese craftsmen building coffins, really beautiful things, ornately carved, made of very fine wood. They kept glancing up from their work at me, the American kid staying with his mother over at the house. Well, one of the craftsmen said something to me (probably "bugger off, na-ku-ning!") that I guess I really didn't like, because I picked up a hammer from a bench and threw it as hard as I could at his head. Fortunately I missed him, but the hammer took a big chunk out of the lid of the coffin, splintered the wood. Boy, did I hear about that one!

Amah didn't like my going out alone, but I became skilled at getting away. Boy it was a long month I had to kill until school started. A couple of weeks passed until I finally ran into a kid my own age named Henry Tinson.[xiii] He was a student at Cathedral School and like many of the British he lived in the Great Western Road area, only a few blocks from the funeral home. Anyway, we rode our bikes all over the International Settlement that summer and got to know the city extremely well. The hot, humid, polluted wind blew in our hair and made our eyes water as we peddled through the hustle and bustle of the city. There were rickshaw accidents, pickpockets, and beggars.

---

xiii Both of Henry's sons are now veterinarians. One lives in Calgary, and the other in Riyadh, taking care of thoroughbred horses for the Saudis.

Beggar in cold winter weather, northern China.

Shanghai beggar boys have been portrayed in books and movies almost exclusively as pleading "no gotti mama, no gotti papa, no gotti whisky soda!" They did say this, but only in the specific circumstance of cars pulling up in front of the theatre in the early evening. Beggar boys would stand around crying this out, hoping to be picked out to guard a car. If you didn't have a driver it was in your interest to pick a boy, because their offer of security implied its opposite action. You would therefore pick the biggest, toughest looking beggar boy to watch over your car.

Henry and I would race along until something caught our eyes, then skid to a stop. The sidewalk dentists were especially fascinating to watch. All over China, in little villages and cities, there were remarkably capable dentists who used the sidewalk as their office. They were available every five or six blocks in pretty much all directions in Shanghai, and they were growing more numerous as war became imminent and western dentists headed for home.

The dentists brought along their entire apparatus: something like a toolkit, a chair, and a stand that stood on three or four legs, with a cable running out the top to a drill. I have no idea how the Chinese dentist may have kept his drills and other aspects of dentistry free of bacteria, because there was certainly no electrical input into the whole affair. There was a fairly large flywheel on the bottom of this structure, impelled by a connected pedal that the dentist pumped his foot up and down upon, spinning the shaft, the cable, and therefore the drill bit. Amazing that he could do this with his foot, sweating like crazy while simultaneously accomplishing the delicate task of drilling out a cavity, and all in front of an audience of onlookers that would usually gather.

You'd sit down because you had a sore tooth. There was no local anesthetic. Instead, the dentist gave you a little bottle. It would be no more than 10 ml of opium, dark brown, readily available anywhere and they came in these little bottles sold in, I think, 10 x 10 or 12 x 12 bottles per box. Opium of course was what the city had been built upon, and so was available everywhere. You could get it in shops, easy as buying a pack of gum.

So, you'd drink it,[xiv] and the dentist would watch your face for the signs of intoxication, then start drilling away, no X-rays, nothing like that. The faster his foot moved up and down the faster the drill went and the quicker he could get his work done. They had all of the accoutrements to fill the hole that they had drilled, to pull a tooth if necessary, and all the

---

xiv I only had this as a one-time experience, but I was about 11 years old, war had begun and there was a shortage of dentists, so I had to go to a sidewalk dentist. The dentist gave me the bottle and just said, "drink it", and I drank it and my gosh within five or ten minutes I was swimming around all over heaven! I have never tasted opium since. It's actually pretty horrible tasting stuff, but certainly very effective as an analgesic (painkilling) agent.

other things that dentists seem to do. Obviously, no high-class reconstitution of dental work could be done, but it was remarkable how efficient these people were. I have no idea of what their training may have been like, but you sat down for 15, 30, or 60 minutes. People would stand around and watch the dentist drilling. These were generally "lower class" individuals who wanted to be amused for a while, to see something a little different. The dentist would move on from street corner to street corner.

The end of August finally came and Rich Hale and my other Hollyheath pals were back from summer camp. School started after Labor Day, but it felt pretty strange, as there were only about half as many students as the previous year, and many of the kids we knew were gone. A lot more Americans were evacuating the area than British, whose home country was in a state of war. Still, we stuck to the old rituals we had established over two years, such as lunch at the Chocolate Shop, which was just a block to the right of the school gates. After school we would stand at the gates and wait for Rich's and the other boys' drivers to pick them up.

We were having all sorts of new adventures on the weekends. War was increasingly on people's minds, both the adults and the kids, and in us it manifested pretty clearly in how we played. We had moved from lead soldiers to shooting at each other with BB and slug guns. (Yes, someone did lose their eye!) One day we were standing at the gate and planning the weekend's battle when Henry Tinson rode up on his bicycle. I introduced him to Rich and the others. The conversation quickly resumed its BB trajectory until everyone had been picked up. I unlocked my bike and Henry and I rode back up towards the funeral parlor. He was interested in our war games, and of course I probably exaggerated just a little, especially about the previously mentioned shooting-out of an eye that definitely wasn't my fault.

Mother and Arthur's wedding was held outdoors on the grounds between the Scott's house and the mortuary on September 14th 1940. After the party Arthur drove mother and me, Amah, and a lot of luggage to his apartment at 1710 Avenue Joffre. The building was made of yellow brick, four stories high and fronted by balconies; pretty standard for the French Concession.

There was no Number One Boy to meet us, nor even a Number Two Boy, so we all carried various pieces of luggage up the stairs to the second floor. Three doors faced the second floor landing on which we stood, while Arthur dug around for his keys. The door to the left, I would learn, was to Ray Uyashima's apartment. He was Japanese by descent, but as American as you can get, to the point of owning probably the only Harley-Davidson in wartime Shanghai, yet somehow he managed to bring in a new one every year. It would sputter and roar mornings when Ray started the engine to go to work. The door directly ahead bore a brass plaque: **Dr. Med. Arthur Peretz**, and was the entrance to his waiting room, which connected to his lab and to his office, which in turn had a doorway to the rest of his apartment, so you could get in through this door, but the proper entrance was to the right off the landing.

There was a long hall that ran through the center of the apartment. We put everything down and Arthur gave us a quick tour. There were two doors to the left: the first to Arthur's office, the second to the dining room and living room. On the right side of the hall the kitchen was through the first door, next there were three closed storage closets, and finally the door to the master bedroom opposite the living room and dining room. Amah and I moved our luggage into the office area: the examination table was to be my bed and she would sleep on the sofa in the waiting room.

While Amah unpacked my things into Arthur's credenza I made a beeline for the lab, and took the cover off the microscope. It had electric illumination, which I flipped on. There was no slide clipped on the stage, but there were clean slides in box, and a dropper, so I plucked a hair, and placed it on a slide, along with a drop of water, then put it on the stage. I peered through the lens and focused, then turned the objective lenses until the lone hair looked enormous.

At the time I was growing vertically much more than horizontally, and as a result my knees were the biggest parts of my legs. I slept best on my side, so this became really uncomfortable. My solution was to put a pillow between my knees and I used to catch hell about it from Amah, who thought this somehow was a bad thing to do. This was an ongoing conflict, and it had been bad enough out at Hollyheath with her sleeping quite a distance away, downstairs and in the servants' quarters. Now she was going to be right next-door! Well, that first night I went to bed with a pillow between my knees anyway. It had been a long day and I quickly fell asleep.

Shanghai was (and is) an incredibly noisy city. I awoke early to honking horns and frequent Avenue Joffre streetcars rumbling below the office window. The early sunlight projected through thin white curtains at a sharp angle on the wall, illuminating Arthur's many degrees. I stared at them, trying to decipher the German words, but made no move to get up. I suppose I was sullen, as it was Sunday and I should have been out in the countryside around Hollyheath Estate with Rich and my other friends. I missed Godfrey, dad, the dogs, and the servants. Eventually there was a knock at the door.

"Dwight, are you awake?" It was Arthur.

"Yes," I answered. He peered around the door and smiled, and again I noticed that fantastic fencing scar.

"Get dressed and come on out. I've got a surprise for you."

I put on my dressing gown and went out into the hall. Arthur was wearing a lab coat and holding the doorknob to the closed door of the largest of the three closets. Mom was standing at the end of the hall with a cup of coffee and smiling at the two of us. Amah was clanking pots in the kitchen. Arthur opened the door and when I saw what was inside the closet my eyes nearly bugged out of my head.

It was a lab to rival my Hollyheath setup. In terms of equipment, I'm not talking about a little chemistry set kit. I'm talking about a full laboratory with Erlenmeyer flasks, test tubes, Bunsen burners, everything I needed. The walls were decorated with a periodic table of the elements, a chalkboard, and other charts. He'd also put some extra shelves in and they were chockablock with chemicals. Being a doctor, Arthur had access to various chemicals from companies like Merck and Imperial Chemical Industries,[xv] and these were invariably in 100 gram bottles. They were beautifully labeled, lovely things. I rushed into my new lab to see what the labels said. It was a small space, so Arthur stood at the door while I checked on everything.

---

xv How important was chemistry in my later life? My Doctor of Medicine thesis at UBC was called "The Biochemistry of the Hallucinogens and A Proposed Etiology for Schizophrenia". Following that, Imperial chemicals made trimethoxyamphetamine for my Master's thesis at McGill University.

A cartoon drawn by a very clever friend of mine of my little lab on Avenue Joffre.

"Dwight, your mom told me about the lab your dad set up out at the house."

I stopped what I was doing, turned and looked at him.

"This isn't a replacement, Dwight. I just thought you might want to have one here too, and then you can run parallel experiments in both labs. This is going to be very scientific, okay?"

"Okay," I said, and he smiled, and I realized we were friends. Then I got to work, and I mean obsessively.

This was an ideal situation as far as my mother was concerned, because it was becoming unsafe for someone my age to be tooling around Shanghai alone. I've stated before that this is strictly a book on China, but even in 1940, before the Internet or cheap airfare, the world was tightly interconnected and events could transmit all over the place. Shanghai, a free port and multinational enclave, was a place where all the tight strands of the world seemed knotted together. The Jewish refugees, who were opening Viennese cafés in Hongkew (and other parts of the city) or otherwise trying to cope, could attest to that. As I've stated, Germany had defeated France early in the summer just past. Marshal Henri Philippe Pétain[xvi] requested an armistice, signed on June 17th 1940, giving up control of northern France to Germany and setting up a capital at Vichy in the south. Henceforth Vichy France existed: now there were three officially anti-Semitic populations in Shanghai.

Now, Japan had very few natural resources, yet had been conducting a long war with China. They had to import steel and, most importantly, 90% of their oil from other countries, namely the United States, which in 1940 provided Japan with 85% of its petroleum.[14] The United States, though strongly isolationist at this time, did not approve of Japan's war with China, both on moral grounds (not recognizing the puppet state of Manchoukuo), and viewing it as a move to usurp western power in East Asia and Southeast Asia, evinced by actions such as the sinking of the USS *Panay*.

---

xvi Avenue Pétain (on which SAS had its address) had been named after the now-Vichy leader for his heroics in World War I as Commander-in-Chief of French forces, such as advocating defensive policies culminating in the Maginot line. Unfortunately he was now running an essentially fascist regime in Vichy France, implementing anti-Semitic policies (such as deportation to death camps) in collaboration with the Nazis to a much greater extent than Mussolini. I'm sure if you name a street after someone it must be an embarrassment when they don't remain admirable for the remainder of their life. Perhaps the rule should be not to name a street after a living person. After the war, Pétain was tried as a criminal and sentenced to execution by firing squad, but Gen. Charles de Gaulle ordered the execution be stayed, on account of Pétain 's advanced age.

In July of 1940, Roosevelt prepared to take action against the Japanese with the Export Control Act. On September 23rd, Japan coerced Vichy France into giving up Tonkin, the northern part of Indochina (Vietnam). From Tonkin, Japan could launch air assaults on certain militarily resistant areas of China. Roosevelt invoked the act, which made it illegal for any American firm to export steel, scrap iron, or aviation fuel to Japan. Japan then signed the Tripartite pact with Germany and Italy on September 27th 1940, which of course meant that Japan, though not at war with the Allies officially, was now a codified enemy.

Japanese aggression towards non-Axis westerners became more pronounced. It was hard to define really, subtle things. For instance, when I was being driven into town from Hollyheath on Monday mornings for school, the guards at the Hungjao railroad checkpoint started to look *into* the car, at the passengers, rather than just *at* the car in general whilst receiving the requisite bow from Driver. We were being slowly and surely drawn into conflict with the Japanese, but my dad kept his flags on the car. The Japanese were not the only threat: as the Chinese suffered more and more and were becoming desperate, there was at least a perceived threat of kidnapping by them. As a result of these vague but growing dangers, it became standard practice not to leave children home at night, even with the servants.

Like many other nine-year olds, I suddenly found myself with a sophisticated new social life the autumn of 1940. Certainly Hollyheath Estate was secure enough for me to stay home, what with all the dogs, the staff, and the fences, so I rarely attended Friday or Saturday night functions with RG, and besides, he mostly led a very quiet life at home. But sometimes dad (and at other times mother and Arthur) would take me to rallies in the auditorium of the British Consulate General, as well as the American Consulate General, where there would be fairly large productions, films, and speeches about Mussolini, Hitler, and Germany. Yet .the next evening I might find myself playing with neighborhood German children.

We went to see Noel Coward's *Private Lives* (which, incidentally, Mr. Coward wrote in the Cathay Hotel, in bed with the flu, while visiting Shanghai some years earlier), and the show started off with God Save the King. There was a lot of that type of entertainment going on. Every movie had the RKO *News of the World* for five or ten minutes beforehand, changing each week so you could see the important news of the week on the theatre screen. I remember Edward R. Morrow and William Shirer in those news reports. In the Lyceum Theatre, before every production there would always be a rendition of:

There'll always be an England,
While there's a country lane,
Wherever there's a cottage small
Beside a field of grain.

There'll always be an England,
While there's a busy street,
Wherever there's a turning wheel
A million marching feet.

Red, white and blue,
What does it mean to you?
Surely you're proud
Shout it aloud.

Britons awake!
The Empire too,
We can depend on you,
Freedom remains
These are the chains
Nothing can break.

There'll always be an England,
And England shall be free,
If England means as much to you
As England means to me.

This royal throne of kings, this sceptred isle,
This earth of majesty, this seat of Mars,
This other Eden, demi-paradise,
This fortress built by Nature for herself
Against infection and the hand of war,
This happy breed of men, this little world,
This precious stone set in a silver sea,

Which serves it in the office of a wall,
Or as a moat defensive to a house
Against the envy of less happier lands
This blessed plot, this earth, this realm
This England

There was all this political jargon going on. Of course at the time it wasn't jargon but the **real thing**, and everybody got behind it and pushed for all they were worth even though the next night you probably found yourself sitting beside the German Consul General for dinner at somebody's home. It would of course never be a British, American, or French home, but if you were in business in Shanghai you were in business with people from all over the world, and received invitations, so this would happen. The very strength of Shanghai that had previously been a model to the world became somewhat embarrassing. People you had dealt with for years became "enemies".

Then a marvelous movie called *The Great Dictator* came out late in 1940 with Charlie Chaplin playing Adolf Hitler. Chaplin had a hell of a time getting support for that movie and in fact footed the bill himself. Many countries threatened to (and did) ban it if it was made, including southern Ireland (Éire). Roosevelt, however, had contacted Chaplin early on and told him to go ahead with it, that he gave him his full support. FDR was an incredibly astute diplomat. I'm not really sure exactly how he manipulated things in such an erudite way with the Lend Lease Bill of March of 1941, but it was brilliant. Beginning with an initial appropriation of $7 billion they could supply aircraft, munitions, and all type of other military equipment (mainly Canadian aircraft) without any payment. Instead, they would get military airports and bases in which to station American troops at various sites in Great Britain for a very long time.

In any case, Chaplin's movie was played one night at the British Consulate General on the Bund, just south of Soochow Creek. It was a large theatre-like affair that would probably seat 100 people and we watched it. It was the most marvelously funny story but of course the German Consulate General objected strenuously to this being shown to so many people in Shanghai and presumably in other Chinese cities. Of course, Axis propaganda was being played in cinemas just as much as Allied propaganda. In any case, as usual, all the sound and fury came to nothing, but we had a hilarious time and stayed up late at night when we got home talking about it. Arthur had photographs of Adolf Hitler and he pointed out to me his gestures, what was behind them, and what the dictator was trying to accomplish. Many comments went around the dining room table about this absolutely scandalous little man. We simply couldn't understand how the German people could possibly put up with him. I suppose it was the same with Stalin in Russia.

Our little family as I now realize was a very sociable, community-oriented, and scientific affair. It seems to me, looking back on it, that we were interested in almost everything. Arthur would tell me to learn everything I could about a given topic by Thursday evening. I would hit the books for a few days then we would have a fine time at the dinner table and then sitting in the living room talking about Chopin, for instance, or baroque architecture. My mother was very happy and the world was expanding for me at an incredible rate.

As to my other family, I saw my dad every weekend, along with the servants, but as usual I didn't see much of my brother. Thankfully, his diary is safe in the archives at Stanford University (his alma mater), because it records his crossing of the Pacific at the time of the attack on Pearl Harbor, and so has considerable historical importance. It is the sort of diary that can be used for several years, and there are entries for 1940. Two entries are quite telling as to what was on his mind:

Saturday, December 7th, 1940
Took Peggy to Alicia's party, gave her my signet ring.

Saturday, December 14th, 1940
Went out with Peggy to the French club, got home at 1:00 am then telephoned her and talked till 6:00 am.

Peggy was the great love of Godfrey's life, and during the war would became his wife in California, but the romance was put on hold when her family heeded the U.S. State Department's October 8, 1940 warning that the 10,000 Americans living in East Asia and South Asia should evacuate. The State Department feared that there would be reprisals from Japanese armed forces against American nationals due to the opening of the Burma road (so nicely covered in Tuchman's "Stilwell and the American Experience in China, 1911 to 1945) to get supplies to Free China, and a related increase of U.S. financial aid to this end. Along with many others, the Allan family evacuated. There had been 60 students in my brother's senior class at the start of September. Of these, 38 would evacuate before the end of the academic year, and only 22 would show up at the convocation ceremony.

I stand on tip toes to inspect a diploma. A small number of Godfrey's graduating class.

The same thing happened in my grade: there were only 18 students in my grade three class compared to 32 the year before. Arthur obviously couldn't go home to Austria so he, my mother and I stayed. RG was too senior at Standard Oil to evacuate, so he and Godfrey stayed too. The Hales and the Scott's also stayed — as did most people with considerable investment and economic interest in Shanghai.[xvii]

Even with the heavy attrition of students, SAS managed to stay afloat. Amah would come and meet me at the gates after school, but sometimes I managed to dodge her and walk

---

xvii It should also be noted that most of the British stuck it out, as well as the French, probably because they had either the Blitz or Nazi occupation to return to, rather than a peaceful isolationist America.

home alone — it wasn't far. To walk to the apartment from SAS, I would take a left out the gates down Avenue Pétain (the spiked wrought-iron fence of the large grounds on my left all the way), take the first left down Route Louis Dufour, then go left again on Avenue Joffre, past the Swiss Consul-General's house and office.

After school on the last day before Christmas break, I had just turned down Avenue Joffre and was deep in thought. I looked up and saw that two kids wearing beanies and armed with BB rifles were coming toward me. We'd seen a lot of newsreels of war footage and for all I knew these were Germans and this was Paris and I was going to get shot. I looked all around for a way to escape, but then one of the "German soldiers" called out to me.

"Dwight!"

"Henry?" I realized it was Henry Tinson. They walked up to me, just grinning, and the kid with him introduced himself in a strange accent that seemed like a composite of many accents.

"Hello, my name is Veikko Tanner, and I would very much like to join your gang, please." He smiled, and rested the butt of his BB rifle on the pavement while we shook hands.

"My what?"

"Your gang, the one you told me about," Henry chimed in, sighting his slug gun at a dead bird in the gutter. Well, me and my big mouth! Henry had no doubt exaggerated my already highly exaggerated Hollyheath exploits to Veikko. I had to figure a way out of this one, and fast.

"I don't know...look, the thing is, only Allies can join. Where are you from, Veikko?" I asked, and started to walk toward the apartment. They followed, and his answer took us all the way to the door.

Veikko was about a year and a half older than I, and had been caught in the crossfire of one of the most mismatched yet fantastically fought conflicts of the war in Europe. After Poland, Stalin had decided on a blitzkrieg of his own, by invading Finland on November 30th 1939. However, two factors made victory less easy than Germany had found in Poland. Number one, Stalin had murdered many of the Red Army's best officers in the political purges, so their existing command structure was poor. Number two, it was winter and the Finns, under Marshal Carl G. Mannerheim, were geniuses of winter warfare. The Finns fought brilliantly, inspiring the Allies. Nevertheless it was a terribly imbalanced battle. Veikko, his sister, and his mother had to evacuate Helsinki as Russian bombs fell within blocks of where they lived. They waited out the conflict at a family farm up north until an armistice was signed on March 12th 1940 wherein the Finns were forced to cede territory, and possibly their best city, to the Soviets.

Veikko's father, who was overseas, was appointed Finnish Consul General to Shanghai in the summer. Veikko, his mother and his sister were to meet him in Shanghai in September, so they had to find a way out of devastated Finland. All the railway lines between Helsinki and Leningrad were blown up from the conflict. Instead, they had to take a ferry across to Tallinn, Estonia, then took the train to Moscow, where they stayed in the Finnish embassy for several days waiting for the next Trans-Siberian train, which they had just missed due to the length of their crossing. Veikko recalled to Henry and I how shocked he was to find, in the beautiful surroundings of the subway stations, that Russian kids stared at him simply because he wore shoes. It seemed that the children of the victors were so poor they had to wear slippers made of felt, or simply go barefoot.

We three arrived at the steps to the apartment at 1710 Avenue Joffre just as Veikko was concluding his narrative of the long train trip across Siberia. Henry opened his mouth, ready to once more broach the subject of the gang, so I quickly invited both of them in. As we climbed the stairs, Veikko finished his story, telling us about their crossing into China at Harbin, and making their way down to Shanghai. I knocked at our door and Arthur answered with a stethoscope around his neck.

"Dwight. I see that though you've managed to skillfully escape your Amah once again, you've been tracked to your lair by a couple of great hunters."

"Soldiers," corrected Henry.

"Oh, my apologies. Soldiers. Well, I believe it is an article of the Geneva Convention that one cannot bring armaments into a doctor's office. It will frighten the patients." Arthur reached out and both boys handed him their rifles, which he stowed in the first closet. Introductions were made, and then the good doctor turned and strode back toward the waiting room.

"Now, what seems to be the trouble, Mr. Taylor," he said, ushering a very pale man in a dark suit, clutching his side, into his office, and closing the door behind.

"Is this your father's lab?" Veikko asked, glancing through the closest doorway at the coveted microscope

"My stepfather's. But I have one too," I said, as we took off our shoes and hung up our coats.

"Can we see yours?" Henry asked.

"You bet." I led them down the hall, opened the closet and turned on the light. Veikko's eyes lit up when he saw what I had.

"May I have a look?" he asked, taking off his beanie to reveal messy yellow hair.

"Sure, go ahead."

He went in and started sorting through the bottles with an expert hand, comparing, inquiring as to which experiments I had run; asking very intelligent questions. Henry was interested too, but not in so specific a way. He kept pushing me about the gang, but Veikko and I were already planning an experiment.

The next day after school I went to Veikko's apartment, as he also had an extensive laboratory and wanted to show it to me. The Finnish Consulate General was about a mile east down Avenue Joffre, then right on Rue Cardinal Mercier. It was on the seventh floor of a building owned by the Catholic Church, and like our place was split into two areas: living and office. His sister Lailai ushered me in, while his father's deep voice boomed from a phone call in the other room. His mom met me and we sat down in a very formal room. We ate cookies, drank milk and visited, but Mrs. Tanner could sense our impatience. She suggested we get to work, then their driver could take me home later. Well, we sprang from the sofa and Veikko turned on the lights in a very fine lab indeed, and we started setting up equipment for an experiment.

We had a tremendous time over the holidays and through the winter into 1941. We made photographic paper, explosives, dyes for dying cloth, and "cosmetics" which my mother very bravely tried. We made batteries with copper and zinc electrodes, and hydrochloric acid or sulfuric acid. Veikko made carbon disulfide, and tetrachloride, draining out some fire extinguishers to purify the tetrachloride. He also made radioactive thorium oxide, powders that glowed in the dark. Arthur helped us equip both labs with so many chemicals that Veikko's shelf broke, the bottles smashed in the sink, which was plugged, and all the chemicals mixed together. Well, I'll tell you, they dissolved the sink pretty quickly!

January of 1941 came and went, I turned ten, and spring was just around the corner. It got warm very quickly, and suddenly there were leaves on the willow trees, and we boys wanted to be outside. 1710 Avenue Joffre had a flat, open roof area, but you had to climb up three fire-escape ladders made of cable to get there, and the Chinese manager didn't like anybody going up top. Veikko and I figured out a way sneak by the manager, jimmy the lock, and get the door open. Finally we could walk out onto the roof in the sunshine.

School finally ended and *The Columbian*, SAS's yearbook, told the tale of the 1940 to 1941 academic year:

> At the end of another year, we pause to look back over weeks full of hard work and new experiences. The evacuation took many of our number away and even threatened for a while to cause the closing of the school. But through the co-operation of all, we were able to complete a successful year. We hope this COLUMBIAN, the Evacuation Special, will be a real joy to you as a remembrance of an unusual year at S.A.S.

Well, what did I care? It was summertime and I had a new interest: radios. Veikko had started dabbling in the field and was an associate member of the ARRL, the American Radio Relay League, his call sign XU8VT. He was experimenting with very short wave transmission at the time (5 meter band, VHF now) and he built two single-valve transceivers. The ARRL's Shanghai group held monthly meetings at the Cathay Hotel on the Bund, and they asked him to demonstrate his radios at one of these sessions. He and I took the equipment down to the Cathay on the appointed evening, and we showed how the transceivers worked by sending signals back and forth from either end of the hotel's very long hallway. No one could believe that we could transmit across town.

I spent a great deal of time down at the bookstores on Nanking road, looking for all the information I could find in order to build my own transmitter. The first book I bought was the *Radio Amateur's Handbook*, which was and is the bible of radio transmission. The 1942 edition came out in the summer of 1941.

Cover of 1942 Radio Amateur's Handbook.

When I had figured out a basic transmitter, I typed out a list of the parts. Arthur went down to the store with me and we bought everything I would need. When we got home from this errand I ran into the lab and started to build.

```
              90 watt 6L6 transmitter
3     6L6
100 mmfd.mica
2     250 mmfd per section.
1     250
2     .001 mica
2     50 mmfd.mica
2     10 mmfd.mica
5     .01 mfd.
1     .1 meg
1        50,000 ohm
1     500 ohm
1  25,000 ohm
1        12,000 ohm
2  25 ohm
RFC
```

SHANGHAI, China, 19 4 1

ARTHUR PERETZ, M.D.
SPECIALIST IN INTERNAL DISEASES
1710 AVENUE JOFFRE, APT. 21
TEL. 79936
IF NO ANSWER, TELEPHONE 87232
9—12 A.M.
4—6 P.M.
SATURDAYS 11 A.M.—1 P.M.

Purchase of parts to build transmitter. Note Arthur's full support through loan of prescription pad. I'm sure this would have confused a pharmacist!

That was our summer, really. Lots of tinkering, transmissions back and forth, mixed with long bike rides when our mothers forced us out of the house. Neither of us went north to summer camp, but we certainly were never bored.

I'm sure Roosevelt wasn't bored either. On July 24th, again with reluctant permission from Vichy France, Japan occupied strategic positions in the south of Indochina. This was particularly menacing, because Japan was obviously closing on the Dutch East Indies, which had no military backup from home since Holland had capitulated to Germany, yet had a great deal of oil it had thus far refused to sell to Japan. It was time for more maneuvering by FDR.

Part of the American isolationist legislation of the mid-1930s stated that belligerent nations had to pay cash for whatever they purchased in the United States. On July 26th, Roosevelt froze all of Japan's assets in the United States, which in combination with the cash-only legislation created a virtual embargo of all petroleum exports to Japan. Holland and England quickly followed suit. The Japanese were now being starved of fuel, so would have to do something decisive very soon if they wanted to remain an industrialized nation.

Once again Labor Day rolled around, but with SAS nearly dead, the decision was made that I attend College St. Jeanne D' Arc instead. Godfrey of course had many tips for me as to how I could best fit in, having attended the school until home leave in 1937. Now, my brother had been the first protestant at the school, and I think I was to be the second, but he told me that when I filled in the form on the first day in school I was to put "atheist" beside religion. Well, I did as he said, and it just about did me in. I of course hadn't the vaguest idea what the word meant and I suppose Godfrey was laughing at home at my predicament. Phone calls went back and forth...school to Avenue Joffre to Hollyheath, back to the school and to Brother Superior...and finally things were straightened out. That is, we were Anglicans, about as close as you can get to Roman Catholic without being sinful. I suspect the only two differences are that the reigning figure in England is not the Pope, but the Archbishop of Canterbury, and we call the pervasive spirit, the "holy spirit" rather than the "holy ghost". Fish on Friday, of course, was not mandatory or, in fact, even encouraged.

As already mentioned, Marist brothers ran College St. Jeanne D' Arc. It was located on a small street just off Avenue Joffre, just off Route Pichon. The brothers all wore long black cassocks even in the middle of summer, which reached 120°f (49c) in Shanghai. This was combined with a black, broad-brimmed felt hat. Wow they must have suffered. The brothers even wore this outfit while on their excursions out to the Zso-Zse hills. The ones I remember best are soft-spoken and little Brother Laurence, tough early Germanic Brother Edward, and Brother "Superior". I never did know Brother Superior's name.

The school itself was housed in a two-story building with a large playground. At one end of what I would estimate to have been a four or five acre (3 hectare) space, there was a covered, blacktopped, 20-foot (6 meter) wide hallway covered but not enclosed. The bicycles generally were left there but only on rainy days. On nice days, the bicycles had to be left along the footpath leading into the school building. There were fruit trees growing along the footpath. One afternoon very shortly after school started, I walked down the path and picked a pear off the tree and started to eat it. Unlike pears elsewhere in the world, in China they ripen very well on the tree in August and September. With sudden, uncanny manifestation, Brother Edward was standing in front of me.

"Do you know what happened to Adam for stealing the forbidden fruit?" he asked, very gravely.

"Yes, Brother Edward."

"Then you know that you should not have stolen that pear. Come to my office. Five lashes."

"Yes, Brother Edward."

I followed him into his office, on whose wall hung about ten canes. With a vague sweep of the hand, he referred me to them. The brothers at least had the decency to allow the offender to pick the cane that was to deliver the lashing. These went from very thin — probably half the size of one's index finger — to quite thick, probably the size of the average index finger. It was said that the one carried less surface and hence damaged less tissue, whereas the other had more surface and gave more pain. I doubt very much if this was true. Most of us, however, took the middle of the line. I had already heard all about it and had come to this conclusion myself before the pear incident, so this was my selection in the brother's office.

This corporal punishment was oftentimes administered in front of the entire class if done during classroom hours. It was, of course, an all-boys school. You came to the front of the class, dropped your trousers, bent over one of the desks, and lowered the waistband of your under shorts down your backside just enough to expose the buttocks. Lord knows the brothers didn't want anybody's underwear torn by the cane! I must say it was a very effective method of reminding one what one should do and what one should not do.

A few weeks later, Godfrey got the good news that the University of California Berkeley had accepted him into their engineering program. He therefore applied to the American Consular General for a visa that would be required for his four-year stay in California. Thus begins the substance of Godfrey's diary:

> *Sunday, November 9th, 1941*
>
> *Still waiting for the visa. Went down to the "Y" in the afternoon, then to see "Zeigfried Girl" with Floyd and Lorry. It was a swell show.*
>
> *Floyd Carman was a classmate of Godfrey's and Lorry was a graduate of 1940, but a very close friend of my brother's.*
>
> *Monday, November 10th, 1941*
>
> *Went to the consulate & asked them if the cable has come yet. They said no so I asked them to cable again. At about 11am when I was at the dentist's dad phoned and said that I'd got the visa. Yippee!!! Yep it's really here and I'm all set to leave.*

My brother was a real film buff so, fittingly, the next evening he went with his friends to see *The Sea Wolf*, starring Edward G. Robinson. The movie opens in San Francisco bay, and I'm sure it excited Godfrey to see his destination combined with adventure and danger on the high seas. They went over to Lorenzo Lo's house after the movie and I'm sure much conversation was given over to whether or not Lorry[xviii] was going to get his visa in time for them to travel together.

> *Thursday, November 13, 1941*
>
> *The Tjibadak is definitely leaving port at 9am. Lorry got his quota number to-day.*

---

xviii Who lives in the Chesapeake Bay area of Virginia now (2005)

Gee it's swell!!! I had lunch with Mrs. Moy & Peter Kim. Bought some more pictures and Christmas cards. Also Peter bought me "Shanghai" by Ellen Thorbecke and also the sea sick pills.

Mrs. Moy was Godfrey's friend Ken Moy's mother, and her husband was a general in the Chinese Army. Some time very early on, or possibly even a few days before the war, Ken moved to the Tennessee area and eventually became a general in the United States Army. As to the *Tjibadak*, she was a coastal steamer about 450 feet long and 7,803 gross tons. Slow and serviceable, making at best 12.5 knots, she would carry Godfrey, Lorry Jorgensen, and Bob Komar down the coast to Hong Kong, then across the South China Sea to the Sea of Mindanao and Manila, where they would board a larger ship bound for Honolulu and San Francisco. The *Tjibadak* was moored at the customs pier alongside the Bund, exactly where our family had arrived back from home leave nearly four years earlier.

Chapter 7

Pearl Harbor War in the Pacific

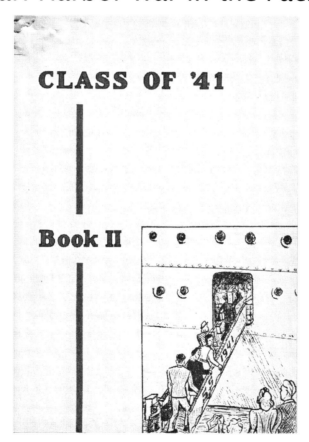

From 1941 SAS Yearbook: The Columbian. Image leads the pages of photographs of the graduating class.

Saturday, November 15th, 1911

Left the customs jetty at 9am. All the kids were down to see us off. It was swell. There was loads of letters to take. Bob Komar, Lorry & I all got in the same cabin. The boat left at 11:30am. Just before clearing I found out that I'd left my keys at home, so I was quite upset. Anyway I found them later in the afternoon. The pilot Capt. Petersen took some letters ashore for us when he left. It was a swell night. I took all the valuables to the purser. Gee it doesn't seem possible that I've really started on the way to the States.

For many aboard I imagine it must have been a great relief to finally be surrounded by the water rather than the Japanese army.[xix] But as the buildings of the Bund, the Public Garden, Soochow creek and the Garden Bridge slipped past the port side of the ship, I bet Godfrey stared down the streets and thought of people he cared about who were still in Shanghai, still in that situation. I can't imagine how torn Godfrey must have felt. They would have cleared the Whangpoo and then the Yangtze by nightfall.

Sunday, November 16th, 1911 — 6:30am.

I just woke up...the sun rays are just coming in the port hole and the sun sure does look beautiful near the horizon. We're pretty near the coast all of the way down. The sea is a beautiful sight with little south Chinese sailing vessels studding it here and there. No moon to-night but the sky was beautiful. It looked just like a pitch black inkwell chockablock full of tiny shiny pieces of silver. After a walk around the deck, Lorry and I turned in at 9pm. We ought to be in Amoy at 11am tomorrow morning.

xix We must understand that from the Japanese point of view, since they were always suspicious of foreigners (maybe justified in this case), that the U.S., Britain, and Holland, having cut of their oil supply, and now, literally, surrounding Japan with the U.S. Navy with a large fleet in Hawaii, to the east of Japan, the Philippines to the south, and now with the U.S. Army strongly supporting the Chinese military all up and down the Chinese coastal area, including the Burma Road, that Japan was literally surrounded. No only that, but the Aleutian Islands to the northeast of Japan were American so, factoring in an ongoing paranoia of and animosity towards Russia to the north and west, they were indeed surrounded. And one can easily imagine the Japanese government expecting the U.S. was about to strike, given the politics of petroleum starvation, so they would pre-empt this by attacking first while still possessing enough fuel to wage war.

They did reach Amoy exactly on time, but Godfrey was about to make a big mistake.

Monday, November 17th, 1941

We got into Amoy at 11am this morning and I took a few pictures of the harbor etc. About half an hour after the boat docked some Jap soldiers came aboard and demanded that I give them my camera for inspection, because they said that they had seen me from their look-out tower on shore taking pictures of the harbor. Finally I let them have the film and kept my camera. They said they'd have the film developed and would return later. Luckily they never did come back. We left Amoy at 4:30pm. There's nothing to the dump, only a few buildings...

Now, my brother was a pretty cool customer. Living as we had in the middle of someone else's war for years, intimidation was something you got used to. And this was of course typical Japanese style, particularly at that time, where they were as usual watching everybody, and to be truthful we were watching them.

Tuesday, November 18th, 1941

Sighted land also 11am. (Hongkong). Stayed in quarantine for about two & a half hours & finally got ashore in Hongkong at 6:30pm. Hongkong has a beautiful natural harbor & a lovely winding entrance to a maze of large islands. Lorry & I first changed $1.00 for $4.00 Hongkong money. Then we went to the Gloucester Hotel & phoned some people who were not in, so we bought tickets for a 9:30 show. We had about 1 1/2 hours to waste so we went up and down the main street & dropped into a soda fountain for an ice cream. Then we saw "Gold Rush Maisie" which was rotten...

They slept aboard the ship that night.

Wednesday, November 19th, 1941

Went into the city at 9am on the tender. I bought some films, books, stamps, and some postcards. We came back to the ship at noon for lunch and then went back again in the afternoon and saw a show. After the show we went and visited Mr. and Mrs. Carman. They took us to the C.I.C. Carnival, to dinner and finally asked us to come and stay the night with them because we couldn't get a tender out to the boat. They have a swell house and a cute little monkey.

Lorry and Godfrey slept aboard ship the next evening:

Thursday, November 20th, 1941

Thanksgiving day and boy did those marines celebrate on boat. They were all drunk when Lorry and I got back at noon, and stayed drunk all day. We woke up at 9am this morning after a swell sleep. After breakfast I played with Floyd's monkey while Lorry wrote his airmail letter to Springfield. After we got back on board I wrote some cards to the kids in Shanghai: Basil, June, Lo-lo, Peter, Bob H. Gino, Floyd, Unk, Marge, Butch, dad & Mom, etc. We were scheduled to leave to-night, but they have postponed it till to-morrow morning at 9am.

On November 21st they set out across the South China Sea for Manila.

Friday, November 21st, 1941

Well we're underway again bound for Manila. We hauled up the anchor at about 4:30am and were out of sight of land at 12pm. After lunch Lorry and I went up to the top deck and lay there for a couple of hours & got nice and red. After tea I straightened out my bags and the cabin and did some washing. Then came down to the dining room and wrote some letters.

Saturday, November 22nd, 1941
Nothing much happened. It was a pretty dry day.

Sunday, November 23rd, 1941

Sighted land to-day at 8am. Arrived at the Customs house at 2:30pm. Mr. & Mrs. Whythe were down to meet me. They took me to the Polo Club and then to their home. After getting settled we went out & saw Mr. Whythe's office, and then went to a show. After dinner that night Evelyne, Mrs. Whythe & myself all played Chinese checkers until 10:30pm. I phoned up Lorry and made a date to meet him at the A.P.L. offices at 10am tomorrow morning.

This was as far as the slow coastal steamer would go, so the boys would have to book tickets for the second passage. A.P.L. stands for American Presidents Line. Formerly it had been Dollar Steamship Line, and there were $$ insignias on the funnels. When I was born the president of that line, a family friend, visited my mother in hospital. His first name was Dwight and she decided to name me after him.

Monday, November 24th, 1941

Went to the A.P.L. and got my ticket. Had lunch with Lorry at a small restaurant. In the afternoon the three of us & Evy and Mrs. Whythe all went to Tagaytay, about 60 miles from Manila & saw the church with the bamboo organ. We all had dinner at the Whythe's and Evy took Lorry & me to visit a couple of kids — Cliff Forster, Jay Fell & the two Seton sisters. We listened on the radio to Charlie McCarthy and Lou Costello from S.F.

They spent a few days sightseeing, socializing with the Whythes and their friends, working out at the Polo Club, swimming, and playing badminton; all of the usual things that Caucasians did. On Wednesday the boys got their baggage off the *Tjibadak*, and arranged to have a cabin together on the Pacific crossing.

Their ship, the *President Coolidge* set off for San Francisco on the usual route via Honolulu. It was a beautiful ship, 650 feet long, sleek, could do about 20 knots and had several times broken the transpacific record. However that speed would never be used. Negotiations between the United States and Japan had broken down on November 26th. In a program codenamed MAGIC, U.S. intelligence cryptographers were managing to intercept and crack the Japanese diplomatic codes. Though they hadn't cracked the military codes and therefore didn't know any specifics, general message activity and traffic indicated the Japanese were about to strike. Whether it was going to be the Dutch East Indies, the Philippines, or some other target was unclear. A war warning was sent out to the U.S. Pacific Fleet on November 27th, and precautions were taken.

Friday, November 28th, 1941

Woke up at 7:00 am and went down for a swell breakfast at 8:30 after a few rounds around the deck. At about 11 am we picked up a cruiser the Luzon to convoy us to the States. The Pierce is also tagging along in the same convoy, and so we're slowed down considerably. But are still making 12 knots which isn't too bad. Anyway we won't get to San Francisco until after my birthday, 'cause we're taking the southern route around New Guinea.

We had a movie to-night: The Marx Bros in...

November 29th to December 7th would be uneventful, the calm before — as it would turn out — two storms. Passing New Guinea there wasn't much to see outside but the odd distant island, so the passengers' attention turned inward. Two movies were shown in first class: *Sleepers West* on the 30th, and a bullfighting film, *Blood and Sand*, with Tyrone Power, on December 2nd.

Wednesday, December 3rd, 1941

We picked up a pilot to-day and are passing through thru the Toro Straits. We will be out in the open sea by to-morrow morning.

Something about the people on board. First of all there's a whole bunch of missionaries on board who absolutely get under everyone's skin. Then the ship seems full of young brats about three years old. We have to listen to them Wa-a-a-ing all day long & all night long. Mommy!!!

Then up in first class there's 50 Chinese flyers who are going to the States to get their training. There is also a panda on board which has been given by Madame Chiang Kai-shek to the States as a present.

This is an interesting passage because it is evidence of the sort of behavior that revisionist historian Robert Smith Thompson says

"…cast doubt on America's true neutrality. The Chinese government had begun to send presents to American officials, especially to President Roosevelt. The U.S. Treasury had begun to buy Chinese silver, granting China a kind of foreign aid. And the Chinese Government had begun to pay money to an American pilot, Claire Chennault.[xx] His job was to reorganize the Chinese Air Force; and although he was retired from the U.S. Army Air Corps, he had plenty of contacts in Washington."[15]

Thursday, December 4th, 1941

We dropped the pilot off this morning and then continued on our way. We're scheduled to get to T.H. on the 14th.

Four days passed. Passengers killed time by writing letters, pacing the deck, leaning on the railing and staring down at miles and miles of dark waves and foam slipping past the long black hull of the ship, which the crew would soon have to paint gray for camouflage. The *President Coolidge* hadn't crossed the International Date Line when the Japanese attacked Pearl Harbor; hence it was Monday on board (and in Shanghai) when the news broke.

Monday, December 8th, 1941

WAR!!! Yes sir, it was announced today at noon that Japan officially declared war on the U.S. and Great Britain at 3:00 am Monday morning. Shortly after there were rumors that we'd turn around and head for Brisbane, Australia. Later in the day we heard that we were going to make a beeline for South America. Over the radio from Japan we heard that Pearl Harbor, Manila and Hong Kong were all bombed. Gee, what will the

---

xx Claire Chennault in fact bought our house "Aqua Vista" at Hollyheath Estate after the war and lived in it for a few years until the communists took over.

folks do in Shanghai? I hope that they're O.K.

I can picture the boys pacing around on deck speculating, above them the smokestacks puffing away, a white wake from the twin screws zigzagging in the deep blue, *The Scott* and *The Luzon* coming and going. It's an odd thing about war, that many of the people you have recently seen alive might be dead. What about Mr. and Mrs. Carman and their Monkey? Or the people in the theatre watching the rotten movie *Gold Rush Maisie?* What about the Whythes and the drunken marines that had sailed as far as Manila?

Tuesday, December 9th, 1941

There are new rumors today that we are stopping at Pango Pango to-morrow. We haven't heard for how long. Also, there was no newspaper today and from last night a strict blackout from sundown is being enforced.

Then another entry for the same date, as they cross the International Date Line.

Tuesday, December 9th, 1941

Meridian Day. We were lucky and got one day cumshaw.[xxi] *The news has been changed now and we're not doing to Pango until tomorrow.*

We picked up on a radio broadcast from Japan that they had sunk the Coolidge & the Scott to-day.

This is another odd thing about war: people you recently saw alive might think *you* are dead.

Wednesday, December 10th, 1941

Well, we're not going to Pango after all. We changed course again this morning and seem to be heading straight for Tahiti. If we are we ought to be there by the 16th and in S.F. by the 21st.

To-night I went up by my self and saw "Blondie Goes to Town" in first class, it was

---

xxi Free: handed under the table.

swell. Later on in the afternoon we changed course again and are headed almost due East. During the day we heard several short news broadcasts from KGEI.

KGEI was a radio station in San Francisco that broadcast on short wave. It must have been tantalizing for Godfrey, hearing voices from his destination.

Thursday, December 11th, 1941

When we woke up this morning the ship was headed almost due north again. Again, there were several short newscasts, nothing very clear. No one this time seems to know where we're going. They say most probably Honolulu. Lorry and I went up to First Class this afternoon and had a pretty good time.

After dinner we got news from Tokyo that the Japs had sunk the carrier Lexington and that before sinking all the planes on board took off. When they got to Honolulu the Japs said that they were shot down by their own men - what a laugh. It started raining this aft & is still raining.

Friday, December 12th, 1941

We're still on the Honolulu course and if we don't change are sure to be there definitely by Tuesday. The whole boat is being painted grey today – gee it's awful but there's nothing we can do about it. Went up to first after dinner and saw "The Wagons Roll by Night." Then we came down again to the lounge & danced.

Saturday, December 13th, 1941

Changed course again slightly and are headed due north straight at Honolulu. Saw "The Wagons Roll at Night" again and then went up first to listen to some music up on deck. Had a boat drill this afternoon.

Then, as they headed toward the metaphorical eye of the war's storm, they encountered an actual storm.

Sunday, December 14th, 1941

Steamed all night last night and all morning and afternoon to-day. Boy, was the sea heavy!!! The Pierce and The Louisville ducked their whole bows under water several times.

The 4 of us (Lorry, Bud, Champka and myself) all dressed up for dinner to-night because of my birthday. We had a real swell dinner and a cake. Then we went forward & saw "A Woman's Face."

Monday, December 15th, 1941

There's no sun out this morning & boy what a sea. There's a terrific wind blowing too. At 10:30 am this morning we sighted an American patrol bomber. Gee, it was a swell feeling to know that finally someone knows that we're really safe. Right after the lunch the cruiser sighted a freighter on the horizon & hurried off to identify it.

And, finally, they reached Hawaii.

Tuesday, December 16th, 1941

Got up very early this morning and saw two Navy patrol bombers fly over us at 4:30 am. Just before 7:30 am the cruiser struck a course East to investigate something. It caught up to us again at 9:30 am.

Just after lunch two U.S. Destroyers came up astern. We got some swell pictures of them.

We sighted Land at 3:00 pm & were in the harbor at 4:30 pm, but were not allowed ashore to-night. They say we'll be let off to-morrow morning.

Got a letter from Pop.

Dad of course had written and mailed that letter before Pearl Harbor.

Wednesday, December 17th, 1941

Well, we got up this morning and telephoned Chuck Riggin at Iolani high school. He came into town to meet us & then took us up to the school. It's kind of small to what I had expected. In the afternoon the three of us went out to Waikiki Beach and walked around that end of town. We had to be on board at 5:30 pm because of the blackout.

Thursday, December 18th, 1941

We went on a tour to-day around Pearl Harbor. We saw the Oklahoma, the West Virginia, Utah, & Arizona sunk in the harbor. In the afternoon we went to the Waikiki theatre & saw "A Yank in the R.A.F." Gee it was a swell show. There were actual live palm trees growing right in the theatre. When we came aboard in the afternoon again they had loaded on 187 wounded men. We talked to one of the Pharmacist's Mates and got the full dope on the situation.

The above mentioned boats were really sunk & lots of damage to other ships. Jap pilots shot down with rings on their fingers & with maps showing the exact location of all the boats in the harbor. The bayonet-stabbing of the Jap pilot by a marine, the strangulation of another by two marines. The corpses out in the sugar cane. Basically 10,000 men lost.

A football team boarded the ship, on their way back home to Willamette University in Oregon. After the attack, the army had pressed the team into service, given them coils of barbed wire to string along Waikiki beach, and rifles to guard water towers and storage tanks from sabotage. The players did this until they could board the *President Coolidge*, whose departure was delayed while she was fitted out with a makeshift hospital below decks.

Friday, December 19th, 1941

The whole ship sure does smell of ether and burnt flesh. We went down & visited some of the men and they seem pretty badly off. According to them some 10,000-odd men were lost in the battle and two more warships than those originally stated.

Boy do those football players take over everything when they get started!!! And can they eat!!!

The *USAT Scott* continued on with the *Coolidge*, and now they were part of a convoy of 8 or 10 ships. No one was allowed on deck even in daylight. The portholes were painted black and closed at night, along with the doors. With the smell this must have been pretty awful.

Saturday, December 20th, 1941

Nothing much happened to-day. The weather is getting a lot cooler now. We're doing a lot of zipping and zapping since we left H., according to the sun we're taking a northern route to S.F. It seems almost certain that we'll get in Christmas day.

Tuesday, December 23rd, 1941

Well, the order's out for all people on board to carry their life-preservers with them constantly. Boy the situation sure does seem to be getting serious.

He had been doing exactly the right thing: keeping busy. It must have been difficult to sleep.

Wednesday, December 24th, 1941

The order came out today that we all had to sleep in our clothes tonight. Boy, is that going to be some job. The water around San Francisco seems to be very dangerous or they wouldn't have made that order.

Lorry & I beat Komar & Lemlke again 4-2.

We're headed West by South now and are due in sometime tomorrow morning.

Boy is there a terrific tension on board tonight, most people are staying awake all night and the rest are sleeping in their clothes. Gee!! Just one torpedo and we'd be blown sky-high. Went to bed at 10:00 pm & got up at 1:30 am. From then until dawn is the worst time so I thought it would be better if I were awake then.

Notice he recorded their course as west by south, which means they were really making some amazing contortions in their course to avoid detection. Having written this, I think Godfrey tried to go back to sleep.

Thursday, December 25th, 1941

Got up again at 2am – shaved then went up to the 1st class smoke room & played 7-up. Won $1.25, played until 7am. We saw the first light offshore at 6:30 am, so we ought to be in by 9:30 am. We stayed in quarantine until 11:00 am & docked at noon. It wasn't until 4:30 that I finally got away from the immigration officers & customs men. Had no duty to pay. Uncle Gus & Phylis & Ron & Johnnie came down to the boat and took me to Johnnie's house where I had dinner then on to Aunt Jean's. We finally got home & to bed about 10:30 pm.

Friday, December 26th, 1941

Went over & saw Alicia this morning. Gee it sure was swell to see someone that you knew back in Shanghai...

And so Godfrey had made it, albeit with a little homesickness. He would go on to study for two years and then join the U.S. Army for action overseas on Okinawa. In the nearer future, however, he would drive down to Stanford and reestablish contact with Peggy Allan, whom he hadn't seen since she evacuated Shanghai.

That such an important American ship was at sea when Pearl Harbor was attacked was a newsworthy item. The following is text from an article in *The Californian*, the student newspaper of the University of California at Berkeley, where Godfrey attended school until he went into the armed forces:

British Student Avoids Subs

Ship Caught on High Seas at War's Outbreak

By Gerald Jacobson '42

A dramatic story of a voyage made through possibly enemy-infested waters was yesterday told by Godfrey Gregg, 18-year-old British subject now enrolled in the University Extension, who was caught on the high seas at the beginning of the war.

On a ship "somewhere in the Pacific" on Dec. 7, both passengers **and crew refused to believe news of the Japanese attacks on Manila and Hawaii, first heard over the Tokyo radio,** Gregg said.

"The same afternoon, however, we heard orders from the captain over all loudspeakers to have a strict blackout and to conserve water because we were at war with Japan.

"Few of the passengers were worried about themselves but many were concerned over the fate of relatives left in China," he recalled.

The ship stopped at Honolulu to pick up sailors wounded in the attack on Pearl Harbor.

"All of the sailors and marines would like to get back on duty soon to get another crack at the Japanese," Gregg declared.

Honolulu itself appears unscathed to the visitor's eye, he reported. Morale everywhere is high and some of Hawaii's famed beach sports are still going on.

The trip took considerably longer than expected as the boat went off its course and repeatedly changed direction, Gregg said. Strict blackouts were enforced all night long.

"We were kind of scared the last **night before docking here,"** he recalled. "**We had news of sinkings of other ships and everyone stayed up with lifebelts ready.**

"We were amused, though, to hear Tokyo radio report that our ship was captured and that a ship that was proceeding alongside us had been sunk."

Born and raised in Shanghai, Gregg plans to study chemistry for two years and then to join the United States Air force. His parents are still in Shanghai.

I might be biased, but I think my brother did a better job of reporting the crossing, and not only in his entries. There is something else in his journal on December 24th. The night he couldn't sleep, knowing that they could be torpedoed at any moment, Godfrey wrote a song:

> *How dear to our hearts is this trip on the Coolidge*
> *When fond recollections recall it to view.*
> *The rush & the worry we might not be on her*
> *But she waited so kindly till all were aboard.*
> *The big sturdy steamer, the cruiser beside her,*

The slow moving Scott that was always behind,
We fussed & we fretted but nothing could push it
The Old Smoky Joe just came poking behind

Chorus: The Pres. Coolidge, the master, the stewards,
the crew and the orchestra carried us thru.

Instead of the course that we often had taken
The ship turned due South where it's hotter through —
We asked & we questioned, but none could enlighten
Emergency measures was all they would tell.
We gazed on the islands & strange constellations
But no one could figure our place on the map
A skipper was with us of long reputation
Who checked on the landmarks to fill in the gaps.

With so many travelers from so many countries
WE all looked around us to see who was who
There were women without husbands & men without families,
Who told of their plans to renew family ties;
but right in among us not few maiden ladies
who deemed not to mention just what they would do
Also babies & Mamas & youth bound for college
when all put together we made quite a stew.

How good to our tummies was the chow on the tables
As three times a day we eat more than we should
Those ample deserts & those heavy meat courses
But oh! what a story the ship's steward told.
Because of the distance, the shortage of water
There was only one shortage that gummed up the works
The ladies efficient just did their own wash up
But try to imagine men ironing their shirts.

Our story at Hawaii was long & uncertain
But "safe, love, & kisses," by cables we sent.
New passengers boarded in fabulous numbers
The old ship is crowded, but still homeward bent.
A Hip, Hip, hooray for service men hearty:
To soldiers & sailors we take off our hats
We've made many friends whom we long to remember
Tho' singing the story have fallen down?

Chapter 8

The Japanese Occupation of Shanghai

Imperial Rescript
on Declaration of War
December 8, 1941

"WE, by the Grace of Heaven, Emperor of Japan, seated on the Throne whose line is unbroken for ages eternal, enjoin upon ye Our loyal and brave subjects.

"We hereby declare war on the United States of America and the British Empire. Men and officers of Our Army and Navy shall do their utmost in prosecuting the war. Our public servants of various departments shall perform faithfully and diligently their appointed tasks, and all other subjects of Ours shall pursue their respective duties; the entire nation with united will shall mobilize its total strength so that nothing will miscarry in the attainment of Our war aims.

"To insure the stability of East Asia and contribute to world peace is the far-sighted policy which was formulated by Our great illustrious Imperial Grand Sire and Our great Imperial Sire, succeeding Him, and which We lay constantly to heart.

"To cultivate friendship among nations, and to enjoy prosperity in common with all nations, has always been the guiding principle of Our Empire's foreign policy. It has been truly unavoidable, and far from Our wishes that Our Empire has now been brought to cross swords with America and Great Britain.

"More than four years have passed since China, failing to comprehend the true intentions of Our Empire, and recklessly courting trouble, disturbed peace in East Asia and compelled Our Empire to take up arms.

"Although there has been re-established the National Government of China, with which Japan has effected neighbourly intercourse and co-operation, the régime which has survived in Chungking, relying upon American and British protection, still continues its fratricidal opposition.

"Eager for realization of their inordinate ambition to dominate the Orient, both America and Great Britain, giving support to the Chungking régime, have aggravated disturbances in East Asia. Moreover, these two Powers, inducing other countries to follow suit, have increased military preparation on all sides of Our Empire to challenge Us.

"They have obstructed every means of Our peaceful commerce, and finally resorted to a direct severance of economic relations, menacing gravely the existence of Our Empire.

"Patiently have We waited and long have We endured in the hope Our Government might retrieve the situation in peace. But Our adversaries, showing not the least spirit of conciliation, have unduly delayed settlement; and in the meantime they have intensified economic and political pressure to compel thereby Our Empire to submission.

"This trend of affairs would, if left unchecked, not only nullify Our Empire's efforts of many years for the sake of stabilization of East Asia, but also endanger the very existence of Our nation.

"The situation being such as it is, Our Empire for its existence and self-defence, has no other course but to appeal to arms and to crush every obstacle in its path.

"The hallowed spirits of Our Imperial Ancestors are guarding Us from above, and We rely upon the loyalty and courage of Our subjects in Our confident expectation that the task bequeathed by Our forefathers will be carried forward, and that the sources of evil will be speedily eradicated, and an enduring peace will be immediately established in East Asia, preserving thereby the glory of Our Empire."

So, were the folks in Shanghai O.K.? We were, initially, because the curse of the Japanese surrounding the International Settlement for four years had become something of a blessing. On November 28th (ironically, the day of the war warning) the 4th Regiment had shipped out to the Philippines, having gained permission to withdraw from Shanghai, citing its indefensibility as the British had over a year earlier. With the British and American military withdrawn, and the SVC not mobilized, that left only a handful of Vichy French and Italian soldiers for defense, and as Axis partners they of course did nothing. The city was essentially defenseless. Without resistance, and with strong Japanese diplomatic as well as military presence, there would be no vicious battle like the one for Hong Kong. Once the order came, very early in the morning, Shanghai time, an advance party of Japanese fixed their bayonets and simply marched over the Garden Bridge past the British Consulate — at which point several Japanese marines broke ranks and took over the building — then continued down the Bund. They rolled several big guns along and placed them in front of the bank façades, taking aim at the mid-channel of the Whangpoo because the river alone held potential for resistance

Two very small Allied warships were moored in mid-stream: one American and one British. Both of these gunboats were positioned there to fly their respective flags, relay radio signals for their consulate generals, and to evacuate diplomatic personnel in the event of an emergency. Knowing this, two groups of Japanese marines motored out in launches from the cruiser *Idzumo,* which was still moored in front of the Japanese Consulate General. The first group of marines boarded the USS *Wake*, overpowered what was essentially skeleton crew (her captain was asleep in the Park Hotel), and took the control of the gunboat. For the duration of the war she would be called *Tatara Maru*.

The second group of marines tried the same thing with the HMS *Peterel*, however her captain had been warned by the British Consulate General and the ship's crew of eighteen were armed. The Japanese tied up, boarded, then demanded Lieutenant Stephen Polkinghorn, the captain, to surrender. He replied: "get off my bloody ship!"[16] The Japanese very politely turned around, got back in their launch, untied and motored away, quickly, because they knew what was coming. Down in the lower decks of the *Peterel*, her crew got busy destroying codebooks.

Once the launch was clear the battle began. Japanese guns along the Bund, on Pootung point, and aboard one of their gunboats moored in front of the Public Gardens opened fire. Then the big guns of the cruiser *Idzumo* boomed as her crew started shelling the tiny British gunboat. The HMS *Peterel* returned fire from two machine guns and put up a pretty stiff fight, but having taken heavy hits in the overwhelming attack, she exploded. Six members of the crew were killed, and several of the wounded were picked up by Chinese sampans.

Moving upstream along the Whangpoo, the Bund became the Quai de France once it passed into the French Concession. Jim Cuming, the wireless operator for the *Peterel*, had been about to board a launch to return to his ship after a night's leave. He was standing on the Quai when the battle began. Luckily for him, he had thus far been unable to find a launch. Seeing his uniform in the artillery flashes, French Gendarmes grabbed Jimmy and hid him in a barrel. However the advance party of Japanese Marines remained a ways down the curvature of the Bund, where the Angel of Mercy statue marked the border of the French Concession and the International Settlement. That they didn't march into the French Concession in respect of Vichy France's position within the Axis was the blessing in disguise of the fall of France.

Once the gendarmes decided the coast was clear, they tapped on the barrel. Jimmy climbed out and slipped away into the city. He would live underground for the remainder of the war, sheltered in the homes of Allied citizens under the alias "Mr. Trees". Free China's people in Chungking would need information as to what was going on in Shanghai, and he had the expertise to broadcast intelligence to them. All he needed was a radio and information.

I personally had no idea any of this was going on because it was Monday morning, and so I was staying miles away out at Hollyheath. I had been up late reading my *Radio Amateur's Handbook*, and in my dreams the telephone kept ringing and ringing. When dad came into my room to wake me up, I was quite groggy and in fact it was still dark, about 5:00 in the morning. He looked very tense and was wearing a dark winter coat, with dark trousers.

"Dwight, I've got to go out for a couple of hours."

"Where?" I propped myself up on one arm; it was cold in the room.

"Never mind where I'm going. You just go back to sleep and I'll be back in a couple of hours, okay?"

"Okay," I yawned, and settled back down on my warm pillow.

"And Dwight?"

"Yes dad?"

"If Driver comes back here without me, have him take you straight to your mother's, okay?"

"Okay," I yawned again and closed my eyes. Suddenly the fact that he wasn't wearing his suit combined in my mind with what he had just said. I sat right up in bed. "What's happened?"

"We're at war with the Japanese; they bombed Pearl Harbor."

"Wow!" I jumped out of bed and stood before him. "What about Godfrey?"

"He should be okay. I don't think his ship has reached Hawaii yet, and even if it has, they would be moored in Honolulu."

"What should we do?"

"The best thing you can do is just stay put. Cook's downstairs. I'll be back in a couple of hours." He patted me on the head, and was gone.

I suddenly wasn't sleepy. I sat on the bed for a while, wondering if there would be even more dead bodies in the river. I walked over to the window and tried to see outside, but it was still dark. Then a dog started barking — probably Blitz, because it was a very deep bark — then the other dogs joined in as a plane flew very low over the house. The dogs kept up their noise until the drone of the engine finally died away. I dressed and went downstairs, but neither Amah nor the rest of the servants were up yet, so I sat in the living room and listened to the grandfather clock ticking away while it slowly grew light outside the big French windows.

Driver, I was to eventually learn, took dad down to the French Concession's waterfront in record time. Standard Oil's smallest and fastest launch was tied up and idling at the jetty along the Quai de France. The car screeched to a halt, RG jumped out of the car, ran down the ramp to the jetty, and leapt aboard. The pilot untied, gunned the engine and brought the launch around, but there wasn't a clear course to take. The Japanese gunboat that had participated in the attack on the *Peterel* was now circling around the slick of oil where she had sunk, spotlight flicking from one piece of debris to the next. My father had the pilot kill the running lights, and they crossed to the far side of the channel, circling a healthy distance around the gunboat before heading downstream.

This course had its risks, because it passed close to the shore of Pootung point and its Japanese gun batteries. Dad scanned the dark channel, which was dotted with the swinging lanterns of Sampans, some of which had helped to rescue the British gunboat's crew, and some of which were probably looking for wreckage of any value. He suddenly had an idea, told the pilot to steer into the midst of a cluster of those lanterns that appeared to be heading back to Soochow Creek. It was still very dark and the small launch almost blended in as it idled slowly downstream amongst the Sampans. Normally the oarsmen would yell at the launch, steer close and beg, or try to sell things, but this strange morning they stayed away and were deadly quiet, just working their oars.

The small flotilla passed Pootung and every gun of the battery seemed pointed at them. Fortunately, the Japanese gunners had their field goggles trained across the river on their troops, who were securing the buildings of the Bund. To these gunners the battle of the river was long over: it was six o'clock am, which in Shanghai in early December is near the start of twilight, and only about forty minutes until sunrise. The sky was beginning to lighten, and just as the *Idzumo* loomed to the left, tied up in front of the Japanese Consulate General, all the Sampans started to change course across the stream, headed for their moorage in Soochow Creek. One by one they cut across until the Standard Oil launch was alone and very conspicuous.

The Japanese cruiser was floodlit and busy with sailors. There were guards posted on all decks and they had rifles. Also, Japanese bluejacket marines were boarding a launch that had pulled up alongside the big cruiser.

"Get ready to power up, full-throttle, on my word," RG whispered, as they idled past, slowly so there would be no wake. The pilot nodded, deep in concentration, as he was following the shoreline much too closely for the given amount of light. In following the curve of Pootung, he was keeping as much distance as possible between the launch and the *Idzumo* on the opposite shore, but at this point the Whangpoo is only about a quarter of a mile (400 meters) wide, and the sky seemed to be getting lighter by the second. Fortunately, like the Pootung gunners, the sailors on the *Idzumo* were more interested in watching the occupation of the Bund than the river. My father and the pilot held their breath.

Finally they rounded the point, just as the Japanese launch sounded its whistle and cast off from alongside the *Idzumo*. Dad bet that the bluejackets were going to be taken downstream to Standard Oil's Installation in order to secure the oil and gas for Japanese military use. His launch would have more speed, but he needed time to do what he had planned. The outgoing tide was also necessary to do what he had planned, and it was beginning to slack, so dad decided to go for broke.

"Okay, full throttle!" he said. The pilot gunned the engine and they raced at full-speed downstream. Dad looked back at the *Idzumo*, expecting to see muzzle flashes from the guns, an explosion of water in his launch's wake, but not one shot was fired. He stood up in the cold winter air as they raced past the wharves of Hongkew on the left, and the industrial wharves on the right, such as those of the Matsui Company, Manyoshia, and Kawasaki.

Standard Oil's Installation was a few miles downstream of Shanghai because it needed to be beside deeper water in order to accommodate huge ocean-going tankers. They moored at the jetty and pumped their cargo into holding tanks. Then smaller river tankers, such as those that had been sunk along with the USS *Panay*, would moor and take smaller quantities upriver. In this way, the Installation was Standard Oil's central distribution center for China, so this gives you an idea of the size of the storage tanks, which held hundreds of thousands of gallons of Kerosene, Oil, and Gasoline.

The sun had almost risen when the launch pulled up to the huge Installation jetty. Dad grabbed hold of the ladder and instructed the pilot to move upstream a few hundred yards in the channel, to anchor and turn off the ignition, and to be sure not to smoke. The pilot shoved off and turned upstream. The Jacobsens were waiting at the top of the ladder, and they led dad to the valve area, where they'd assembled the mainly Chinese staff, one man per valve. Dad stood before them.

"Is anybody smoking?"

"No!" They all cried in unison.

"Good. Everybody ready?"

"Ready!"

"Kerosene tanks A and B. Open them up!"

The men on those valves used their whole bodies to turn the enormous iron wheels. There was a roar over the side of the jetty as the big pipes poured kerosene into the river, and the air filled with the smell.

Tank after tank they emptied into the Whangpoo, and it all started to drift out to sea. Obviously from an environmental standpoint this was a bad thing to do, but war is a special case. RG didn't want the Japanese to be able to use this fuel to wage war against the Allies and kill Allied soldiers.

By the time all the tanks were empty, the white winter sky had grown bright. Dad stood on the jetty with a cup of coffee Mrs. Jacobsen had brought him before she and her husband had motored off in their own launch for the French Concession, where they would stay with relatives. Having told the Chinese workers to clear out as soon as possible, he was alone, waiting for the Japanese marines, whose slow launch was finally catching up, chugging down the middle of the channel. It didn't matter if the Japanese captured him; the last of the oil was well on its way out to sea. Dad had done his duty.

The pilot made signs that he should bring the launch in, but RG waved him off. Instead, dad walked up the jetty well away from the pipes, lit a smoke, closed his eyes, and listened while the engine of the launch got louder and louder. Then, miraculously, the Japanese launch bore away from the middle of the channel toward the Riverside Power Station, which was across the Whangpoo and slightly downstream from the Installation. Dad waited until they were on the other side of the channel before he waved at the pilot to weigh anchor and bring the launch in. The pilot worked quickly and soon the launch pulled alongside. RG climbed down the ladder, hopped in, and they motored back upriver. There was no point in stealth, so they just went up the middle of the channel, past Japanese warships and gunboats at anchor, and tied up back at the wharf in the French Concession.

The dogs started barking again at about eight o'clock when the Packard rolled up the gravel drive. I ran out to the porch then down to the car. RG got out and scooted me back in the house, then started making telephone calls on the phone in the entrance hall. I tried to stand near him as he talked, but he waved me off. The household was just waking up, the servants getting to work. Number One Boy came in from the back yard and handed a small sheet of paper to dad, who read it while wrapping up his conversation with one of the Standard Oil bigwigs.

"Many outside," Number One Boy said when dad hung up the phone.

"I know. A Japanese plane dropped leaflets all over the city. Dwight, have a look at this while I go change," dad said, handing it to me before he hurried upstairs. It was a proclamation that Japanese forces were going to occupy the International Settlement at ten o'clock sharp. The paper was wet with dew.

"Where did you go this morning?" I asked dad when he came back downstairs in a suit and tie.

"I can't tell you," he said, putting on his overcoat and hat.

"Why not?"

"It would be neither in your best interests, nor mine," RG said, with a finality I knew not to question. "Now, regarding your best interests, have you eaten breakfast?"

"No."

"Well I'm afraid it's too late as we've got to get moving."

"Will there be school today?"

"No, but you are going to get a very valuable lesson. Go and get your things." He took the leaflet back and I ran up the stairs.

Amah no longer was coming with me on weekends, so I had to pack my own knapsack. I did this quickly as I could, then ran back down the stairs and out the front door past Number One Boy and Coolie, who was showing off a damp wad of leaflets he had gathered from the grounds. Cook was rattling around in the kitchen, working on the breakfast we weren't going to eat. I didn't take the time to say goodbye to any of the staff. How was I to know that this was the last time I would see them?

Outside, dad was sitting in the Packard while Driver wiped mud from the race to the river off the fender. It was a cold, overcast morning. Driver opened the door for me then went around back and stowed his rags in the trunk. Putting on his hat and gloves, he went forward and got behind the wheel. Just as Driver started the engine, dad leaned forward and spoke into the microphone.

"Driver, I think it might be prudent to take the flags off the fenders."

Driver actually spun around in his seat when he heard this. He looked like he'd just been slapped.

"You heard me," dad said. "Take them off."

Very slowly, I suppose hoping to stall so dad could change his mind, Driver got out of the car. Dad turned to me. "Lesson number one, probably under the heading of Minor Strategic Decisions. We have neither the Seaforth Highlanders nor the 4th Division here anymore, so the Japanese are absolutely superior both in numbers and firepower. Never stand your ground against a superior enemy except when you have no alternative. These flags don't ultimately matter to us, but they will provoke the Japanese, so we must remove them. Do you understand?"

"Yes."

"Good." We sat there while Driver fiddled around in the trunk, searching for tools or something. After too many seconds of this, dad opened the window and stuck his head out. "Just go up front and break them off!"

RG wasn't normally one to lose his temper, so this really made things happen quickly. Driver slammed the trunk shut and hurried up front on the right side. He wrapped the Union Jack several times around its pin with his white-gloved hands, gritted his teeth as if bracing himself for great pain, and pushed. A stiff snapping sound resounded through the steel chassis as the flag pin broke off the fender. Driver winced as he slipped the flag on its pin into his pocket. We watched him trudge around the grill past the shining hood ornament and do the same to the Stars and Stripes. Now we could go into the city.

Of course, we had to clear the checkpoint at the railway crossing first. Dad sat on the edge of the seat and stared ahead, but it turned out to be the usual Monday morning scene, with no more Japanese soldiers than normal. There was the usual traffic jam of peasants with their wares trying to get into the city, although there were slightly fewer cars lined up to get into town. I'm sure many executives who lived out in the countryside were either advised by their offices or consulate generals not to come into work, or made unilateral decisions to take the day off.

Going in the other direction, there was no traffic heading out of the city. You'd think people would be making a run for Free China, as the Japanese occupied the coast for only about 200 miles inland. However you must understand that the roads hardly extended out of the city so you couldn't drive the distance. The trip could only be done on foot. To do it, you would have to have adequate provisions to cover the distance, be in tremendous physical shape, and possess a fantastic knowledge of Chinese because you would need a lot of help along the way. Several days after the occupation of the city, there was a question and answer session between journalists and the Japanese military. One correspondent asked if Allied nationals were to be interned. The Japanese Army's public relations officer replied: "The International Settlement is in itself a sort of concentration camp."[17]

Very soon we were at the head of the line. Driver had to get out and perform his usual bow. The soldier closest to our car looked through the window at dad and me, but there was no more scrutiny than usual.

"Driver, put a little speed on," dad said as we pulled away. And so we drove down Great Western Road and past the SVC guard post, which was unmanned, into the International Settlement. The streets were very quiet, far fewer people milling around than normal. I didn't see any streetcars. Leaflets dotted the damp pavement, had fluttered onto the rooftops of big houses behind high fences, and were lodged in leafless hedges.

As we got into the business district, what appeared to be big flakes of black snow started to blow over the windshield and past the car. Driver turned right onto Szechuen Road and after three and a half blocks pulled over opposite Standard Oil's offices. The black snow was all over the sidewalk and in the gutters, blown there by passing cars.

"Well, this brings us to lesson number two," dad said. "Are you ready?"

"You bet!" I answered. Boy it was exciting: I was downtown with dad at the office at the start of the war!

"Good. Leave your books in here, and let's just step out and have a look," he said, as Driver opened the door. I followed him out onto the sidewalk, where we stood amidst the slowly falling ash. The businessmen who walked past were hurried, but not panicked, even though there were already a few Japanese military personnel milling around at major intersections.

"Where's the ash coming from, Dwight?"

"It's coming from the tops of the buildings," I said, squinting up past the grey buildings at the fluttering sky. "They're burning paper!"[xxii]

"Well done. Lesson two: bearing lesson one in mind, you still have to make it as difficult as possible for the enemy. All of our companies and consulate generals have codebooks and very detailed maps. The Japanese could use this information against our military forces, so we've got to make sure they don't get it."

"Why aren't the Japanese stopping this then?"

---

xxii Apparently the first paper shredder was invented in 1935 for Adolf Hitler, but they weren't yet in widespread use by 1941. Many companies in Shanghai such as Shell, Standard Oil, and others had incinerators on their roofs for the destruction of sensitive documents. Also, many offices and especially the consulate generals had fireplaces.

"They don't have enough men. They don't really know what to do with Shanghai," RG said, brushing a bit of ash from my hair. "Now, I want you to listen to me, because we might not see each other for quite a while. Are you listening?"

"I'm listening," I said, though it took me a second because my head was clouded with what he had just said.

"Good. Lesson three: war is never absolute. Do your duty continuously and without doubt and you'll find there is freedom and room to maneuver right at its centre. This is the most important lesson. Do you understand?"

"I think so."

Dad nodded.

"Now, your mother is worried sick about you, so Driver is going to take you back to her and Arthur."

"I want to stay and help."

"Dwight, your duty at this point is to ease your mother's worry. She's already got one son out in the middle of the Pacific to worry about, so you need to go and be with her." We were both still facing the Standard Oil building. If anything the paper ash was coming down more heavily. He squeezed my shoulder. "Go on," he said, and gently urged me into the car. I knelt on the back seat as we drove off, and watched RG cross the street of ash and go to work along with all the other men in fedoras.

He was right of course. Mom hugged me pretty tightly when I got home. Arthur had rushed over to the Shanghai General Hospital in case there were casualties in the occupation, so we had a late breakfast alone. After we ate, she made several phone calls to the American Presidents Line office to find out the whereabouts of the *Coolidge*, but their line was always busy. Amah just went about her ordinary day, washing the clothes I had brought back from Hollyheath.

I went out on the balcony at ten o'clock and looked up and down Avenue Joffre, but nothing was happening, in fact things looked quieter than normal. I went back inside and did a little work in my lab, but kept going out and scanning up and down the street, following the gleaming tram tracks off to the east and then to the west, hoping to see a Japanese tank or two, though none appeared. Respecting Vichy France as an ally, the Japanese didn't enter the French Concession that day or for many hundreds more to come. I felt oddly disappointed as the afternoon wore on.

In the International Settlement the occupation was calm and orderly. The Japanese marched in and took over targets in a very strict order; they had to because they didn't have a tremendous number of men. I would estimate the Japanese had 20,000 or 30,000 troops in Shanghai, which sounds like a lot, but in a city with millions of people, it was a drop in the bucket. The best way to control those millions was to control their money, so the banks were the top priority.

One bank took precedence over all others, as it was *the* symbol of western domination and *the* depository of wealth generated by that domination: the Hongkong & Shanghai Bank. The marines took over the bank's palace-like head office on the Bund at exactly ten o'clock that morning, and promptly froze all assets of enemy nationals. That was the practical part of the maneuver. In terms of the symbolic, down came the Union Jack and up rose the rising sun. By nightfall the lions that guarded the doorway had been broken from their mountings and carted away.[18]

I went to school the next morning. College St. Jeanne D' Arc was French and so the Japanese left it alone, though it was situated right on the border between the French Concession and the International settlement. Actually, I'm pretty sure all the schools continued to operate. Shanghai American School had opened as usual the morning of Pearl Harbor and half the kids showed up for school. By December 15th, about 80% of SAS students had returned to school.[19] For the most part businesses continued to run too, and life carried on. Veikko and I continued our experiments, worked on our radios, and walked between each other's houses in the French Concession without any trouble at all.

The movie *Empire of the Sun*, though fairly accurate about life in camp, over-dramatized the actual act by the Japanese of occupying of the city. It also depicted Allied citizens being interned right away whereas, in reality, mass internment wouldn't occur for about fifteen months. Until then it was easier for the Japanese to let us take care of ourselves. I want to make it clear that the Japanese were not even close to omnipresent, and had nowhere near complete control of the city. Therefore they had to channel the limited force they could exert in ways that could achieve maximum control.

To this end, the Japanese shut down pretty much all Allied publishers, radio stations, and newspapers right away. The radio station XMHA, which Arthur's friend Elroy Healey ran, was one of the first to go. *The North China Daily News* disappeared right away (not to return until after the war), but not the British-run *Shanghai Times*, which had been deeply indebted to Japanese creditors for some time. This lower-brow paper became the mouthpiece of the Japanese occupation force, issuing edicts almost daily, along with news of Japan's spectacular military victories, which were also illustrated in huge "war situation" boards affixed to the sides of buildings. The journalist weren't really to blame they had to eat.

One of the first published edicts was that the banks would reopen on December 11th for withdrawals by Allied nationals limited to 500 yuan,[xxiii] and with a monthly cap of 2,000 yuan. This placed most Shanghailanders at a similar economic level to Chinese. I think the cap had practical reasons of control, but the Japanese also put it into place in order to humble westerners. Mother, Arthur, and I were fine because Arthur, being "German", had access to his accounts. RG didn't however, so he had to let all of the house's staff go except Number One Boy and Driver, who was paid for by Standard Oil.

Another of the initial edicts was that all Allied nationals had to register at the new Japanese headquarters downtown in Hamilton House. The deadline was Saturday, December 13th, and the office was only open from 9 to 5, so there were huge lineups there and also at passport photo shops. Essentially you had to fill out forms regarding your level of income, all property, dependents, etc. In return, the Japanese gave you a photo identification card that allowed you to travel around the city and through the checkpoints they had setup at major intersections.

Mother and I took the streetcar down late in the week, had our photographs taken, and lined up out in the cold and the rain outside Hamilton House for a whole day. It was miserable. Still, this was the first I had seen of the Japanese occupation, and I was interested to watch the soldiers guarding the doorways to office buildings. They stood so still and stern, saluting their superior officers who arrived in jeeps and strutted up the front steps in order to take over whichever Allied company was inside. A funny thing was that a certain amount of paper ash was still coming down from rooftops, and would for several days. I watched it from the lineup on the sidewalk beside Foochow road. We

---

xxiii Really 500 fapi, but people still called a fapi a yuan out of habit.

were just around the corner from dad's office, so I mostly craned my neck to see if I could spot him. Chinese people walking past just gaped at us. The faces in the lineup were not happy.

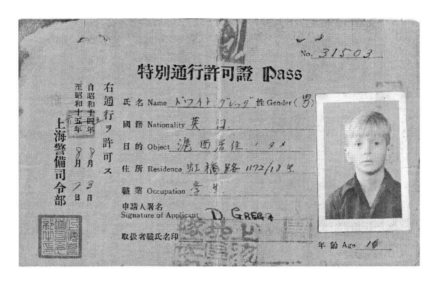

My wartime traveling pass through the city, to be presented when stopped.
I tried to make myself a year older by writing under the picture.

Our identification cards were only good roughly during business hours. The Japanese had immediately imposed a curfew of 6:00 pm (or earlier, at nightfall in winter) until 8:00 am. If you were spotted out during curfew hours you would be shot. At this point there were no armbands, so there was no way the Japanese could visually distinguish a German or Italian citizen from American, Dutch, British or Canadian, so Caucasian Axis citizens had to stay indoors too.

It got very claustrophobic staying indoors, because we were also ordered to cover our windows for blackout purposes and to keep glass from flying inward due to exploding bombs. We pasted sheets of the suddenly-despised *Shanghai Times* to the glass using flour and water. Especially prominent in these pages were cartoons by the artist Sapajou. Like the newspaper in which he appeared, Sapajou was a turncoat. It seemed that the very *hour* that

Pearl Harbor was struck, he went from being an Allied cartoonist to an Axis Cartoonist. It was a remarkably rapid change in allegiance and he was not forgiven for this, dying in obscurity.

Sapajou puts Roosevelt, Churchill, and Stalin in chains.

I'm not certain just how effective the "blackout paper" was, but I guess it must have cut down the glow from the city at least slightly. This was supposedly demanded by the Japanese to prevent our bombers from seeing too much of the areas of the city, but at the beginning of the war the U.S. Air Force didn't have airstrips near enough to launch strikes against Shanghai. The "blackout" was probably just another aspect of psychological warfare on the part of the Japanese.

It could be argued that the Japanese thought the possibility of bombing was real because they also forced the various Allied resident's associations to build "bomb shelters", which were just culverts sunk vertically into the ground. These obviously provided no protection from direct hits, but the idea was that you could dive into one in order to avoid flack traveling horizontally outward from nearby explosions. Then again, this also was demoralizing for us, not only being forced to build them, but because later in the war, in monsoon season especially, the shelters filled up with water, snakes, oil, everything you can think of, and you had to dive in whenever the siren went off. If you didn't dive in, you would be shot. Sometimes there was so much disgusting debris in the culvert you seriously considered just taking the bullet.

After about a week of the war, the city became eerily quiet. Shanghai was and is a serious contender for noisiest city on earth, but the Japanese had taken over all the gas stations very early on. Some people simply drove their cars until they ran out of gas. Many others, such as Veikko's dad, parked their cars with whatever was in the tank, ready for any sort of emergency. Then the Japanese issued yet another edict on December 18th, this one stating that only people engaged in essential services could operate automobiles. Fortunately for dad, the Japanese really needed him and other executives in the office at this time in order to keep the remains of Standard Oil running. They let dad keep his car and Driver and even provided the gas.

Buses were also withdrawn, leaving only trolley cars. Mornings in the week before Christmas I would wake up to silence, punctuated by the infrequent passing of a trolley car, rather than the usual dull roar outside the window of Arthur's office on Avenue Joffre.

School broke for two weeks for the holidays. With the harbor essentially shut down and fuel rationing in effect, shortages of food and just about everything else started to manifest very quickly. Christmas Day came with bad news, not a whole lot of food, and no word on Godfrey. The bad news was that Hong Kong had surrendered to the Japanese, and so we all felt pretty low when we went to bed that night.

Finally, next afternoon the phone rang. Arthur answered, and he handed it to mother. It was dad. He had received a telegram from San Francisco through Standard Oil channels stating that Godfrey had arrived safely. Mom started to cry. That night I lay awake in bed thinking about my big brother. Godfrey was a swimming champion, and I decided before falling asleep to go for a swim at the Cercle Sportif Francais the next morning.

I got up early and set out towards the French Club, which was about a mile (1.6 km) east of our apartment, on the same street as Veikko's, but left instead of right at the Cathay Theatre. Well, what a horrendous fifteen-minute walk that turned out to be! Because of the cold, beggars and the poor who lived in hovels had died in the night. This was a "normal" thing in Shanghai, not a characteristic of the war. Nevertheless, this was the coldest winter in decades; a hardship compounded by general shortages so the corpses were really stacking up. "Over the previous year the cemetery had picked up 29,440 bodies in the streets; of those 20,720 were children."[20]

The morning light revealed corpses covered by straw mats on the sidewalk at just about every intersection and often slumped against a building somewhere in-between. People had carried or dragged their deceased from the minor roads on which they lived to Avenue Joffre, ready for when municipal workers would come by in their truck. One worker would take the wrists of the corpse, the other its ankles, and they would swing the corpse back and forth a few times until there was enough momentum to get it over the side and into the box on top of several others. The workers would then add the straw mat to a tidy pile of straw mats belonging to the other corpses. This same procedure was repeated at intervals down the street. When they had a full load, they would take the corpses out of the city and burn them, then sell the mats.

Walking to the gym that morning, scarf wrapped around my neck, seeing my breath on the air, I stepped gingerly over the dead, quietly as possible, as if they could be woken.

Chapter 9

Espionage in Shanghai:
The Rescue of Jacques Marcuse

The Japanese culture deplores any sort of secrecy, and during the war this manifested as a sort of spy-mania. In early January of 1942, the Japanese showed up at Hollyheath in the middle of the night and arrested dad, not for dumping the oil and kerosene into the river, but because he was Worthy Grand Patron of the Order of the Eastern Star. This was a Masonic organization and because of its secretive nature, with the special handshakes, late-night initiations, etc., the Japanese assumed it was, or at the very least *could be used as,* a system of espionage. So they played it safe and rounded up all the major people, beginning with RG, the leader of this potential nest of spies.

Number One Boy and Driver of course were ordered to clear out, which they wisely did, vanishing into the night. I don't know what happened to the dogs, which is probably a good thing. At any rate, the Japanese tagged everything inside the empty house that could be appropriated for use at a later date, then put a paper seal on the front door, declaring it the property of their empire. Then they pulled away with dad in the back of the jeep, stopping to padlock the gate. Dad never really told me the particulars of that night (not even long after the war), but I'm sure he paid very close attention to where they were headed. And I'm sure his heart rose when they pulled up to the Custom's House wharf, because this meant that he wasn't being taken to Bridge House. Instead, they took RG in a launch across to Pootung, where he would be interned in an old cotton warehouse.

Frederick J. Twogood, dad's boss, wasn't so lucky. I don't know whether Twogood was arrested because of the dumping of oil and gas, but I highly doubt it. If the Japanese had known about such a large-scale act of sabotage, dad, as chief engineer, would most certainly have been implicated, and his fate would have been much harsher than internment at Pootung. Quite simply, Twogood was chief of the company that symbolized American dominance in China, and I think the Japanese wanted to punish him for this, so they took him to Bridge House.

Bridge House was the headquarters of the Japanese secret service, a very nasty group of spies and killers called the Kempei Tai. They operated from two locations. The main branch was situated in its namesake, an apartment building called Bridge House about a block from the Garden Bridge on the Hongkew side of Soochow creek. The satellite branch occupied the "requisitioned" Union Jack Club next to the racecourse.

Just after Pearl Harbor, the Kempei Tai had remodeled the interior of the Bridge House apartment building by knocking out walls to create three large rooms, then building several small wooden cages within these large rooms. This was the first step towards their goal of creating a sort of hell on earth.[21] They then went on a spree of arresting enemy nationals, both men and women, whom they suspected of a wide range of crimes against the Japanese Empire. Conditions for the prisoners were deplorable. It was cold in the cages, yet the prisoner's were stripped upon arrival and given only a light cotton gown to wear. There was only a single bucket for a washroom in each cage, which contained maybe a dozen people, and it wasn't emptied often enough. With the crowding there wasn't enough room in the cages to lie down, so people had to sit upright for days, sometimes weeks on a cement floor while they waiting to be interrogated. The food was wholly inadequate so people lost weight, compounding the obvious health problems created by sitting on the cement floor for such a long period of time. Basically their buttocks would wear away.

When it finally came time for questioning, the prisoner was called out and dragged to a nearby cement room whose door was left open so the other prisoners could hear the screams. The cement room housed all that was needed for the horrors that people with a little power can inflict on others: canes for beatings, pliers to extract certain body parts, electrodes to be applied to genitals, and water torture apparatus.

The water torture was probably the worst, if relative relationships can still exist at such extremes. Guards trussed the prisoner on a steel table then forced a steel spout connected by hose to a large container of water into his mouth. The spout was small on the open end and grew wider, so when shoved into the prisoner's mouth it would force his teeth open, or simply break them. This accomplished, the guards hoisted the tank high to create a great deal of pressure, opened the valve, and water flowed into the prisoner's stomach, into his lungs, up his nose, and he would find himself drowning on the steel table. The guard might choose to sit on the prisoner's stomach, bounce up and down a little, and water and blood would spew out and the prisoner would more often than not lose consciousness. At the point of unconsciousness, the guards would hang up the prisoner by his feet for drainage. After a few repetitions of this, the most innocent of men would sign a confession, no matter how ridiculous. The pressure of the water would often break men apart inside, causing internal bleeding and toxic poisoning.

Frederick Twogood likely underwent the full range of torture at Bridge House because he died from his injuries in the United States after being released and repatriated. A Standard Oil press release on May 1st 1944, Mr. Twogood's date of death, states that he "was imprisoned by the Japanese in Bridge House jail in Shanghai, where he spent 109 days of incredible hardship and privation." You can see now why RG was perfectly happy to be interned. When I heard the news about dad, my sadness was tempered by the fact that at least he wasn't in Bridge House.

The Kempei Tai were also of course arresting many actual spies, but it was a hydra-headed problem for them. They picked up the head of British intelligence very early, but then a prominent Shanghai businessman named Michael Moses Moore instantly took over this position. Moore was the result of the marriage of a Chinese mother and British father, and had gone to Cambridge University. Dressed in the correct fashion, and socializing in the correct places, he passed absolutely as an Englishman. Dressed as a Chinese he could be totally mistaken for a Chinese man, could move between Shanghai and Free China, even by train, virtually undetected. Given what we know about Arthur, it will be no surprise the two men were close friends, and Michael Moses Moore often came over to our apartment for short visits.

The head of American intelligence had a better fate than his British counterpart, managing to escape to Free China. It fell to Elroy Healey (just by coincidence another of Arthur's close friends!) to take over the top position. Healey had come over to our apartment very frequently for dinner before the war. Conversation at the table was always lively and intelligent and we all enjoyed ourselves very much. Elroy was about the same age as Arthur, a very witty guy, quite thin. As these evenings wore on there always came a point where the men would take two glasses of wine and excuse themselves to Arthur's office, where they would have a private conversation. Mother wouldn't allow me to go near the office, which of course was my bedroom, so I would fall asleep on the sofa with my head on her lap.

Since Pearl Harbor we hadn't seen Elroy at all. I suppose he assumed his arrest was imminent and felt it would be in bad form to have the Kempei Tai move in on him whilst visiting friends. He had simply and openly gone about his necessary business through December 1941 and into January 1942, expecting to be nabbed any second, but it just wasn't happening. Perhaps, not having his predecessor to interrogate, the Kempei Tai simply didn't know he was now the top American spy. Then again they did know he had been general manager of radio station XMHA until the outbreak of the war, and they were seriously pursuing one of the stations former broadcasters, a French journalist named Jacques Marcuse.

Marcuse had been one of Arthur's patients for about a year, and in connection with Elroy Healey had also become a family friend. He was a compact, urbane man from Paris with *a lot* of women in his life. Every time I saw him he had a different beauty on his arm. Not to minimize his considerable panache and social ease, Marcuse's magnetism was also due to the heroic public stand he had taken against Vichy France. Up until Pearl Harbor he had been a journalist for the Agence Française Indépendante, but he had also hosted a weekly radio program on XMHA. In his program, Marcuse reported events in Europe from a Gaullist perspective and encouraged the French to believe in the eventual liberation of their country. He did this in conjunction with the British Press Attaché's office, headed by John Alexander, a family friend from Hollyheath who had been nabbed at the start of the war and held under arrest at Cathay Mansions with all the other Allied diplomats until repatriation could be arranged. These broadcasts made Marcuse probably the most prominent member of the Free French group in Shanghai, and of course enraged the Vichy council of the French Concession, along with the Axis nationals. They had had to tolerate this annoying man for some time, but as soon as a state of war existed in the Pacific theatre he was marked for assassination and probably worse.

Knowing this, Marcuse left Shanghai the morning of Pearl Harbor and joined with Chinese guerrilla troops who were moving around the city and gathering refugees; mostly Allied nationals who wanted to make the journey east to Free China. Because the Japanese army didn't have enough men to patrol all of occupied China at all times, their soldiers moved up and down the frontier at irregular intervals of days, hoping to catch groups of would-be escapees. Basically the goal of the guerillas was to gather as many refugees as possible, find a hole in the Japanese patrol best guaranteed by the soldiers just having passed, and rush through that night. Complicating this was the flat terrain and general lack of cover around Shanghai. It was like a large-scale game of chess played over a period of weeks and months.

Michael Moses Moore, an exceedingly capable intelligence agent, got word to Marcuse and the guerillas that several U.S. Marines captured on Wake Island had escaped from a Japanese prison camp and wanted to get back their own signaling unit via Free China. Then the employees of the Shanghai Power Company threw their lot in too, having had enough of working for the Japanese, and all were told to meet in a small town south of Shanghai. Unfortunately Marcuse had injured his leg several days before and it got severely infected on the walk to the town. Hoping he could get better and still make the journey to Free China, Marcuse wrote a letter to my stepfather, "AP", describing the injury and appearance of the infection, then gave it to one of the guerillas who specialized at moving into and out of Shanghai.

I guess I must have been at school when the guerilla, named "George", arrived at our apartment. He knocked at the door to the good doctor's office, and when the door opened to Arthur's face, which bore the told-of fencing scar, George unscrewed the top of his bamboo walking stick, and pulled out the letter from Marcuse. Arthur read the letter, mulled over the details, then retreated into his office, returning with antibiotics, label peeled from the bottle, and written dosage instructions, both of which George carefully stowed in the top of his walking stick.

"I wish you hadn't brought that message past the Japanese," Arthur said, while the guerilla carefully tightened the bamboo cap. "It has my name and this address on it, and if the sentry had stopped you it would have been very bad for me, my family, and your group."

"George never caught," the cheerful man proudly countered before tromping back down the staircase. And he wasn't caught on that particular journey; he got the medication to the patient. Unfortunately for Marcuse, the infection was too advanced for the dosage and number of doses the walking stick could conceal, so his leg deteriorated and he had to leave the small town. Marcuse was fortunate in leaving, because the Japanese sentries at the railway crossing stopped George the next day, took his bamboo walking stick, and figured out how to open it. It contained another letter to Arthur, but George tore the small, still-folded piece of paper out of the sentry's hands, put it into his own mouth and swallowed. This really very brave act saved us, but the Japanese interrogated George and they struck the town pretty hard.

Marcuse made his way slowly and painfully back into the city. As to what was happening back in Shanghai, the city had definitely settled into the rhythm of war, though the news seemed to always be bad. Singapore fell on February 15th. Well, let me tell you that the Japanese were in the mood to celebrate their victory the following day. All of the International Settlement was flapping with Japanese flags, and the trolley cars that came into the French Concession were bedecked with flowers. This day of celebration was also my eleventh birthday, so I pretended it was all for me. The Dutch East Indies capitulated to the Japanese on March 9th. Dad was still in Pootung.

It was a rainy Saturday in the middle of March that Elroy Healey finally showed up at the apartment. Mom and Amah were out trying to scrape up some fabric for mending clothes, and Arthur was seeing a patient in his adjoining office. The patient was a fairly high-ranking Japanese officer. You see, because Arthur was such a well thought-of doctor, and also because he was "German", he had become the *de facto* official physician to Japanese officers. The enemy held him in such high regard that when Wang Ching Wei was shot (either in the arm or the shoulder) in the middle of the war, Arthur was the doctor they flew out to Nanking to treat the Chinese puppet leader. It didn't matter that Arthur was a kidney specialist; they wanted him and no one else. The situation was decidedly odd for me: Japanese officers, with their various complaints, were stretched out for examination during the day on what by night was my bed.

Note from S. Sirasaki, Japanese administrator of The Country Hospital,
telling Arthur that he isn't billing enough. A show of respect for the good doctor.

I was in the kitchen taking a break from the lab, making myself a peanut butter sandwich accompanied by an ice-cold glass of milk. There was a knock at the front door.

"Dwight, could you get that?" Arthur called from his office. The walls were quite thin.

"Sure." I tromped out of the kitchen, opened the door and there was Elroy in a peacoat and black toque, looking much thinner than usual. He opened his mouth to say hello, but I put my finger over my lips while darting my eyes quickly at the other door to the office. Elroy understood and went quiet. I stepped aside so he could get into the apartment quickly, closed the door, and led him into the kitchen, then out the back door, which led down some really quite rickety wooden steps down into the back yard.

"How are you Dwight?" Elroy said once we were outside on the landing, and the door was closed.

"Good," I said, but nothing more because I had no idea what to say. This was a man wanted by the Japanese, so he had taken on mythic proportions.

"Listen, I need you to give Arthur a message for me. Tell him that Marcuse's leg has gotten worse, so he's back in town, staying at his girlfriend's place. Okay?"

"Okay, but which girlfriend? The big one with the small voice?"

"No, not that one." Elroy chuckled. "The small one with the big voice. Does Arthur have office hours tomorrow?"

"No, not on Sundays."

"Good. Can you tell him that I'm going to lug Marcuse up the back steps tomorrow morning at eight-fifteen sharp?"

"Yes."

"Topnotch. See you then." Elroy went quietly down the steps and left out the back way.

I passed the message on to Arthur once the Japanese major left and he was very excited to hear that both Marcuse and Healey were alive and at large. The two men appeared at the back door to the kitchen the next morning and Marcuse looked to be in very bad shape. He was pale and sweaty and skinny from wandering around the countryside. Healey had gotten him to our place by hiring one of the new pedicabs, converted rickshaws attached to half a bicycle to answer the shortage of gasoline and the banning of vehicles for private use. Seated and pedaling either behind or in front of the passengers, depending on the type of pedicab, the rickshaw coolie had made a rare and enormous jump in caste from a sort of horse to a sort of driver.

Marcuse, pale and trembling, with Arthur and Elroy under his arms for support, hopped on his good leg through the kitchen. His bad one had swelled to the point there was no fabric left to his pants. I ran ahead and opened the door to the office.

"Can I help?" I asked, as they sat Marcuse down on the examination table.

"No thanks Dwight. Just close the door," Arthur said, as he held the feet of Marcuse. "Ready Jacques?"

"Ready," said Marcuse, though it held no conviction, and was followed by a terrible groan as Arthur swung up his legs onto the table. I closed the door so mom wouldn't wake up. Arthur had told me not to tell her, as she might worry about having a fugitive in the house. Amah wasn't in, as we'd cooked up a bunch of errands for her to run. This is why I had offered my assistance: I felt a part of the team.

Arthur worked quickly to clean the wound after setting up Marcuse with an I.V. to counter the infection. Unfortunately the work was more extensive than Arthur had imagined, so mom woke up before the work was complete. She came out in her dressing gown and asked me where Arthur was. I couldn't lie to mom, so I told her he was with a patient.

"He can't be; it's Sunday," she corrected, but then there was another groan from the examination room. Mom proceeded toward the sound's source, opened the door, and was treated to the horrifying sight of Marcuse's leg, which actually was salvageable, though didn't look it at the moment. She then was charmingly greeted by both the owner of the leg, by Elroy Healey, and by a sheepish Arthur, his lab coat a real mess. She turned around and marched me out to the balcony. It was a fine spring day, everything turning green.

"Dwight," she said, holding both my shoulders and looking deeply into my eyes, "I need you to promise me you won't tell anyone at school about this."

"I promise."

"Not anyone, not even if they are Allies. Do you understand?"

"I understand." Of course I did: I was eleven years old.

When you're that age, nothing ever strikes you as particularly strange, perhaps because most things in the world still are new. The war isolated Shanghai and by summer there were definite new things going on. About half the factories had shut down. By July, there was a rice shortage in the city. Rationing was put into effect and smuggling became widespread. General shortages caused inflation and on June 30th 1942 the Japanese replaced the fapi with a Japanese-backed Central Reserve Bank of China dollar. We lined up and traded our old money in, two dollars of the old for every one dollar of the new. For Allied nationals on a limited income, this inflation was very bad news. Americans, British, and Dutch had to organize themselves and pool resources on a large scale. For instance, the British Resident's Association (BRA) set up at the old cathedral on Kiukiang Road, where rations were collected and sold, as well as basic general supplies. Up until the war, these associations were basically just welcome wagons set up to form a sense of community, but with Pearl Harbor their organization became the framework upon which nationals could organize themselves financially, and were a lifeline for many people. For instance, they took up collections for people who had no work or savings.

Whereas the BRA was the financial lifeline, the Swiss Consul-General was the mediator between Allied nationals and the Japanese on official matters. They performed tasks such as issuing identification. Here is my mother's identification card:

BRA card for cereals. Japanese tolerance amidst shortages.

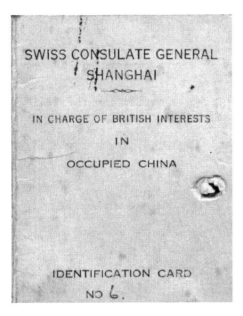

Mother's Swiss Consulate identity card (cover). Note the telling detail:
"Occupied China". The Japanese had only taken a small portion of the whole country.

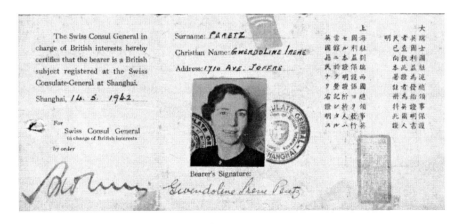

Mother's Swiss Consulate identity card (inside).

With the great heat of summer I got sick with a recurrence of malaria. I was actually fortunate to get it at that point, only three months after the fall of the Dutch East Indies, because a certain amount of quinine was still available. Then there was a cholera epidemic, and Arthur was swamped. As soon as I was feeling better, I started to work in his lab doing hemoglobin and white blood cell counts. He taught me how to count the white cells: lymphocytes and leukocytes. I would look down the microscope and see them: basophiles, and eosinophiles (allergy response white cells), and record the information. It never dawned on me that a boy my age doing this sort of work was unusual.

Over this period Marcuse steadily improved. We got the news from various girlfriends with whom he was staying. One day Arthur was asked if he could go and see Marcuse that night. Mom, Amah, and I sat up and listened to the radio (short spurts of music interspersed by many outlandish reports of Japanese victories and American losses) while Arthur went on his errand. He had an armband that indicated he was a physician, and as long as he wore it he could be out on his bicycle after curfew without being shot. He also took along his blackjack, a leather-handled pouch filled with shot that was good for knocking out assailants and would-be thieves without killing them.

Arthur knocked on the door and waited with his doctor's bag ready, but the only medicine to be practiced that night would be hypothetical. Marcuse answered the door and was in fine shape. Elroy Healey was waiting inside, in order to relay an idea John Alexander had had regarding Marcuse (of whom Alexander, like Healey and Arthur, was very fond). Rumor in John's circles had it that a ship would sail out of Shanghai in mid-August in order to repatriate British diplomatic personnel. By this time everyone in Shanghai was talking about repatriation. One ship, the *Conte Verdi*, had already sailed from Shanghai in order to meet the Swedish *Gripsholm* for an exchange of Allied nationals for Japanese nationals. Both ships were painted white with crosses and the word **DIPLOMAT** painted boldly on the side and funnels, floodlit at night so that U-boats could see these markings through their periscopes and not attack. Lourenço Marques, the free port, was chosen as a rendezvous point. The formula of exchange was one human being for one human being, really very egalitarian on the face of it, as neither rank nor social position supposedly mattered.

Mind you, this egalitarian concept of one human life for another was tinkered with on both sides. The ship that was to leave in mid-August, the *Kamakura Maru*, came to be known as the "Wangle Maru" because of the incredibly complicated political and social maneuvers that prominent Shanghailanders made to get on this ship. Furthermore, neither side wanted to hand over someone who could be useful in the enemy's war effort. So Japan, and I'm sure the Allies too, sent home many people who were terminally ill. John Alexander knew this, and had told Elroy Healey, who put the question to Arthur:

"Can you make Jacques appear to be terminally ill?"

Arthur thought about it for a moment.

"I can give him acute myeloid leukemia."

"Good."

Healey contacted John Alexander with the news, who applied to the Japanese to have some Free French exchanged too for Japanese nationals living abroad. The Japanese accepted.

The following night Arthur went back to Marcuse and gave him a typhoid vaccination, as well as injecting milk intramuscularly to get his body temperature up as much as possible. When Arthur came home, he created a fake blood count and inserted it into a chart very openly headed with Marcuse's name. He must have done all this in his lab, as I was asleep on the examination table.

The next day at Shanghai General, Arthur searched for X-ray pictures that would fit the disease. Unfortunately, all he could find was one of a female patient that showed very clearly the outline of her anatomy. There was no getting around it: an X-ray was needed for the chart and this was the only one in which the glands were prominent enough for clear diagnosis. Arthur attached it to Marcuse's chart, hoping for the best.

The good doctor went to see his "patient" over the next few nights and the injections were having the hoped-for effect: Marcuse was becoming very ill. Moving him to the hospital was the tricky part. The girlfriend he was staying with had to agree to surrender Marcuse, which would be an admission on her part that she had been harboring him. She very bravely agreed to tell the Japanese that Marcuse had been at her apartment for several weeks, and that he had been very ill upon arrival so she couldn't really turn him away. She did this, though to what personal consequences I have no idea.

This arranged, Arthur called again the next morning then telephoned the hospital, which sent an ambulance, accompanied by two Kempei Tai men on motorcycles. These thugs had heard the name over the radio and given chase. One went inside to question Marcuse's girlfriend, while one followed the ambulance back to Shanghai General. Arthur sat in the back with a delirious and raving Marcuse, taking his pulse, frowning in very real concern, because his friend was actually quite ill.

No sooner was Marcuse admitted than Arthur received telephone calls in his office at the hospital from the Japanese Navy and a senior officer of the Kempei Tai. An intelligence officer of the Japanese Navy visited that afternoon and asked very politely and very correctly how Arthur came to know Mr. Marcuse and where the fugitive had been all this time. As prearranged, Arthur told the officer that Marcuse had been very ill for several weeks and had been in the lady's apartment. Because he was so ill, he had actually been unable to surrender to the Japanese. Asked why he did not report Marcuse's whereabouts, Arthur simply told the Japanese he had to protect the name and the illness of a patient and that it was beyond his professional calling to report anyone, unless he was a criminal, to any authority. Well, the Japanese Navy went for it hook, line, and sinker. This was face-saving news for them, the only reason why they hadn't captured this annoying Gaullist Frenchman.

This explanation was not good enough for the Kempei Tai, who did not use Arthur's medical services to nearly the same extent as the army and the navy, nor revere such a rare intellect in the same way. These were brutal men. An interrogator called at Shanghai General the next morning, closed the door to Arthur's office behind him, and started pacing back and forth. One "most troublesome point we would like you to clarify" led to another, and the good doctor was subjected to an entire day's worth of questioning and threats. However, Arthur stuck to his story and by eight o'clock the interrogator finally seemed to be satisfied.

Word of the interrogation had gotten back to my mother from one of Arthur's colleagues at the hospital. She had been sick with worry all day long. I got home from school and she told me as soon as I stepped through the door. We simply didn't know what to do. Finally, about two hours after dark, Arthur arrived home. Taking off his armband, he acted like it was nothing, like there was no problem. Later that night, after we had gone to bed, the phone started to ring. It was the interrogator, who felt it would probably be in the patient's best interests to get a second opinion, and to expect a Japanese doctor to arrive at 10 o'clock next morning in order to examine Marcuse and have a look at his chart. Arthur agreed, said goodbye and hung up. None of us got much rest that night.

Arthur was there at 8 o'clock in the morning to see that everything was in order. Just to be sure, Marcuse received another typhoid vaccine injection. His temperature soared to 104 degrees Fahrenheit (40°c). Arthur checked on all the charts to make sure all the blood tests were there. Any nurse who could have possibly noticed something was sent to another floor. Two hours after the appointed time, the Japanese doctor appeared, without finding it necessary to apologize for his tardiness. Marcuse really looked ill, absolutely lived up to the picture of his ailment. Arthur went to the nurse's desk, took the chart out, and showed the Japanese doctor the patient's leukocyte count, a blood count that matter-of-factly told of an acute myeloid leukemia.

Nodding his head as he scrutinized the numbers, the Japanese doctor demanded to see the X-rays. With a heavy heart, Arthur took the picture with his left hand, covering the outline of the female breast with his thumb, and pointed with his right hand to the enlarged gland. The Japanese doctor frowned, hummed and hawed but then nodded and seemed satisfied. He concurred with Arthur's diagnosis and the very bad prognosis, then very curtly left.

Later that afternoon the Kempei Tai telephoned and relayed the report from their doctor stating that Marcuse was terminal, but could probably be made to live until mid-August. Did Arthur agree? Oh yes indeed, Marcuse could very possibly live until mid-August. Everything seemed to be going all right.

Coming down from his 104 degrees Fahrenheit temperature, Marcuse was glad to hear the news, and quite naturally protested against any further "treatment". However, the required symptoms were so severe they could not be simulated in any way but through actual manifestation, so they would have to continue with the injections exactly the same way until the day the exchange ship departed. Knowing the alternative—torture in Bridge House—Marcuse made the decision for one sort of suffering over another.

This was one of those impossible decisions war foists upon people, and Arthur would have to make one too. The Japanese quickly made it known that were going to exchange this practically dead man for a useful and healthy Japanese national held somewhere by the Allied Forces. Arthur was to do his best to keep this man alive. Yet every day closer to departure, Arthur had to take Marcuse a little closer to death, because the typhoid vaccine was building up a cumulative effect. By early August, Marcuse was a very, very sick man, and for all intents and purposes might as well have had acute myeloid leukemia. If the ship didn't sail soon, he would die. Arthur faced the unpleasant choice of stopping the injections in order to save Marcuse's life (for death in Bridge House), which would probably give the game away and therefore condemn himself and perhaps my mother and me to particularly nasty fates, versus letting Marcuse, a very close friend, die. Finally, on the morning of what appeared to be Marcuse's last day on earth, word came that the ship was departing. There was no typhoid vaccination that day.

Unconscious, Marcuse was taken by ambulance down the Bund to where he was carried by stretcher aboard the *Kamakura Maru*. Everything seemed to be all right. We went down to watch the ship depart, and were more than relieved to see them steam out of the harbor. However, this wasn't the hoped-for end to our anxiety. Marcuse's health improved dramatically through the journey with treatment from the ship's doctor, and as soon as he landed in Lourenço Marques, the British authorities shipped him to New Delhi in order to resume his broadcasts. John Alexander protested that this would harm us, but to no avail. Marcuse's words came across the airwaves once again. Now the Japanese (and the Germans) knew they'd been deceived.

This was a period of real worry for Arthur, mother, and I as we assumed it was only a matter of time until the Japanese would arrest and torture us for misleading them. However we didn't know we had an ace up our sleeves. Whereas an aspect of Japanese culture, suspicion of secrecy, had condemned RG, another aspect of their culture, saving face, saved us. The Japanese wouldn't cause one of their own nationals, the Japanese doctor who had so lackadaisically inspected the X-ray, to lose face over diagnosing a healthy man as being terminally ill. I would also theorize that they depended on Arthur's services far too much to follow through on any sort of direct retribution. Instead, the Kempei Tai pursued indirect retribution. They arrested Elroy Healey in late September and locked him up in Bridge House.

Caption for following two pages:

Jacques Marcuse attests to Arthur's heroism. After the war practically everyone wanted to emigrate to the United States. Notice that Marcuse plays up his own involvement in the planned escape of the American engineers, perhaps to this end. Also, notice that Marcuse doesn't mention that Arthur had to make him ill, avoiding the issue by indirectly stating that no Japanese doctor verified the diagnosis. Marcuse knew that Arthur wanted to emigrate to the United States. I can only surmise he covered up the milk and typhoid injections so as not to endanger Arthur's chances of being a doctor in the United States. The Hippocratic oath states that above all a doctor should do no harm. Who knows at the time how the American College of Physicians would have viewed such an act from the outside and no real awareness of the alternative in Bridge House. Great hero, bad doctor? At any rate, the letter shows the major point: that Arthur really stuck his neck out.

May 14th 1946

TO: AMERICAN CONSULATE GENERAL,
    SHANGHAI.

          Following my conversation with Mr. Latrabh at the American
Consulate General here this morning,I wish to put the following statement
on record:
          1. Prior to the outbreak of the Pacific war, I was a resident of
Shanghai where I was engaged both in news reporting on behalf of the
Agence Francaise Independante,85 Fleet Street,London,England, and on
propaganda work on behalf of the Free French movement whose spokesman I
was in this city. My official work was carried out in close co-operation
with the British Press Attache's office and included a daily broadcast
over the American owned XMHA station. Dr. Arthur Peretz,whom I first met
in the early months of the year 1941 had been recommended to me as a
physician by several of my friends in the Free French movement.
          2. Shortly after Pearl Harbour,I, together with a party of
Allied nationals,left Shanghai and joined a group of pro-Chungking
guerillas outside. Sometime in March 1942,I returned to Shanghai with
instructions to organize the escape of a number of American engineers
employeed by the Shanghai Power Company. As my health was bad, I called
on Dr. Peretz whom I knew I could trust. Dr. Peretz,who was aware of my
position,offered every possible assistance without any thought for his
own personal safety.
          3.At a later date, one of our guerilla guides having been
caught by the Japanese and found in possession of incrimating evidence,
I was compelled to go into hiding in Shanghai. The Japanese gendarmerie,
together with the Municipal Police of the French Concession which was
controlled by Vichy,tried to arrest me. They began a very thorough search
for me and questioned a number of my friends whom they suspected of
knowing my whereabouts. During this period,which lasted over four months,
Dr. Peretz helped meuninterruptedly both as a physician and as a friend,
thereby putting himself in a very dangerous position.
          4.Early in July of the same year,the British Press Attache,
Mr. John Alexander,who,although interned with other Allied diplomats,had
managed to remain in constant communication with me,informed me that he
might succeed in putting me on the exchange ship which was due to leave
towards the middle of August,provided I were not in hiding and I were in
a dying condition. It was,of course, very much of a gamble,and it could
only succeed with the full co-operation of a medical man. Once more,
Dr. Peretz volunteered to help. He made the necessary arrangements for me
to move seemingly openly,that is under my own name,but discreetly to the
Country Hospital to which I moved from my hiding place during the month
of July. In order to carry out our scheme,Dr.Peretz had to produce
faked blood-tests and X-ray pictures. He came to see me every day and was
my only contact with the outside world,apart from a few very intimate
friends. There is no need to point out that had the Japanese sent one of
their own doctors to examine me I should have been found to be enjoying
perfect health and that Dr. Peretz would have been made to pay for his
courage and his devotion to the Allied cause with his life-presumably
in a particularly unpleasant manner.

- page 2 -

5. At the very last moment, my name was put on the exchange list, and after Mr. Alexander had informed the Japanese Consulate General that he would himself refuse to leave on the exchange ship if I were not put on board, and Dr. Peretz had certified that I had no more than a few weeks to live, our plan finally succeeded. I should like to emphasize that I had, at the time, no other means of leaving Shanghai and that I consider that I owe my life to Dr. Peretz. This is also the view held by Mr. Alexander who can easily be contacted through the British Foreign Office.

6. I was to learn later that Dr. Peretz also helped in various ways several other Allied nationals during the Japanese occupation of Shanghai without ever taking into consideration the grave risk which he was constantly running on behalf and for the welfare of others.

7. Finally, I should like to make quite clear the point that no question of money was ever involved and no fee ever charged by Dr. Peretz, and that Dr. Peretz gave his full assistance to those who needed it, including myself, in a completely disinterested and altruistic spirit. Out of all the extremely dangerous work which Dr. Peretz did for the Allies, he never derived any profit, material or otherwise, for himself.

(signed) Jacques E. Marcuse
Far Eastern Manager,
Agence France-Presse

American Consulate General
Shanghai, China.

Subscribed and sworn to
before me this 14 day of
May, 1946
William M. Olive
American Vice Consul
Shanghai, China.

Formerly accredited War Correspondent U.S.A.
Forces, China Theatre.

Fee No. 4489

American
Foreign Service
$2.00
Fee Stamp.
WMO
cancelled American Consulate General.
May 14, 1946

State of California)
) SS.
County of Alameda   )

I, Morris E. Bruner, a Notary Public in and for the County of Alameda, State of California, duly commissioned and sworn, and residing therein, HEREBY CERTIFY that I have this 11th day of February, 1947, compared the above and foregoing with the original and find the same to be a full, true and correct copy thereof.

WITNESS my hand and seal this 11th day of February, 1947.

Morris E Bruner.
Notary Public in and for the State of California, in and for the County of Alameda.
My Com. Expires Apr. 25, 1950

173

Chapter 10

The Kempei Tai Take Mother
And Arthur in to Bridge House

The Japanese issued red identification armbands to enemy nationals in late September of 1942. Each armband bore a four-digit identification number below a large letter denoting nationality: A for American, B for British, N for Dutch. Partially this was an attempt to humiliate us, but if this was the goal, the color was very poorly chosen, as red is very auspicious with the Chinese. Also, it lent to the wearer a vaguely militaristic air. Like many boys my own age, I looked forward to turning thirteen, old enough to wear one. (A photograph of mine is on the back cover.) Adults knew better: this was the first step towards internment.

More steps followed, some just to destroy our moral, and some more tangible. For instance, later that fall, the Japanese issued an order that enemy nationals could no longer go to the movies. Then, on November 5th, several hundred very prominent enemy national males, mainly executives, were taken from their beds in the middle of the night and interned in the old barracks of the U.S. Fourth Division Marines on Haiphong road. This became a sort of holding ground for those the Japanese suspected of espionage, and many men were taken from Haiphong to Bridge House, to be returned a few weeks later, if at all.

Elroy still hadn't been released by early January of 1943, nor had my dad, and we were naturally very worried about both of them. The worst part was knowing that you couldn't do anything. Then, for some reason, the Kempei Tai started to allow Allied nationals to send food into Bridge House twice a week. I suppose that with general food shortages and a growing number of prisoners, even the starvation diet was becoming difficult to provide. I doubt any individual contribution made it to its intended recipient, but was just sort of divided up and distributed in general. Mother sent packages of food intended for Elroy twice a week.

Many of the men held at Haiphong were taken in to Bridge House for questioning then returned to camp a few weeks later in a really bad state. Some of the men interned in the camp were doctors, and they treated those returning who were in moderately bad condition, but they had no facilities to treat those seriously injured. The seriously injured were sent to external hospitals and Arthur took care of some of them. Having seen the condition they were in, not just due to torture, but also due to malnutrition, he wanted to take extra precautions with Elroy. So, one morning when mother was making sandwiches, Arthur and I ground up some vitamin B1 (thiamine) tablets in the lab. Then we took the mortar-full into the kitchen and sprinkled the fine powder on the peanut butter that mom had just spread on the bread.

I was to find out something was wrong when I walked through the gates of College St. Jeanne d'Arc after school that day. It was raining pretty heavily and I was keeping my head down, but a car horn honked, which was an odd thing to hear in those days, so I looked up to see where it came from. Well, it came from what was probably the most spectacular car in town: a bright yellow Studebaker "President" four door convertible with a tan top. At that time, a yellow car was really shocking, as this still wasn't long after Mr. Henry Ford had said, regarding the Model T: "You can have any color you want so long as it's black." Well, this amazing automobile belonged to Carlos May, a good friend of Arthur's. Flamboyant and quite fat from good times, Carlos was a Frenchman (though definitely not Vichy), the Far East representative for Coty and Hennessy brandy. He'd probably managed to keep his car because the Japanese officers considered his line of fine alcoholic beverages an essential service. Lily Green, Carlos's "friend", rolled down the passenger-side window.

"Dwight, get in the car before you're soaked right through."

"Gee, thanks!" I said, glad to get out of the rain. I assumed they had just been driving by and spotted me. I opened the passenger door, which opened front-first, and piled in.

"Dwight, we've got some bad news," Carlos said, putting the car into gear and pulling out.

"What?"

"Arthur and your mom have been taken in by the Japanese for questioning."

"Bridge House?"

"We think so. You're going to have to stay with us for a while."

"I don't want to," I said. My eyes were suddenly burning, and my face was wet, but it was just rain. "I want to go home. Where's Amah?"

"She's at the apartment, but it's not safe for you there. They might come back."

"I'm sorry Dwight, I really am," Lily said, turning around in her seat. Her makeup was running from her eyes, and it wasn't just rain on her face. We drove to their apartment quite near to the Bund in silence, except for the rain drumming on the canvas top, and the windshield wipers beating back and forth.

Good times in the past. Carlos May, Lily Green, Arthur, and Mother out at a dinner club.

We hung up our wet clothes when we arrived. There was a room off the main hall of Carlos's quite luxurious apartment that was paneled with exquisite Southeast Asian silks. I was gawking through the door at this incredibly opulent room, and Lily noticed.

"My 'quarters'," she explained, and ushered me through to the kitchen.

We had dinner and listened to the radio for a while until it was time to turn in. Lily got up from the sofa and went into "her quarters". Carlos sat staring at his feet for a while, yawned, and grunted as he got up. He patted me on the shoulder as he passed, and followed her into the same room.

It's funny how the mind works, how we cope. As I lay under a blanket on their sofa, I found myself wondering about the domestic arrangement in this palatial apartment just as much as worrying about mom and Arthur. I mean, Carlos and Lily were sleeping in the same room, but *they weren't married!* Focusing on this odd situation probably saved me from going crazy with worry, as I fell asleep to it.

Carlos drove me to school the next morning. I sat through the lessons but it all went in one ear and out the other. It was the longest day of my life. Brother Edward just droned on and on and on and I stared off into space. Finally the bell rang, I rushed outside, and my mother was standing at the gate. She looked very tired but otherwise alright. I ran into her arms.

"But where's Arthur?" I asked after a long hug.

"He's fine, just making his rounds, but he'll be home soon."

Arthur and mother told me the story over dinner, and it was hilarious.

All the trouble had been over the package they sent to Elroy. The Kempei Tai had taken apart one of the peanut butter sandwiches and found the white powder. Well, this was out of the ordinary, and the suspicious mind always assumes the worst. The guards guessed the powder was some kind of poison with which Elroy Healey was going to commit suicide. They sent a car to the apartment to pick up mother, and another to the hospital to pick up Arthur. Fortunately both of them were taken to Bridge House at the racecourse, rather than the main branch by the Garden Bridge. This meant they didn't have to spend the night in a holding cell, though they did have to spend it waiting in a windowless interrogation room in the basement. The problem was that neither Arthur nor mother knew the real reason why they had been brought in. They assumed the Marcuse affair had finally caught up to them, but the room likely was bugged, so they could only stare at each other with grave concern.

Finally, early the next morning, the locks turned and the heavy door opened. Carrying a thick file, Colonel Ogamino sighed deeply as he sat down. Arthur had heard of him. Ogamino was very high up in the Kempei Tai organization; probably only answering to General Konishita, who ran the whole show, so to have such a big shot for an interrogator was either a very good or a very bad sign. Probably the latter. Ogamino started to ask questions in rapid fire without looking up from his documents. He spoke fairly basic English as virtually all Japanese officers did, but it was slow-going.

As usual, the questioning began with the very general: "Who are you, how long have you lived in Shanghai….", and moved in tighter and tighter orbits toward the central issue. Arthur answered all the questions and Ogamino never attempted the standard technique of separating his interrogatees. Likely this was due to the standard disdain of the Japanese male for the female in important matters. How could this mere woman know of the male code of honor, suicide in the face of dishonor, etc.? At best she might be useful if she were to burst into tears and thus humiliate Arthur.

The questioning went on for hours and hours without any mention of Marcuse. Still, it had to be coming. Arthur prepared for the worst, but he had an ace up his sleeve. The first time Ogamino had looked up from the very impressive file, the good doctor diagnosed a seborrheic dermatitis on the colonel's face. Finally, well after lunch, Ogamino dropped the bomb that Arthur had been certain would pertain to Marcuse.

"Doctor Peretz, how many years you know Elroy Healey?"

"Several years," Arthur began, then he leaned forward in his chair, squinting, as if just noticing. "Ogamino-san, please pardon my interrupting, but do you know that you have sebhorreic dermatitis on your skin?"

"Oh," Ogamino stammered, thrown off. "Yes. I know. Deborraic sermatsisis."

"Well, I could cure that for you. No more. Gone."

"Really?" Ogamino said. His eyes had literally lit up.

"Really."

Well, the colonel sat there for a second until he appeared to have made a very definite decision. He nodded his head, got up and left the room. Mother looked at Arthur with raised eyebrow, and he winked at her. Just then Ogamino came back in with one of Elroy's peanut butter sandwiches on a plate. He plunked it down on the table.

"Is this poison for your friend…for hara-kiri?" Ogamino asked, but he was shaking his head "no!" vigorously as he said it.

"No, this is not poison."

"Not poison. Good." And Ogamino started to smile, but his smile vanished as Arthur reached out, grabbed the sandwich and bit into it. The look of terror on the colonel's face: suicide in his office! But then mom burst out laughing.

"See, not poison," Arthur said, chewing away. "Vitamins. Healthy." And he took another bite, as he probably was hungry from the long wait and interrogation. Then he handed it to mom, who turned up her nose and put it back on the plate.

"Ahhhh! *Not poison*," said Ogamino-san. Mother and Arthur were sprung from Bridge House in minutes, but with a promise.

"And here's where I will require your assistance, Dwight," Arthur said, taking a sip from his wine after telling the story over dinner.

"What would you like me to do?"

"Well, the bacteria that causes this problem generally is responsive to sulfa drugs. I need you to deliver a sulfa-drug ointment to Bridge House tomorrow. Okay?"

"Okay," I said, and pretended like it was nothing for the rest of the evening. Boy, I'll tell you, that was the second night I lost sleep. **BRIDGE HOUSE.** We boys used to play a game by the same name, reenacting what we thought went on inside, though we really had no idea and our imaginings weren't nearly as bad as the truth. Nevertheless that night I lay awake in the vigil of a condemned man. At sunrise I heard activity in the laboratory. I pretended to be asleep when Arthur came into the room to wake me.

After breakfast I took the ointment, which was in a paper bag, got on my bike, and rode down towards the racecourse. It had stopped raining the night before and the morning was very cold and dry. I pedaled slowly, but got there too quickly. Well, of course you can imagine I was out of my mind thinking about approaching Bridge House. I locked my bike against a lamppost in front of the YMCA, quite a ways away from the building, because if I went any closer my hands would be shaking too much to do it. My knees were practically knocking together and I felt like I might fall down as I approached the stone-faced sentry standing at attention on the top of the front steps. Arthur had instructed me to deliver it personally to Ogamino, so I had to get inside.

"Uh, hello," I said to the sentry, bowing deeply. He didn't bow back or even reply. He just stared straight ahead, over my head actually, toward the centre of the racecourse. Boy, did his bayonet look sharp! "Uh, delivery for colonel. Ogamino-san?" The sentry didn't move or blink. The only sign he wasn't a statue was that his breath steamed rhythmically into the cold morning air.

A Japanese officer pushed past me to enter the building. The sentry saluted and moved aside, then stayed put in his new peripheral position. It was now or never. Heart pounding in my throat, I took a step, fully expecting to be skewered. It didn't happen, and the sentry continued to stare at some imaginary point in the middle of the racecourse. I took another step, with the same result, so I took two more and pushed through the heavy, ornate door.

Inside was a rather opulent lobby with Japanese officers milling around, but no sign of Allied nationals. Maybe they went in the back. Now, it was an old gentleman's club, so there was a front desk for members to check in. Behind it stood a junior officer, and I approached him.

"Delivery for Colonel Ogamino," I said, placing the bag on the counter. Where the bag was rolled up was really creased from my grip, and damp from my sweat in spite of the cold.

"Excellent. He has been expecting this." The young officer replied in perfect English, taking the bag and putting it behind the counter. He then started writing in some sort of ledger and I no longer existed.

"Uh, sorry, but I'm supposed to give it directly to Ogamino-san."

No response, nothing. He scribbled away. The longer I stood there unable to speak again the more my knees shook and the faster my heart pounded. Finally I lost my nerve and stumbled back out through the heavy doors, almost knocking that statue of a guard from his plinth. I ran down the street, struggled with the lock, hopped on my bike and rode like hell away from there.

That night Arthur asked me how my mission had gone. Little did I know it at the time,

---

but he was testing me. I lied and told him I had handed the bag to Ogamino. Arthur was pleased, and this was a source of guilt and worry for me for some weeks, culminating in a visit to our apartment by Ogamino and his wife. Arthur and mother had invited them for dinner one Friday evening and the whole day I was really biting my nails. What if the colonel showed up with the dermatitis on his face?

Well, I answered the door and my expert diagnosis was that he didn't have dermatitis anymore. To make a long story short, after dinner, Colonel Ogamino got up and made a little speech. It seemed he had been practicing his English.

"Dr. Peretz and Mrs. Peretz, I must say, beautiful dinner, beautiful people. I thank you from the bottom of my heart. And my wife's bottom also." Well, of course, I started to giggle, and much to Arthur and mother's chagrin. I just couldn't help it, having been so tense all through the evening that Ogamino would somehow expose my lie. Still, the feeling of goodwill in the room was too strong for my giggle to ruin. Ogamino had had the seborrheic dermatitis for 20 or 30 years and the sulfa drug took it away. Well, the sun once again rose and set on Arthur, and again, little did Ogamino know that Arthur had anything to do with the American, British and French intelligence. Little did I know that I would soon be involved in Arthur's secret world.

Before that, though, I would have to go to camp. News of general internment came in early January of 1943, over a year after the war had begun. Why did the Japanese suddenly change their minds? With the June 1942 Battle of Midway, the August 1942 landing of U.S. Marines on Guadalcanal (the first battle of the "island hopping" campaign), and the January 1943 defeat of the Japanese landing forces in New Guinea, the tide of the war had shifted. The notion of Shanghai as a sort of concentration camp in and of itself had depended on the city's extreme isolation. Whereas it had initially been easiest for the Japanese to let us continue to run industry as well as it could be run, and to therefore feed and clothe ourselves, when the U.S. Army began to advance, Allied nationals became a threat. We were potential soldiers either through abandonment of the city to an ever-closer Free China, or through a disbursement of weapons by U.S. troops that might attack Shanghai. This in mind, the Japanese decided that the difficulty and expense of housing and feeding us in internment camps was worth the strategic safety of locking us up all in one place.

There would be three major concentration camps, named Civilian Assembly Centers (CACs), aside from Pootung: Lunghwa (mainly for British); Chapei (mainly for Americans); and Yangchow, which was a day's journey out of Shanghai. From early March to the summer of 1943, enemy nationals were to be interned in 35 separate batches. You had to provide your own necessities for camp, and you could store anything in your house not stickered for Japanese use in a Swiss godown run by Scharpf, Gunther, & Company. The day of internment you'd struggle out the front door with your camp gear, lock up your house, and put a paper seal the Japanese had provided across the doorway.

The first group of internees went into the Pootung CAC in late January, several weeks before the first of the main groups. This group was comprised of males without families. They assembled downtown at the BRA headquarters in the cathedral on Kiangse road, where they supplemented their own supplies with those gathered by the association. The rule was that an internee could take as much as he could carry into camp, but no more. It has been described[22] that the internees resembled one-man bands as they carried their loads of pots and pans and bedding the two blocks from the cathedral to the Customs House jetty, where they boarded tenders that took them across the river to camp. RG must have been like an original settler to these new arrivals, a sage, though I cannot comment on his experience in camp because he never talked about it.

I don't really want to talk about it either. Our time came on March 11th; mother and I were not exempt just because she was married to an Axis citizen. To give you the basic facts, our group assembled at the racecourse. We then set out for Chapei Camp, which was an abandoned university about two miles north and slightly east of Hollyheath Estate on Chung San Road. Mother and I shared a 6-foot by 8-foot cubicle, partitioned by a curtain from others in the main dormitory building. Yes there was barbed wire, yes there was hunger, and yes there was hardship, but I have to give the Japanese civilian administrator real credit for making it as bearable as possible, given the shortages and the situation. Perhaps we were fortunate in that he had gone to university in England, had practiced law there for years, and was a real anglophile. For instance, the university had an excellent library and he made it clear to us that we were allowed to take out books. My favorite books in the library were Arthur Conan Doyle's various books, individually, like the *Hound of the Baskervilles.* It was easy to read and very exciting to me.

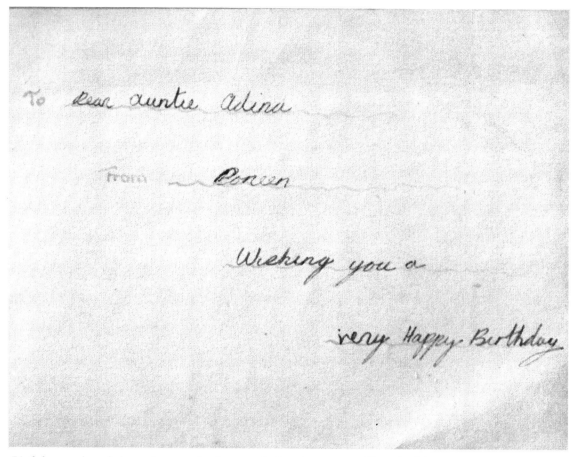

Birthday card made by an internee for her aunt in Lunghwa camp. (Note the faint stamp) Many things like this could be exchanged around and out of camp with Japanese discretionary agreement.

The administrator also allowed a camp newsletter and many other projects that kept us busy and kept up moral. Also, much of the faculty of the Shanghai American School, along with many of the students were interned in Chapei, so the administrator allowed internees to set up a provisional school for us children. Mother and I only stayed for a few weeks until Arthur managed to pull some strings and get us out.

That's all I really have to say on the matter. Perhaps my vision of camp is skewed because I wasn't there for long (I went in a second time, but again for a very short period), and this is a good reason not to detail the experience. More importantly, I feel the subject of life in the camps has been documented exhaustively and often (due to exaggeration) *exhaustingly*. Therefore the reader will have to go to other books for a description of life inside the camps. *Empire of the Sun* is the best known, both as a novel and a movie, but the most accurate description I have ever read on this subject (and I have read 40 or 50 such books) is by David Nicoll, called *Young Shanghailander*. I would love to recommend this book to the reader, but I don't think it has been published. At the very least, I heartily recommend its publication.

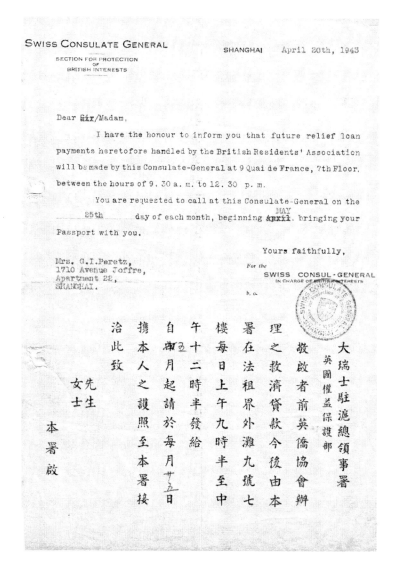

SWISS CONSULATE GENERAL

SECTION FOR PROTECTION
OF
BRITISH INTERESTS

SHANGHAI   April 20th, 1943

Dear Sir/Madam,

     I have the honour to inform you that future relief loan payments heretofore handled by the British Residents' Association will be made by this Consulate-General at 9 Quai de France, 7th Floor, between the hours of 9. 30 a. m. to 12. 30 p. m.

     You are requested to call at this Consulate-General on the __25th__ day of each month, beginning MAY April, bringing your Passport with you.

                       Yours faithfully,

Mrs. G.I.Peretz,
1710 Avenue Joffre,
Apartmant 22,
SHANGHAI.

For the
SWISS CONSUL-GENERAL
IN CHARGE OF BRITISH INTERESTS

b. o.

大瑞士駐滬總領事署
英國權益保護部
敬啟者前英僑協會辦
理之救濟貸款今後由本
署在法租界外灘九號七
樓每日上午九時半至中
午十二時半發給
自本月起請於每月廿五日
攜本人之護照至本署接
洽
此致
先生
女士
本署啟

With its personnel in camp, the BRA was no longer effective in its role as collector and distributor of financial aid. The Swiss Consul-General took over. As evinced by the date, mother and I were out of Chapei camp very soon.

Shortly after our release, very suddenly, the Kempei Tai released Elroy Healey from Bridge House. He was transferred to Haiphong Road camp. We all breathed a sigh of relief because he had survived, but also because he hadn't given away Arthur's involvement in saving Marcuse. That was odd, because everyone talks under torture, and why wouldn't they ask who else was behind the escape of Marcuse? Ogamino may have instructed his Kempei Tai interrogators not to ask such questions, but I can't be sure of that.

It's surprising to find there is room to breath and to maneuver in the middle of the war. Spring rolled along and Veikko and I would go up on the roof of my building and stay up there two or three hours in the evening, watching people go by on the street three floors below. Our expertise in radios was progressing rapidly, and to further our experiments we ran an antenna wire down from the roof to a disused room in the basement of the building, which became the radio room. From there I could talk to Veikko, who was on his father's setup at the Finnish Consulate General.

Out the window of my radio room was the back yard of the building, which was on the north side, and therefore in shadow. There was a moderately large area, probably 25 x 25 feet (7.6 x 7.6 meters) that was what we would call a lawn, but there was hardly any grass on it. I dug up this area and planted potatoes, which grew extremely well, and I made some money from selling them (mainly to my parents!) Across the backyard and my potato patch was a Chinese girls' school. Our interest was definitely moving to girls, as I was nearly thirteen and Veikko was fourteen. It was very interesting to us to watch these girls doing various things in their school where they couldn't see us because we were two floors above them. This of course caused us certain revelries, which I'm sure are experienced all over the world.

Summer came in spite of the war. Though there wasn't a recurrence of the previous year's cholera epidemic, malaria became a BIG problem in the summer of 1943. With the flow of quinine from the Dutch East Indies now having been cut off for more than a year, Shanghai's supply for civilians was completely used up. Also, with overcrowding and inadequate mosquito netting for most internees, the disease was particularly rampant in the camps. Arthur was visiting the camps often, and it really bothered him that all these people were suffering, and many dying. He resolved to do something about it.

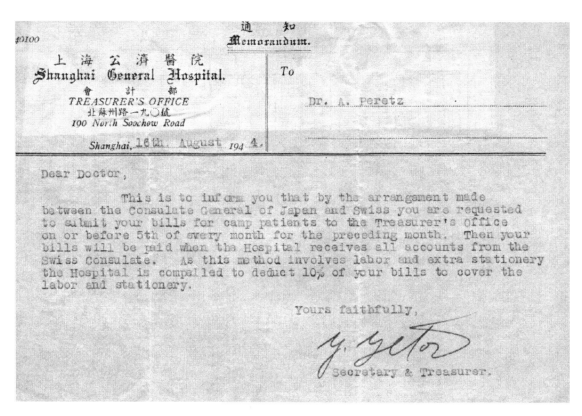

Arthur and other non-Allied specialists often assisted American and British doctors interned and practicing in the various camps. The Japanese insisted the consulting "Axis" physicians bill for this work.

Arthur started into a routine of overwork that was awe-inspiring. On top of doing his rounds both in Shanghai General and in the camps, he worked very late into every evening trying to find an alternative to quinine. School was out and I worked in his lab through the summer, doing blood cell counts. I worked very hard too, staring through the microscope until I started having dreams about microscopic things. I was happy to do it though, because it helped Arthur, and he in turn found an alternative malaria treatment with a substance called bismuth violet, which was nowhere near as effective as quinine or any of the products available today, but nonetheless was still effective in a basic way against malaria.

Unfortunately, bismuth violet meant exactly what the name says, VIOLET. When you took this medication, which seemed quite innocuous from the patient's point of view, you literally turned violet, that is, your skin became violet, the whites of your eyes became violet, your urine became violet, and this stuff came out through the skin and stained all of your clothes violet; not a nice scenario. Then again, it was the only thing available and was therefore used, particularly around Shanghai, both as a preventative agent as well as a treatment agent. Arthur actually had a paper published on this in the *Shanghai Medical Journal*. This was a quarterly publication written in English; really quite an amazing phenomenon in the middle of China, and shows again the collaboration and mutual appreciation between both the Chinese and na-ku-ning that is often ignored in histories of colonialism.

As to the fate of colonialism in China, it was sealed in August of 1943. 101 years after the Treaty of Nanking came into effect, granting foreign powers land and trading rights in China; Britain, France, and the U.S. surrendered their rights in a new treaty with Chungking. Wang Ching Wei took over the administration of a unified Shanghai, and the French Concession was finally controlled by Japanese military. They rolled into our part of town. Once again, I don't want to give the impression that the streets were swarming with the Japanese, as they now had to fan out over an even larger area, and therefore were thinner on the ground than before.

We did have a scare though, in that the Japanese had been operating radio triangulation trucks in the International Settlement, and they picked up our signal one night when Veikko and I were talking. We hadn't thought of this possibility before, as the Japanese simply hadn't been able to enter the French Concession with this sort of equipment. At any rate, they worked in teams of two trucks and each could find the direction from which a signal was coming, but not the distance. The men in the two trucks talked to each other, giving their position and heading of the signal, and by drawing their respective lines together on the map they got a pretty accurate position at the point of intersection. At any rate, they showed up at our door and, once again though the goodwill Arthur had built up, we got off lightly. The story we gave was that I was just playing around with a radio I had built, but obviously I was just a little kid so it was harmless. (I was probably a bit small for my age due to the food shortages. Indeed, for this reason I never grew to the same height as Godfrey, though in just about every other way we were very similar.) At any rate, the

Japanese just made me take the wire down. I don't think they knocked on Veikko's door, perhaps due to the fact they knew they had triangulated the Consulate General's office of a supposed ally.

But the situation of alliances was changing too. With the September 1943 capitulation of Italy, the Italians of Shanghai suddenly had to wear armbands too, marked in the same pattern as ours, with a large letter I above a four-digit number. Theirs were the probably the nicest armbands anyone has been forced to wear in the history of warfare. Basically the Italians tore down the beautiful deep-red velvet curtains in their Consulate General and made their armbands from the fabric. Many were interned in spite of still siding with Mussolini, but scuttling the graceful *Conte Verdi*, as well as one gunboat in the Whangpoo. The great white liner rolled on its side, but the river was too shallow for it to sink out of sight. Japanese engineers set right to work to salvage the *Conte Verdi*, but Chennault's "Flying Tigers" came in low from the west and strafed the superstructure, slowing recovery operations.

Obviously the Italian liner couldn't be used in the next Gripsholm exchange. Instead, the *Teia Maru* sailed from Shanghai on October 15th, 1943 to meet the *Gripsholm* in Goa. Once again, an exchange of one human for one human was made. People marched in orderly lines down the gangplanks of both ships, passed one another as "enemies" on the jetty between, then up the other gangplank to sail home to their respective ports. Rich Hale and his family were aboard this final sailing. According to the *New York Times*, they reached New York harbor on December 1st 1943.

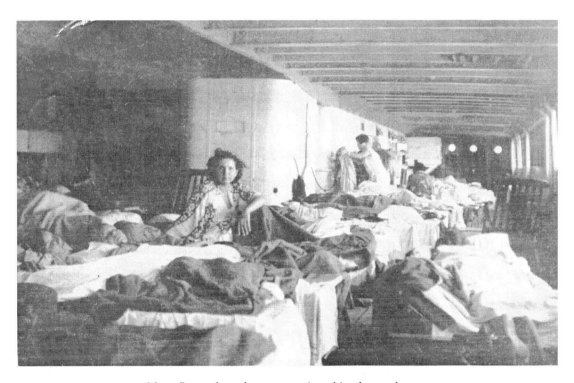

Mary Scott aboard an evacuation ship, date unknown.

Mother and I, on the other hand, had to go back into Chapei camp, though we once again only stayed a few weeks until Arthur managed to get us out. RG was transferred to Chapei shortly after we left. Now that dad was out of Pootung, Arthur and mother could send food and supplies to him, which they did as soon as they could. They did this for many others as well, both British and American.

Mother and Arthur send RG supplies. Mother and I had witnessed some pilfering of aid packages by Japanese guards, mostly chocolate, but the majority of aid got through.

Chapter 11

Radio Transmissions to Free China, Bombing Raids, and Final Victory

Arthur's intelligence work increased in both depth and scope as the war progressed. The indicator of this to me was that he would often be on the telephone at night, having conversations in which he kept switching languages every couple of sentences. As I've said, this had always been a parlor trick of his and he'd shown it to me before, but now as he did it he wasn't smiling. If he knew I was in the room, he stuck to fairly innocuous (or perhaps coded) stuff for the English segments.

The Flying Tigers and other groups like it were flying small-scale missions further and further north from the Burma road area (the hump, the pilots called it) and closer to the city. Strafing the *Conte Verdi* is a good example of the sort of work they were doing. Of course, pilots were often shot down, and it was very difficult for those who survived to get out of enemy territory in once piece. Elroy Healey had been getting this information before he was captured, and through the Office of Secret Service (the OSS, American Intelligence's precursor to the CIA), he helped to form the Air Ground Aid Section, or AGAS.

The AGAS was a rescue network, mainly involving guerillas, for pilots downed in enemy territory. One thing they did was to set up a reward system for the safe return of pilots. On the back of the book you'll find an American flag with Chinese text. This was sewn on the back of the Flying Tigers' fur-lined leather flight jackets in case they crashed in Asia. The same message was printed in five languages, essentially saying that the wearer is an American airman who is fighting the Japanese and if you get him back to us in Free China or anywhere else, you will receive a handsome reward.

Now, not only was Arthur having to meet the demands of coordinating a lot of this in Healey's absence, he was also providing free medical treatment for guerillas and Allies injured in operations both for AGAS and general intelligence, sabotage, etc. All this action was on top of his work in the camps, his private practice that was swamped with demanding Japanese officers, and his office and hospital hours. The needs of the guerillas even permeated his hospital hours, as many would check in with mysterious illnesses in order to confer with him. The good doctor was stretched to the limits.

Furthermore, intelligence demands were increasing as American forces made progress in their island-hopping campaign. Soon, either through capturing air bases within the range of existent bombers, or through development of the new B-29 bombers, or both, the U.S. Air Force would drop ordinance on the industrial and Japanese military areas of Shanghai, the harbor, and especially warships. But first, the U.S. Air force needed targeting information.

As I've mentioned, Arthur's office and the ward in which he worked in the Shanghai General Hospital had a bird's-eye view of what had been called "Battleship Row" before the war, due to all the Allied warships moored there, and now was the moorage for Japanese warships. It of course fell to Arthur to gather intelligence, but there simply wasn't time, so he delegated. He found three nurses he could trust (interestingly, one of them was a German nun) to write down Japanese warship movements as they observed them out the window in the course of their work. Late in the afternoon they passed the observations which included details such as the number of troops boarding which ships, and their times of departure to Arthur, who would pass them to guerillas checked in to the hospital with phony illnesses, or would take them home and hand them to George's courier successors who stopped by.

Unfortunately, by the time the information got to U.S. Air Force command, about 200 miles (300 km) away, it was mostly out-of-date. Furthermore, with the French Concession now occupied, this system of manual delivery was becoming extremely dangerous. Something had to be done.

"Hello Young Master," Michael Moses Moore said to me in his perfect Oxbridge accent, standing on the back steps looking for all the world like an archetypal Chinese peasant. Amah was messing around in the kitchen behind me. She never said hello to him, because she was thrown-off by the disparity between his appearance and what came out of his mouth.

"Hello Mr. Moore."

"Is Dr. Peretz home yet?"

"No, he and mother are both out, but they should be back soon." It was a rare Sunday Arthur had taken off. Suspicious, really.

"That's alright and in fact preferable, because I came here to have a little conversation with you. Can I come in?"

"Well sure!" Of course I let him in. I knew who Michael really was and to have the chief of British Intelligence want to talk to me? Fantastic! We sat down in Arthur's office, and MMM apprised me of the intelligence situation in a long lead-up before he got to the point.

"Your stepfather tells me you are something of a tinker with radio transmitters."

"I built one just before the war, but we're pretty short on parts these days." Ooh, I liked where this was going. I moved forward onto the edge of my chair.

"Could your transmitter send a signal two-hundred miles?"

"You bet." I jumped up to get it before he could even ask me. The transmitter was actually in the cabinet underneath my "bed", which continued to be the examination table upon which Japanese brass complained about their ulcers and kidney stones. If only they knew!

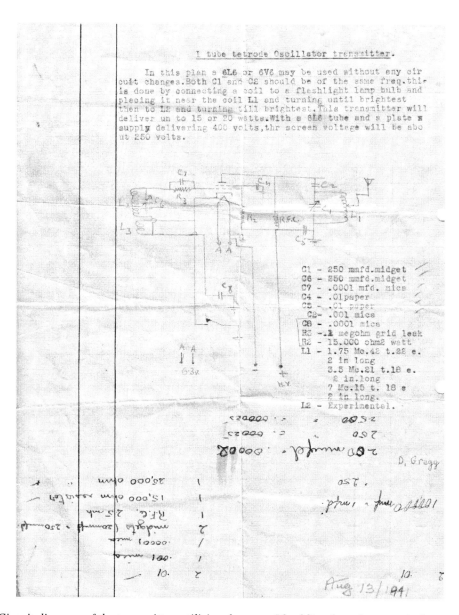

In this plan a 6L6 or 6V6 may be used without any circuit changes. Both C1 and C2 should be of the same freq. this is done by connecting a coil to a flashlight lamp bulb and placing it near the coil L1 and turning until brightest then to L2 and turning till brightest. This transmitter will deliver up to 15 or 20 watts. With a 6L6 tube and a plate supply delivering 400 volts, the screen voltage will be about 250 volts.

C1 - 250 mmfd. midget
C6 - 250 mmfd. midget
C7 - .0001 mfd. mica
C4 - .01 paper
C5 - .01 paper
C2 - .001 mica
C8 - .0001 mica
R3 - .1 megohm grid leak
R2 - 15.000 ohm 2 watt
L1 - 1.75 Mc.48 t.22 e.
      2 in long
      3.5 Mc.21 t.18 e.
      2 in.long
      7 Mc.15 t. 18 e
      2 in. long.
L2 - Experimental.

Circuit diagram of the transmitter, utilizing the parts I had listed on the prescription pad.

"This is just what we're looking for. Nice and compact," he said, turning it over in his hands. "Are there any disadvantages to the design?"

"This one is easy to triangulate because of its frequency, so you can't broadcast for long before the Japs home in on you."

"What would you need to build a better one?"

"Well, let me think about this. Uh, maybe some of the higher frequency tubes. The 9003 and the 9004, and some other ones I can't think of right now." As I said this, I could see he had mentally noted the numbers.

"And in what way would these tubes be superior?"

"Well, the higher frequency allows the transmission to go right up to the stratosphere and transmit several hundred miles before coming down, so it'll be harder for the Japs to triangulate from the ground."

"And they are small, could be easily hidden?"

"Oh yes, in a bamboo stick, whatever. About as big around as the end of someone's thumb." I was an old hand at this stuff!

"Excellent. Give me some time and I'll bring them to you. Until then, may we use your transmitter?"

"Sure. What do you want me to transmit?"

"Well, in fact there is a radioman at large in this city whose services we wish to utilize," MMM said. I felt very disappointed, until he continued, having observed the expression on my face with a certain cold, clinical way he had: "We were thinking instead of a more dangerous role for you, a utilization of the skills you developed as a courier of ointment to one Colonel Ogamino."

"Oh...what do you want me to do?"

Speaking quickly, MMM explained the plan he and Arthur had worked out, and my chest just swelled with the responsibility. He'd just handed the radio back to me when we heard familiar voices and a key in the main door to the apartment. Michael shook my hand and waited until Arthur and mother could be heard in the hallway, heading for the living room. He snuck across the hall and out the back way through the kitchen. Amah shook her head, but I think she knew not to cross him by telling mother about the visit.

"Hello my lovely son!" Out in the living room, mother made space for me on the sofa.

She was just ecstatic at having spent the afternoon with Arthur. I sat next to her and she gave me a hug, while Amah served tea.

"Tell me Dwight, how goes the war?" Arthur asked me, with a very meaningful look.

"A-1," I replied.

From then on through the winter of 1943 and pretty much until the end of the war, I became a courier. Twice a week after school I would go home and take my books out of my school bag, place them under the examination table, take the radio from its secret corner in the same cabinet, and put it into my schoolbag. Then I would ride my bicycle to the hospital and go up to Arthur's ward.

No one suspected anything about my daily visits because of the work I had already done with blood levels and my well-known interest in medicine. Arthur would take me on his rounds and teach me all sorts of fascinating things, which was a huge upshot to the whole scheme. When we finally ended up alone in his office, he would hand an envelope to me, giving verbal instructions where to go. I would put the envelope in my schoolbag, slide it in next to the radio transmitter, and ride the elevator down to the street, sometimes standing beside a Japanese officer or two, staring at the numbers.

Usually the addresses Arthur told me to bicycle to were houses in the French Concession. I would leave the bag outside the gate or front door of the given address, ride away, come back 10 or 15 minutes later, and the bag would be there, containing only the transmitter. I would pick up the bag, ride home, and put the radio under my "bed". Miraculously, the radio would sometimes vanish from the cabinet on days I wasn't a courier, so I think someone else was delivering it and messages to the radioman as well. Because of the system I never set eyes on the radioman, so I can't say for sure that it was Jim Cuming from the HMS *Peterel*, however I'm not sure how many Allied radiomen could possibly have been at large in Shanghai throughout the war.

In a novel called *The Lonely Battle* about Jim Cuming's time at large, Desmond Wettern tells a slightly different story. A British agent named 520 (who bears a close resemblance to Michael Moses Moore) delivers a large radio in a suitcase to Jim to use. However, I don't believe for a minute that such a large item could be smuggled into Shanghai, as MMM had enough trouble just getting the tubes through, though he did, and I ultimately built a better transmitter. Also, Wettern claims familiarity with Jim Cuming, the implication being that they sat down and wrote the book together, yet its descriptions of transmission techniques are completely out to lunch. For instance, at one point in the narrative Jim lays a wire on the ground in a big loop as an antenna through which broadcast, but anyone who knows about radio knows this simply could not work. For this reason and because of its sensationalist, narrative-for-boys style, I strongly distrust Wettern's book.

I would be lying if I told you I wasn't scared on those delivery and retrieval missions. I was scared all the time, because having a radio and intelligence papers on your person was a first-class, express ticket into Bridge House. Maybe the Kempei Tai would have had leniency on a child, but I strongly doubt it, and anyway that never occurred to me. At the very least Arthur and mother would have been killed. So yes, I was scared, but that's what courage is, doing something even though you're scared. Courage is not "not being scared".

As if the elevator descents in the hospital weren't bad enough, I had to ride my bicycle past Japanese soldiers at guard posts on these excursions. Once I got nervous and didn't watch where I was going. I hit the curb and crashed right in front of them. It was raining incredibly hard, and I struggled and slipped in the mud. A sentry watched me; I must have looked like a newborn fawn trying to stand. He frowned and started to walk towards me; it was like he could read my mind, like he knew. Well, my legs just gave out completely. Then he smiled, and very kindly helped me up, picking up my bag and bicycle, and handing them to me.

In the comfort of an easy chair in a (locally) peaceful world, the reader might wonder just what the hell Arthur was thinking putting me at risk like that. Speaking from my own perspective, I have to say that this little job and many other things I experienced both before and during the war...well, they made me who I am. It was very important work, and because children were in a way invisible to, or at least not taken seriously by, the Japanese, this was the best way to do it under the circumstances. If we judge actions by outcomes, let me tell you about the sequence of bombings that interspersed my deliveries.

According to the COMBAT CHRONOLOGY OF THE US ARMY AIR FORCES [23], the following actions occurred in and around Shanghai. On July 5th, 1944, five B-24s dropped mines in the harbor. A group of thirteen B-29s bombed the city on both November 21st and December 19th, 1944. On January 17th 1945, one hundred and eighty P-40s, P-51s, and P-38s hit a multitude of targets-of-opportunity on airfields in the Shanghai area. Local airfields were attacked by thirty-two P-51s on January 20th, 1945, leaving twenty-two Japanese aircraft burning on the tarmac or on nearby fields. In the darkness of the night between March 4th and 5th, 1945, eleven B-29s dropped mines into the confluence of the Whangpoo and the Yangtse delta, plus the narrows of the Whangpoo at Shanghai. Two weeks later, on March 28th, 1945, a group of ten B-29s dropped mines in the mouth of the Whangpoo River.

Note that at that point in history, the Air Force was still a division of the Army. As to the mining of the harbor and the confluence of the Whangpoo with the Yangtze, as well as the bombing of shipping in general, it was Arthur and his nurses who provided much of the targeting information. Especially the nighttime mining by the B-29s, which would have been risky and therefore based on very solid information about imminent ship movements. I felt good about the work we were doing, very proud, and it bolstered my courage.

The US Army Air Force Chronology for some reason omits most of the raids, and I can't imagine why. The only reason I can think of is that they only recorded the most strategically important raids for posterity. The fact is, huge groups of B-29s pounded the periphery of the city daily for long stretches. Let me tell you, it wasn't pleasant having to jump in those flooded bomb shelters through the winter, but when the siren stopped and you hauled yourself out, shivering and wet, you could at least hope that the air strike had brought the end of the war a little closer.

Following the March 28th attacks, clear but cool weather held into the weekend, so Veikko and I decided to take an excursion out into the country on Sunday, April 1st. Having built radios for Michael Moses Moore (and really gone to the extremes of our combined knowledge), we were once again getting interested in chemistry, though supplies were of course very limited at the time. Mercury was necessary for an experiment we wanted to run, but pretty much impossible to come by. Then I had a real brainwave: the clock in the house out at Hollyheath Estates had mercury in its counterweights. We could break in and steal the counterweights, smuggle them through, drain the mercury out, and run our experiment.

The problem was how to get past the sentries at the torture pond and out of the city. Veikko and his family had lost impunity due to politics. Between September 1944 and April 1945, Finland had driven Germany out of its territory in the "Lapland War". Finland signed an armistice with the Allies on September 19th, 1944. On September 22nd, 1944 they broke off diplomatic relations with Japan, and on March 3rd, 1945 they declared war on Germany, retroactive to September 15th, 1944. Veikko was now a theoretical enemy of Japan, yet he still didn't have to wear an armband, due to his father's diplomatic status. I wore one though, and with a great deal of pride, having turned thirteen in February of 1944. Maybe I was feeling a bit too cocksure of myself from the radio deliveries, but we hatched a plan wherein I would take my armband off, hide it in some bushes, and we would simply ride our bikes out of the city. I probably don't need to tell you the punishment for taking off your armband was severe, instantaneous, and involved a bayonet.

We cooked up a story for our parents, packed a lunch, and set off early in the morning. It was the first really warm day of spring, and the prospect of getting out of the city was absolutely tantalizing. Maybe the mission was less about the mercury and more about a little freedom. For me personally it was also about seeing home again.

We pedaled like mad and headed west out of the French Concession with the heat of the rising sun on our backs. As we jumped off our bikes and started to walk them across the tracks and through the checkpoint, the sentry turned and stared at us. We were a pair of blonde boys, could have been from anywhere, so I guess he thought he would at least question us.

"Whistle the Soviet anthem," Veikko whispered to me from the side of his mouth.

"What?" I couldn't hear him over my heart, which seemed to be pounding in my ears.

"Comrade, *Vistle zee Soofviett Antheem*," he said a little louder, with a really cornball Russian accent, then started to whistle it. I knew it a little too from some kids at school, but not like Veikko, who knew it well, I suppose as an aspect of "Know Thine Enemy". So he started whistling the anthem and I followed, and I'll tell you, to the sentry we became two Soviet kids out for a bike ride, and he turned away, and we made it past, whistling for as long as we could before we burst out laughing and jumped back on our bikes.

The Soviets were at war with Germany, but they hadn't declared war on Japan, though at the Yalta Conference, held on February 4th to 11th 1945, Stalin had promised Roosevelt and Churchill that he would do so three months after Germany's surrender, in return for territorial concessions in the Far East. I suppose Japan didn't want to provoke the Soviets and open up a huge extra front in their war, so the theoretical ally/enemy thing was out the window in this special case. Thus, Veikko and I could make our way as Red Russians out to Hollyheath.

I think there's a saying to the effect that, "You can't go home again." This is quite true. The gate to the house was wide open and weeds grew up from the driveway. Leaves from the previous fall, and maybe the one before that, covered the front steps. An unbroken paper seal adorned with Japanese characters crossed the door. No signs of life, but as a precaution we left our bikes outside of the yard, leaning against the fence and pointed toward the main road ready for a quick getaway. Then we snuck around to the back porch area, lay flat in the long, overgrown grass, and peered up over the ledge from which I had enjoyed jumping what seemed a million years before. The backyard reflected in the panes of the three main windows to the living room, but the lower panes of the rightmost window reflected less light, just the dark side of a small tree, so we could see inside. There didn't seem to be any movement, but we waited a long time just the same.

Eventually we got up and very gently tried our luck with the doors to the solarium. Nope, locked. Then we started to jimmy the top of the window behind the bush, and by golly it opened! I shaded my eyes and I could see the clock through the window: the pendulum hung very still. Veikko tapped my shoulder and cupped his hands to make a step for me. He boosted me up and I was just getting a hold of the window when I saw movement in the hall. Someone shouted inside, there were footsteps but I didn't see who it was because Veikko's hand, which had heretofore been supporting my foot, no longer did. I fell, but got up so quickly I was right behind him and we ran around the side of the house, while whoever was inside could just go through to the door and cut us off, so we really sprinted to our bikes. As I was getting on mine, in what seemed like slow motion, like in a dream when you can't run no matter how hard you try, I kept imagining a hand grabbing me by my shirt, but it didn't happen and I started pedaling like crazy.

We rode as fast as we could out of the estate and through the main gates, then I made a quick decision.

"Veikko, go left!" I cried and he followed me when I turned west on Hungjao Road, toward the open county rather than east and back toward the city. My fear was that we could get caught between whoever was chasing us, and the guards at the checkpoint. I think Veikko was thinking the same thing, because we just pedaled and pedaled and pedaled at top speed without talking or looking back. Actually, we couldn't talk; we were hardly getting enough oxygen as it was.

We raced past the fields, which were still being farmed, same as they ever were. After we'd gone about five miles, I realized we were at the Hungjao airstrip, which was of course held by the Japanese, and also very bad news for us. We slowed down, casually as we could, considering we were in the line-of-sight of concrete gun emplacements, and sentries with rifles guarding fighter planes.

Gun emplacement at Hungjao airstrip.

Veikko and I turned around and rode back slowly. We were completely winded and very thirsty. It was becoming a particularly hot day and we hadn't brought along any water. Stupid! We pedaled and panted for about a mile. Heat waves came off the road and big, buzzing dragonflies paced us, darting suicidally around our spinning spokes. We'd gone about a mile and a half back toward town before I got my big idea.

"Veikko?"

"I know, I know, we forgot the water."

"Yeah, but there's a place nearby where we can get it. Let's turn right at this next road; I know a house there."

We turned down Keswick Road and then up to the gate of Elroy Healey's abandoned summerhouse, taking the same precautions as at Hollyheath, leaning the bikes against the fence for a quick getaway. Well, when we entered the yard we knew it was a different story altogether, because someone had boarded up the windows. The grass was really long and it wasn't flattened from anyone walking on it. It looked safe. Unfortunately, the front door was boarded up just like the windows.

"Maybe there's an outside tap for watering plants or something," I said, shielding my eyes and looking up at Elroy's water tank, which was atop quite a high tower around the back of the house. Sweat was rolling down my forehead and stinging my eyes now that we'd stopped moving. Veikko and I set out in search parties of one around opposite sides of the house and met up at a tap in the wall around back, just below where the pipe from the tower ran into the house. I turned it wide open but all this produced was a really annoying squeaking sound.

"There must be a shutoff valve inside," Veikko said, wiping his eyes with his t-shirt. "Hang on a minute, I've got a brilliant idea."

"Up we go?"

"Up we go." He went up the ladder first then I followed, trying not to look down, until we reached the catwalk with a railing that encircled the tank. The tank did have a tap on its side—maybe it had been originally intended for use on the ground—but we had to struggle to turn it. Finally it gave and out poured water that was metallic tasting and warm. We were thirsty though, so we went ahead and drank, taking turns on the catwalk around the tank's side, cupping our hands and splashing water over our faces and necks, washing away the salty sweat.

We took off our packs and ate our sandwiches, munching away and clomping around on the catwalk to take in the view, which stretched for miles in all directions. I looked back toward the east at the city; the big brown cloud of smog that had floated above Shanghai before the Pearl Harbor and the war was gone. Suddenly the air raid siren at the Hungjao airstrip started to go off.

"Dwight, come here quick!" Veikko cried from around the other side of the tank. I clanked around to his side and I was just in time to see several Japanese fighters taking off: Zeros. They climbed in unison at a very steep rate, and were initially heading toward us until they made a quick turn to the north. We were probably lucky the Zeros made the turn, as they might have seen our blonde hair and strafed us. But why were they going north?

We watched them disappear. The sirens kept going for a while, then the answer as to why the Japanese were going north came with a deep sound of horsepower coming from behind us, to the south. We clanked around the tank and met on the other side.

"Mustangs!"

"Yeah, P-51s!" Veikko cried, but we could barely hear each other over the noise as four of them flew over us, two breaking to the left toward the airfield and the rest staying on the northern track to chase the Zeros. We hurried back around the catwalk to the airstrip side and watched as the Mustangs strafed the field and obviously hit a lot of hardware on the ground because there were several explosions and a lot of smoke. My jaw dropped open and so did Veikko's as a Zero was taking off, just above the tree line and gear going up, when one Mustang swooped in and cut it down. The Zero's wings folded up and the whole fireball streaked below the tree line and out of sight with a deep boom.

The Mustangs circled around and around and did much damage, their wing vortices swirling the smoke all over the place. We had front row seats. Then the two fighters were coming straight toward us and we started to wave our arms in the air and shout. They came over low, then broke to the right and left of the tower, and I guess they saw our blonde hair, because they waggled their wings as they roared past!

"Did you see that!?" We turned and asked each other in unison. "HOLY COW!" we both cried, then starting laughing with the purest of joy. Veikko grinned and whacked me on the back as we watched the fighters, which had turned north, vanish very quickly in pursuit of their own group.

I think we both somehow knew that the war was going to end soon when we saw those Mustangs inflict the damage they did. Off in the distance to the south, we could see an attack at Lunghwa airstrip too. Still, we very prudently decided to get off the tower, because a straggler Zero could come back and strafe us in reprisal. We climbed down the ladder then rode our bikes home, ready to play at being Soviets again. It worked like a charm and we got home safely, barely able to withhold our stories.

The United States Army Air Force Chronology summarizes the attack we'd witnessed as twenty-three P-51s strafing the airfields around Shanghai. According to the report, a group of thirty-two P-51s returned the next day to do the same. A military depot at Shanghai took direct hits by bombs from B-24s on April 23rd, and the B-24s returned on April 26th, 1945 to hit more general targets.

There was a lull in bombing raids between April and the summer of 1945, as the U.S.

Army was in the process of invading Okinawa, wherein the Air Force provided a great deal of support for the ground troops. Godfrey was there, having enlisted after two years at Berkeley, and he was in the middle of the vicious battle, which produced losses both military and civilian that were *much* worse than Iwo Jima. By the end of June of 1945, when the island was secure, Godfrey became administrator of the hospital at the airbase. The airbase was the real prize, the perfect point for launching heavy-bomber attacks on China. It was from Okinawa that a proposed infantry invasion of Japan, called "Operation Downfall", was to be staged.

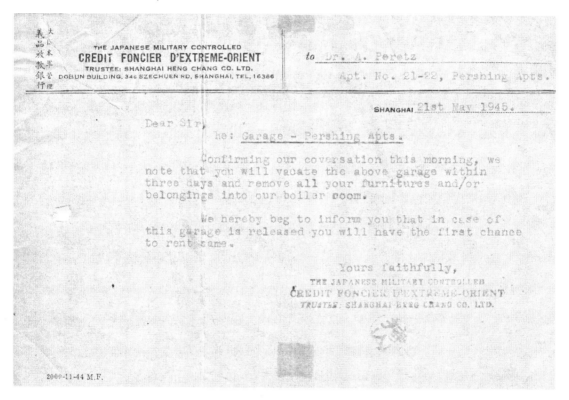

Even though they were at this point clearly losing the war, the Japanese were quite civilized in commandeering property. Note that they went through an intermediary, the apartment building's property management company, to take over our garage.

I will never forget the last really massive bombing run on the area around Shanghai. The USAF combat chronology documents Wednesday, July 18th, 1945 as follows (emphasis mine):

WESTERN PACIFIC [Far East Air Force (FEAF)]: In China, **about 150 B-24s, B-25s, and A-26s, covered by 54 P-47s, hit the Shanghai area, airfields at Chiang Wan, Wusung, and Lunghua, Shanghai docks, shipping on the Whangpoo River, and airstrips on Chusan Island.** Other P-47s attack various targets of opportunity on Kyushu Island, Japan and P-51s attack communications lines, bridges, shipping, towns, and other targets throughout Kyushu and the Ryukyu Islands…

Funny how departmental language can obscure the true nature of things. Have you ever seen 200 aircraft in the sky all at once? If not, I think it might be difficult to imagine. At any rate it was a hot, clear day. I was alone at home, doing some work in the lab for Arthur when the air raid sirens started to go off. Probably not the wisest thing to do, but I ran out of the apartment, hurried up the chain ladder to get to the roof of the building, and just gaped as this *armada* of bombers flew from the north, from Woosung and heading over Hongkew at high-altitude. The anti-aircraft batteries on Pootung point started firing, about four and a half miles from where I stood. Crack! Crack! Crack!, placing puffs of smoke in the sky from shrapnel, and the bombers kept roaring along. Off to the west and south, near to the airbases outside the city, American fighters were zipping and zapping, I suppose to engage any Japanese fighters unwise enough to take off.

The bombers left behind a broad white streak in the blue sky; their combined contrails. I was about to witness a "carpet bombing", meaning that when the bombers were over their target, they started to drop thousands of bombs, several from every aircraft, so the sky was literally blacked out with the falling ordnance. Rather than targeting specific things, they just targeted broad areas, and covered (carpeted) every square inch of the ground with bombs. It sounded like a thunderstorm even from where I stood, and this is a major understatement. And if what seemed like a cloud of bombs fell, well, the smoke that rose was far more massive. I think I was in a bit of shock, because I stood there for some time after the bombers turned off to the east. Maybe my eyes just were adjusting, from the microscopic to the macroscopic, biological to historical.

There was no more action in the sky through the rest of the week, aside from the towering dark plumes of smoke from persistent fires on the docks and the rivers. Then, on Sunday, July 22nd, thirty-seven B-25s droned across the sky, again from the north, hitting shipping, railway shops, a destroyer, a gunboat. Thirty-four P-51s and several P-47s assisted the heavy bombers in pounding these and numerous other targets. Two days later, on Tuesday, July 24th, there was another heavy attack on Shanghai, involving over 100 B-24s from Okinawa. A lull of two weeks ensued, until a small attack on Monday, August 6th, which involved no heavy bombers, only fighters. This was the last air attack on the area around Shanghai, because the war was about to end.

As to what ended the war, I'll leave it to the Air Force chronology. In this case, the report's administrative language, in not attempting to qualitatively describe what happened, is the best way to mark an event I did not witness and which was, contrary to many stories, not visible from Shanghai:

MONDAY, 6 AUGUST 1945
CENTRAL PACIFIC [US Army Strategic Air Forces in the Pacific (USASTAF)]
Twentieth Air Force: The world's first atomic attack takes place. At 0245 hours, Colonel Paul W Tibbets pilots the B-29 ENOLA GAY off the runway at North Field, Tinian Island; at 2-minute intervals, 2 observation B-29s follow (Major Charles W Sweeney's GREAT ARTISTE and Captain George W Marquardt's Number 91. At 0915 hours (0815 hours Japan time) the atomic bomb is released over Hiroshima from 31,600 feet (9,632 meters); it explodes 50 seconds later. 80+% of the city's buildings are destroyed and over 71,000 people (Japanese figures (US figures say from 70,000 to 80,000)) are killed. The ENOLA GAY lands on Tinian at 1458 hours, followed within the hour by the 2 observation B-29s.

THURSDAY, 9 AUGUST 1945
CENTRAL PACIFIC [US Army Strategic Air Forces in the Pacific (USASTAF)]
Twentieth Air Force: The second and last atomic bomb of World War II is dropped on Japan; Major Charles W Sweeney pilots a B-29, BOCK'S CAR, off the runway at North Field, Tinian Island, Mariana Islands, at 0230 hours; he is followed by 2 observation B-29s-the GREAT ARTISTE piloted by Captain Frederick C Bock (who has exchanged planes with Sweeney for the mission) and another B-29 piloted

by Major James I Hopkins (who loses contact with the other 2 B-29s); the primary target, Kokura, is obscured by bad weather; the attack is made against the secondary target, Nagasaki. The bomb, dropped from 28,900 feet (8,809 meters) at 1158 hours (1058 hours Nagasaki time), explodes about a minute after release. Japanese reports claim nearly 24,000 killed; US figures estimate about 35,000. The attacking B-29s refuel on Okinawa, and return to Tinian by 2339 hours.

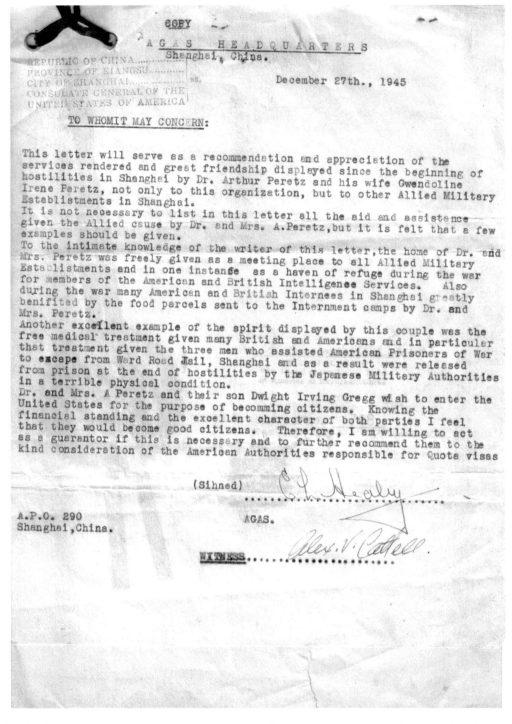

COBY

A G A S   H E A D Q U A R T E R S
Shanghai, China.

REPUBLIC OF CHINA
PROVINCE OF KIANGSU
CITY OF SHANGHAI
CONSULATE GENERAL OF THE
UNITED STATES OF AMERICA

ss.

December 27th., 1945

TO WHOM IT MAY CONCERN:

This letter will serve as a recommendation and appreciation of the services rendered and great friendship displayed since the beginning of hostilities in Shanghai by Dr. Arthur Peretz and his wife Gwendoline Irene Peretz, not only to this organization, but to other Allied Military Establistments in Shanghai.
It is not necessary to list in this letter all the aid and assistance given the Allied cause by Dr. and Mrs. A.Peretz, but it is felt that a few examples should be given.
To the intimate knowledge of the writer of this letter, the home of Dr. and Mrs. Peretz was freely given as a meeting place to all Allied Military Establistments and in one instance as a haven of refuge during the war for members of the American and British Intelligence Services. Also during the war many American and British Internees in Shanghai greatly benifited by the food parcels sent to the Internment camps by Dr. and Mrs. Peretz.
Another excellent example of the spirit displayed by this couple was the free medical treatment given many British and Americans and in particular that treatment given the three men who assisted American Prisoners of War to escape from Ward Road Jail, Shanghai and as a result were released from prison at the end of hostilities by the Japanese Military Authorities in a terrible physical condition.
Dr. and Mrs. A Peretz and their son Dwight Irving Gregg wish to enter the United States for the purpose of becomming citizens. Knowing the financial standing and the excellent character of both parties I feel that they would become good citizens. Therefore, I am willing to act as a guarantor if this is necessary and to further recommend them to the kind consideration of the American Authorities responsible for Quota visas

(Sihned) ....

A.P.O. 290
Shanghai,China.

AGAS.

WITNESS.............................

Michael Moses Moore attests to intelligence work that members of our family did during the war.

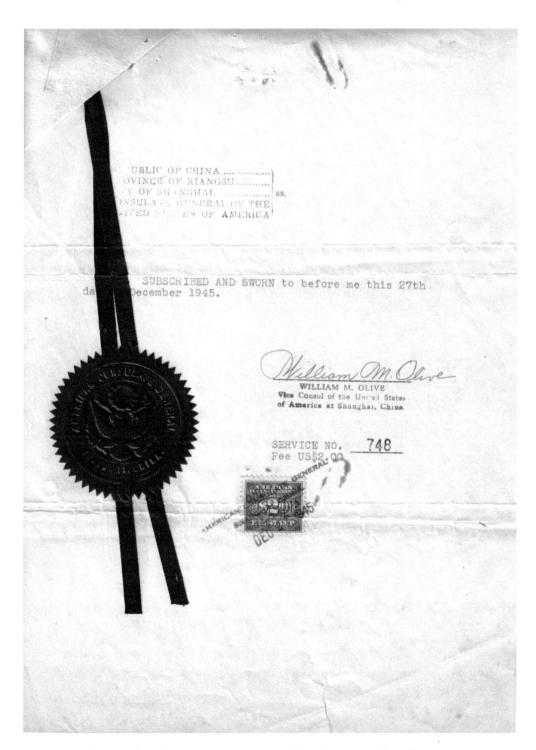

Elroy Healey's letter to American consul testifying to Arthur's heroism.

```
COPY                    British General Liaison Office
                              27 Peking Road
                               Tel; 15803
                                Shanghai


                          December 24th., 1945



        TO WHOM IT MAY CONCERN

   I have read Mr. Elroy HEALEY'S letter of November 27th., 1945
   re; Dr. and Mrs. PERETZ and fully endorse the statements
   made therein.
        I also wish to thank Dr. and Mrs. Peretz for the help
   extended to me during the Japanese Occupation.


                          (Signed)
                            M.M.MOORE
```

Elroy Healey's letter to American consul testifying to Arthur's heroism.

Chapter 12

The Parachute, Passing Muster, and Two Uses for a Colt .45

The war was over officially with Emperor Hirohito's unconditional surrender on August 14th, 1945, which took us all by surprise. Up until the atomic bombs had been dropped, the general belief was that we would win but it would take a long time and a lot of bloodshed through a conventional infantry invasion of Japan. President Truman decided to opt for the atomic bomb instead of losing tens, maybe hundreds of thousands of American soldiers in such an endeavor. The atomic bomb quite possibly saved my brother's life.

Because there was no traditional invasion of Shanghai by the U.S. Army, there was a great deal of confusion after Japan's surrender. Victory and loss were sort of academic. What I mean is that the Japanese were still clearly in charge in Shanghai—they had the guns—yet they were the losers and we were the winners. A very confusing situation indeed. It wasn't until September 7th 1945 that the Japanese handed their authority over Shanghai to the United States. Even then, Japanese troops stayed on duty under Allied orders.

An odd thing was that though the Japanese guards left the internment camps the day of surrender, most of the internees stayed in the camps. They had to, because they had nowhere to go. Odder still, on the face of it at least, the internees asked the Japanese guards to come back to the camps. The reason was that people in camps were oftentimes better off than many Chinese peasants out in the nearby countryside, so what little food and other items internees had were in very real danger of being looted from the outside. People stayed for quite some time, and in fact a shuttle bus between Chapei and downtown was soon up and running.

RG wasn't one of the unfortunate people who had to stay. He was finally about to have some luck after what had been a long, hard war for him. The New York office of Standard Oil recognized that he had stayed in Shanghai with war being imminent, had destroyed company documents, and had sabotaged Japanese attempts to use the company's assets against the United States. They paid for a room in the Cathay Hotel, then made sure he got on the first evacuation ship to Hong Kong and on to England, where he could gain some weight and recover. Head office took care of the sale of the house out at Hollyheath to Claire Chennault. Moreover, they paid RG's salary for all the time he had been interned. Without any expenses deducted, this was a princely sum. A few years later, when my mother, Arthur, and I had settled in Vancouver, dad moved to Victoria, only about 60 miles (100km) to the south of us. In his retirement he returned to his boyhood passion of fishing; his heart was always on the water. When Sue and I got married, dad's gift to us was a large freezer filled with salmon he had caught in the Strait of Juan de Fuca.

Dad had already left Chapei camp when Arthur, mother, and I went out there to deliver food and supplies to friends, and to just visit people in general. Well, we had a lot of people to see. Mother and I had of course made new acquaintances while interned, and there were many old Shanghailanders living there in the absence of other options. Actually, it was pretty amazing how many people remained, and they were edgy because the Japanese guards had left, but had not yet come back.

The children of Chapei camp, taken the day of liberation.

Things pretty much looked the same in camp as I remembered, though there weren't any guards and there were leaflets all over the place. Prior to our visit, an American Douglas C-47 Skytrain (two engines, the military freight version of what was to become the legendary DC-3) that had been circling over Shanghai passed over the camp. A tethered officer opened the rear door just ahead of the tailplane and threw handfuls of General Wedemeyer's *Notice to Allied Prisoners of War and Civilian Internees* into the port engine's wake. The leaflets fluttered down.

NOTICE TO ALLIED PRISONERS OF WAR AND CIVILIAN INTERNEES

The Japanese Government has accepted the Allied peace terms set forth in the Potsdam Declaration. Final negotiations are being concluded.

An official representative is on his way for humanitarian purposes and liaison with this headquarters. He will be an initial, pre-Allied occupation representative in the interest of welfare needs and general conditions in the area or camp to which he is sent.

He will coordinate with the Red Cross and Japanese Military and Government, all plans to assure the security of the personnel concerned, to take emergency action to properly house, feed, clothe and furnish medical assistance to such personnel, and to assist in maintaining order in camps awaiting occupational forces.

He will not have authority to act for the Allied Forces in the rendering of any decisions, military, civil or otherwise. Until such time as allied occupational forces arrive to accept the surrender of Japanese military forces, those military forces are responsible for all such control and decisions in conformity with the terms of surrender and the dictates of the Supreme Allied Command.

(Signed) A. C. WEDEMEYER
Lieutenant General, U.S.A.
Commanding

The end of our war, dropped from the sky.

The other side of the leaflet. The war ends for the Chinese too.

I was visiting a couple of my friends inside the main building when there was a roar of airplane engines, big ones. Naturally we boys ran outside, and a bunch of B-25 Mitchells flew over the camp very, very low, perhaps only two hundred feet above the ground. Their bomb bay doors were open, and steel cylinders that looked very much like bombs started to roll out of the bays just before they passed over our heads. A big yellow parachute snapped open behind each as it fell clear of the fuselage. My stomach dropped, because the parachutes didn't seem to be doing much. Boy they were moving! Probably 200 miles per hour when dropped, and there was nowhere to run, so I just stood perfectly still as the bombers roared over and the canisters thudded against the ground all around me, kicking up dirt and rocks into my eyes, clattering as they hit railings and the sides of buildings. These canisters contained a lot of food and were refrigerated, so were very heavy, probably about 300 pounds. Imagine refrigerators, or motorcycles, or bathtubs falling from the sky.

I didn't close my eyes while waiting to die, but I wish I had, because a canister—it's chute spiraling really rapidly because it was only partially open—bowled into one of my friends, only about 30 feet from me. The thing had probably only slowed down to about 150 miles per hour, and I'll leave it to your imagination as to how little was left of my friend, whose name I'd prefer not to mention. He was in pieces. When all the canisters had hit the dirt, and the last one rattled to a stop, having spun like a top on a bit of pavement, people screamed and came running.

I stood there, just staring at the mess. My mother suddenly grabbed me, and walked me away very quickly. I was calm, but mom was crying. She marched me into the main building and up to our old cubicle, which was vacant, made me lie down on the empty cot, and wrapped me in a blanket, even though it was really hot and I wasn't shaking or anything. Then she turned out all the lights and left, presumably to find Arthur, or get me a hot drink or something. I got up the instant the door closed and looked out the window, down on the central area. An ambulance had arrived and they soon carted off my friend. The parachute, however, remained where it was.

I probably was in shock, because I then did something quite interesting. I cracked open the door and mother nowhere to be seen. I snuck off and borrowed some scissors from a woman in the last cubicle down the hall; she knew me from my two brief stays. Then I went back outside, and I remember walking toward all the blood on the grass and the parachute, which people had superstitiously left alone. I remember thinking, "boy, I really want to remember this," as I untwisted the lines, then cut out the part with the drop instructions that the pilot had ignored. I folded the swatch of fabric and put it in my pocket. There is a photograph of it on the back of this book.

Ideally, the canisters should have been dropped from an altitude of at least a couple of thousand feet. Nevertheless, I can understand the American pilots' mistaken logic. It was windy that day, but the internees needed the food so the drop couldn't wait. If the B-25s had dropped too high, the aid canisters would have drifted on their chutes for many miles. The bombardiers likely weren't trained to adjust for windage in such slow descents, and such training probably wouldn't have helped much because the wind is a *very* complicated thing, varying in speed at different altitudes due to friction with the earth. To hit an area as small as the camp with the canisters from a safe altitude would have been impossible. By the time the internees had set out into the fields and retrieved them, that is, if they could be found, I bet the canisters would already have been broken open and raided by the Chinese, and quite understandably so. In other words, confusion and the lack of local authority I've alluded to were probably the root cause of this tragedy, having necessitated the low drop.

Then there was the confusion of Japanese troops, or maybe it was just pride. A couple of days after the accident at Chapei, Arthur told me that two Free French intelligence officers (DGER) wanted to go to Lunghwa camp and he asked me if I could guide them. I had been to the pagoda, which was right beside the camp, several times, so I knew the way. Just as we were getting ready to leave, Arthur gave me a Colt .45 handgun to bring along for any contingencies. God knows where he got it. As this type of gun was, and still is, the standard-issue sidearm for US forces, I would have to assume Elroy Healey smuggled it into our apartment at some point very early in the war.

Well, I didn't care where the gun came from! I belted on the holster then got on my bike feeling like a real big shot. We got rolling and went down Chungshan Road, then cut off into Lunghwa. Just as we cut off to Lunghwa, nature called and I told the DGER agents in my best College St. Jeanne D' Arc French about the pressing matter at hand, and that they should just carry on; I would catch up. They assented with very Gallic shrugs, kept pedaling and puffing on their cigarettes while I pulled off the road and went down into a drainage ditch to take care of business.

When I was climbing back out of the ditch, pushing my bike before me, I saw two very young Japanese soldiers about a hundred yards ahead of me, just kids about my age. They had unslung their rifles and were taking aim at the backs of the French officers. I fumbled a bit with the holster but managed to pull the Colt .45 out, pointed it at the Japs, thought better of it, and fired several rounds into the air. Luckily for me it scared the hell out of them. They didn't turn around, but ducked down and ran for it, across a ditch and into a field. I got back on my bike and raced to catch up to the agents, whose position was marked by two bicycles thrown down on the road, wheels still turning. They had their sidearms out and were crouched down in the ditch, still smoking, mind you. We watched the Japanese vanish out of sight, and the DGER agents were suddenly a whole lot more respectful of me. One of them offered me a cigarette, which I politely declined. We climbed out of the ditch then proceeded down to Lungwha, returning that evening without further incident. About a year later, the government of France offered me a medal, which I politely accepted.

That was an odd period between the Japanese surrender and the arrival of the US armed forces. What if I'd shot the soldiers in what was, effectively, peacetime? Would there have been any repercussions for me personally? I think the answer lies in point 2 of General Wedemeyer's *Proclamation to Allied Nationals* (image on following pages) regarding "...the extermination of all reactionaries." At any rate, though it seems I had carte blanche, I'm glad I fired into the air. My life has been about prolonging and improving lives, not taking them.

PROCLA

ALLIED N

The United States Army Air Ground Aid Section organ
established at Shang-Jao in Kiangse Province and office at Shun-
Japan. Following the Japanese defeat and surrender Shanghai ha
to intensify mutual help between the armed forces and civilians of
been established. All Allied nationals are expected to fully under

1. That following the decision made at the conference
States and for upholding justice and supporting the world peace st
towards the liberation of all allied nationals from war sufferings.

2. That the allied armies have returned to Shanghai to
tion, all allied nationals are expected to cooperate in the eliminatio

3. That as long as war time conditions remain in Shan
cooperate in maintenance of peace and order should help to guard
actionaries.

4. That from to-date this office shall promote the relie
the name of this office for selfish ends or offending the law shall be

The offender will be severely dealt with by the Allied H

Sept 1945

高告作冒慰滬　　之隊安希態　　　一進僑民已
當本其充問美　　蠢一，互期　　　切肅胞眾重
局處他本救國自　動，切共間　（　反清務一返
嚴當不處濟僑即　。切同相，　三　動軸希切上
懲即法名工民日　　信愛防凡　）　份心竭痛海
不呈行義作及起　　譽護止我　　　子殘力苦，
貸報為在同本　　　，，，在　　　。餘協，
西　古上　　如者盟本　　　及協同本　　　　協，
歷　拔海　　外　處　　　破同盟　　　　　　　
一　路辦　　　　　　　　　　　　　　　　　　
九　一事　　　　　　　　　　　　　　　　　　
四　○處　　　　　　　　　　　　　　　　　　
五　六（臨　　　　　　　　　　　　　　　　　
年　｜　　　　　　　　　　　　　　　　　　　
八

MATION
O
NATIONALS

nized by the United States Military Authorities has its headquarter
An in Chekiang Province for the prosecution of the war against
as been liberated.   With the view to extend closer cooperation and
the United States and China, the Shanghai Post has per order
stand and cooperate towards the following points:

among China, The Great Britain, Soviet Russia and the United
tructures, the United States government pledges to fully cooperate

liberate all people from the sufferings due to the enemy occupa-
on of any Axis influence and the extermination of all reactionaries.

nghai all allied nationals with the view to extend mutual aid and to
against any impair to the allied armies reputation and the re-

work towards United States citizens.   Any one found abusing
e immediately reported to this office.

igh Command.

U. S. ARMY
AIR GROUND AID SECTION
SHUNAN OFFICE
SHANGHAI POST
(Temporary address: 106 & 149 Rue Amiral Courbet)

告同盟國

駐華美國陸軍陸空
戰地總部淳安分處上

間，總部於浙江上饒，本處在同盟樞紐
處敗於江西淳安，由美國在中樞
推展中美輔助勤務協助海，
華軍民中美軍民，
命在上海同盟設立勤務辦
將有關上海同盟設立僑辦務
點，昭告於下：

各國僑胞於現同
助共同努力水火救
安全機構起見擁護見決正，去
針美國為行會議正
歷次舉行（一）過去

（一）
（二）

My mother dated Wedemeyer's proclamation as September 1945, and this is really when US authority took hold of the city. On the 7th of the month, the Japanese surrendered authority over the city, but Japanese troops stayed on for the time being under Allied orders. Then the US Navy returned to Shanghai on the 17th of September. We all waited on the Bund and cheered as Admiral T.C. Kinkaid's flagship, the USS *Rocky Mount,* steamed around Pootung Point, leading the U.S. 4th, 6th, and 7th fleets into port. They anchored mid-channel in the Whangpoo, and the fleet looked just like "battleship row" which had been such a signature feature of the city before 1941. Any sort of ambiguity over authority was over. Now it was the Japanese who were forced to wear armbands. They also were confined to Hongkew until, eventually, all 5 million Japanese living abroad in Southeast Asia were forcibly repatriated to their homeland.

With the return of authority came organization and a huge backlog of paperwork. All the intelligence work that had gone on during the war had to be accounted for and cleaned up. Elroy Healey was slowly gaining his strength back, but in too rough of shape to do much, so Arthur took care of a lot of this. A Colonel Hart of SHAD (I have no idea what this acronym means) from the China-Burma-India (CBI) theater of the war, arrived in Shanghai to debrief Arthur, and I suspect mother. He never talked to me. The three of them took the colonel's car and went on a long tour of the countryside. Life in the Chinese countryside was much the same as it had been for millennia.

Mother and several Chinese in front of Colonel Hart's car in Chinese countryside.

*Colonel Hart (US Army - SHAD) and Arthur pumping water from a lower rice paddy
to a higher rice paddy.*

By the start of October, Elroy was feeling better, reports had been filed, and it was time to celebrate. AGAS held a party and we received an invitation that puzzled me. I knew that Elroy was a military man, yet his rank wasn't beside his name on the list of attendees.

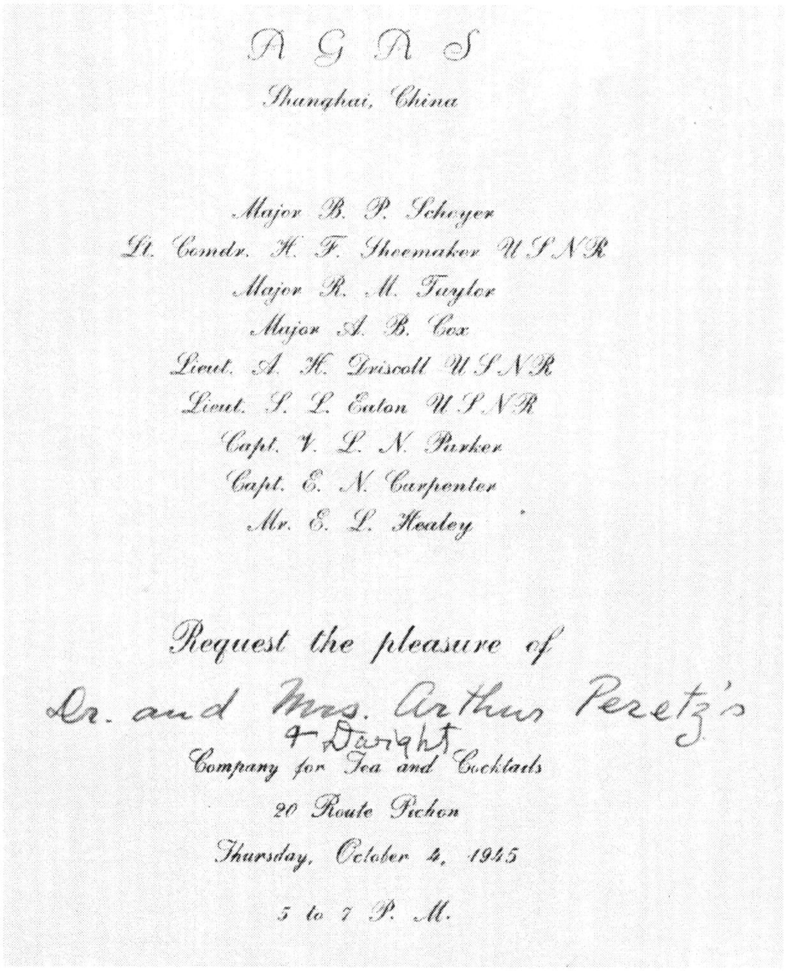

A G A S

Shanghai, China

Major B. P. Scheyer
Lt. Comdr. H. F. Shoemaker USNR
Major R. M. Taylor
Major A. B. Cox
Lieut. A. H. Driscoll USNR
Lieut. S. L. Eaton USNR
Capt. V. L. N. Parker
Capt. E. N. Carpenter
Mr. E. L. Healey

Request the pleasure of

Dr. and Mrs. Arthur Peretz's
& Dwight
Company for Tea and Cocktails

20 Route Pichon

Thursday, October 4, 1945

5 to 7 P. M.

Our invitation to the Air Ground Aid Section party.

Arthur, mother, and I went to the party, and once I'd overcome my shock at how skinny Elroy was, I asked him about this. He told me in hushed tones that he was a Commodore, but wouldn't tell me why it wasn't on the invitation.

Another party in a time of jubilation, this time at our apartment. Our guests included both friends and virtually the entire Allied intelligence corps in Shanghai just after the war. Michael Moses Moore is standing in the extreme left of the photograph, wearing a white suit. Arthur wears a white suit as well, and mother links arms with him. Not to be left out of this white suit club, I'm sitting on the floor next to Alva Scott. Mary Scott stands behind my right shoulder, and R.O. Scott stands behind her left shoulder (white collar, grinning). Elroy Healey sits in front of me with his legs crossed. I knew all the rest, but only for a short period of time, and have forgotten their names.

Two months after the Japanese surrendered, Godfrey came back home. He flew in from Okinawa with his friend, Major Hayes, and stayed with us for a week. They came over in a B-17 and of course at my age, fourteen years, I was absolutely boggled by this aircraft and my brother landing out at the Hungjao airstrip, which the American engineers had repaired from strafing damage. My mom was of course bawling and nearly squeezing the life out of him while the propellers spun to a halt. He stayed in Shanghai for a couple of weeks and we had a marvelous time. The city seemed not to have changed one bit, and we went back to the French Club, all of the various theatres, and it was if he had never been away.

Taken just after Godfrey flew in on a B-17 from Okinawa, a short journey.
This is in our apartment on Avenue Joffre.

Godfrey had a close friend from the University of California at Berkeley who was one of the officers aboard an American naval vessel that was moored in battleship row. My brother introduced me to this officer, and I was invited to come aboard whenever I wanted to. This was an absolutely magnificent opportunity for me, still so interested in radio, to get introduced to the radio, electronics, and photography departments on the ship. The officers aboard the ship of course wanted to accommodate their confrere, my brother's good friend, and made great efforts to entertain me. The U.S. Navy jitney would pick me up at the Customs House dock and take me out to the U.S.

Navy vessels. I was going to return to Shanghai American School soon, but it didn't open until October 15th, so for the first half of the month I went down to the ship pretty much every day.

I would spend several hours down in the electronics area (of course, nothing like today) and they would literally give me anything I wanted to take home. Over several days I took a great deal of equipment off the ship which Veikko and I used to build superb radios. At the end of each day, as the jitney came back alongside the pier, everyone aboard had to pass muster past U.S. Navy personnel to get back into Shanghai. They simply assumed that I was a young sailor off the ship. It certainly boosted my ego tremendously to be offered, in fact, to be TOLD, that I had to take a "prophylactic", which in those days was the name given to condoms, in order to pass muster.

So, here I was, aged fourteen, being told to take a condom out into Sin City. This of course was something almost completely unknown to me. I knew what they were for but nobody had ever offered me one, and I had never seen one. Anyway, it always made my day, passing muster. It made me curious though. How would I measure up? One day I went into the washroom to check, to sort of try things on for size. Well, yet again I passed muster!

Godfrey's friend Major Hayes gave me his leather bomber jacket as a present at dinner the evening before the first day of school. It was an AGAS jacket, had the American flag with the rescue instructions on the back. I must say that I absolutely strutted back through the gates of Shanghai American School, my first time back in over four years. It was a funny situation at school though, because the war had aged me beyond my fourteen years. I did the work and did well, but my heart was in radios and on the ships and all the military excitement in the air.

As an amateur radio operator in Shanghai, probably the city's youngest when Veikko and I started to build radios just before the war, I actually had obtained my own Chinese call letters, which is sort of a passport into the rarified circles of the radio world. My brother had another officer friend from Berkeley, this time in the US Army, who was an amateur radio operator. The day before Godfrey flew back to Okinawa, he introduced me to this friend, who had rented an apartment in Shanghai since he was going to be in town for several months working in the military administration. The apartment was in the French

Concession, just three blocks down the street from where we lived, and the biggest piece of furniture he moved in was a U.S. military transmitter. It was a BC610, a very large transmitter and receiver made by Hallicrafter, a superb technical producer of radios, and when told he had one of these, I think I actually drooled.

When I first went to look at it, I must say it surprised me my brother's friend had managed to get it up to the second floor. This wasn't the type of thing that an amateur could carry around. It would probably take two strong men to lift a BC610 and move it just a foot or two in a room. The case measured about two-and-a-half feet tall, about three feet wide, and about three feet thick, and it sat permanently in one place like a safe.

At any rate, because of his friendship with my brother, he literally gave me a key to his apartment and said I could use the transmitter from after school at about 3 until he got home from work at 6 or 7. Veikko came with me pretty much every afternoon until he had to leave Shanghai, when his father was reassigned. The transmitter used a dipole antenna stuck out the side, 2 feet up and one foot down from the main stem, and sent power through both at once, therefore transmitting simultaneously on the 10 and 20 meter bands. The dipole had great power for a short antenna. Using Morse code (telegraph) and phone (voice), we could communicate with people all over the world, which was a real thrill after being in a city under siege for so long. I had several conversations with the crown prince of Denmark, who was also an enthusiast.

Veikko and I would rush over after school and basically be glued to the transmitter until the officer tapped us on the shoulder, his throat-clearings having had no effect at all. Obviously we boys were fascinated, and our myopic focus was compounded by the fact that the BC 610's immutable location was in the corner of the living room. Therefore our backs were always turned on a beautiful Chinese lady who lounged around the place all day, referring to herself as his "apartment cleaner". I think she was offended by our preference for looking at the large, luminous dials rather than her.

The officer who owned the transmitter told me to use his call letters: W6 QEE, which are Californian, where he was from. While I was writing this book I was racking my brain trying to remember the officer's name, though I remember his rank of captain.

Of course, only one person should be using one set of call letters and this captain, as I've said, was using W6QEE, so it was a simple matter of finding out who held the callsign in 1945. So I tried to get hold of him, even thinking that he may well be dead, because he certainly must have been 25 years older than I was, placing him at about 100 years old today.

I wrote to the FCC, the official American group that assigns callsigns to both commercial and amateur radio operators. They had no problem whatsoever in bringing me the data I needed. And it turned out that Mr. Arnold H. Hills, who is still very much alive in his early nineties, has personally held W6QEE for at least the last 80 years. I picked up the phone to call him, and asked him if he'd ever lived in Shanghai, to which he replied in the negative. I had the wrong man as, apparently, Godfrey's friend from Berkeley had been using the wrong callsign. *However*, Mr. Hills had indeed been an officer in the US Army in World War II, and had landed on Okinawa. Recall that my brother Godfrey was also on Okinawa, as the hospital administrator. Now, this seems rather remarkable, but in our phone conversation, Mr. Hills told me that he had met my brother on Okinawa as a result of being in hospital with a broken arm! Such a small world.

As to the second use for a Colt .45, the need arose on a hunting trip Arthur and I took late in the fall of 1945. An American lieutenant got a jeep and we three drove down the road to Hangchow, about 60 miles south of Shanghai. There's very good deer hunting down there. We had U.S. Army rifles and, I hate to tell you, machine guns too. I sat in back with all the weaponry and ammo, the lieutenant drove, and Arthur sat in the passenger seat, with his leg stretched out on the outside fender; it was a fine day.

Hangchow is a beautiful area with a large lake with several promontories out of the lake with houses and a great resort site; literally right on the East China Sea. Unfortunately, the road approach at that time was fairly dangerous. It was a single track atop a dyke, of sorts, 60 or 70 feet high, so if another car came along, one of you would have to back up to let the other pass. On one side was the Pacific Ocean and on the other side a small(ish) river.

Well, it rains there a great deal, and we managed to pick the first fine day following a long period of rain. There was mud everywhere and the jeep slipped off the single-track road into, fortunately, the river. Arthur was sitting on the passenger side with his leg outside the jeep on the mudguard and we rolled over three times on the way down into the river. I don't remember it even happening, and neither the officer nor I were hurt. We found ourselves upside down under water, having to swim for it.

Fortunately the Chinese garrison was very close by to where we landed and they saw the whole thing. A good number of soldiers came running and dragged us up onto the land, including the jeep too. However, because the engine had been inverted for a good while, as well as immersed in water, it was impossible to start. It was getting too late to go to any sort of hospital, we were cold and wet, and Arthur was too tough to complain, so we slept in the garrison.

Well, I awoke at a very early hour of the morning with—you'll find this hard to believe—*thousands* of cockroaches in my sleeping bag. I then found out, hurrying to the washroom, they quite literally carpeted the floor. Cockroaches crunched underfoot. Then I had to haul them out of my sleeping bag. Poor Arthur couldn't really move, but then again the lieutenant had given him a great deal of scotch to kill the pain, so I don't think he noticed.

Next morning they had repaired our jeep's engine and got us onto the road to Hangchow. My father's leg definitely required assistance, so they took us to an ancient French hospital that had an equally ancient X-ray machine. Very quickly we ascertained there were three breaks in Arthur's leg. That was how we knew that the jeep had rolled three times in our descent down the embankment! It would be very uncomfortable for him to sit in the jeep all the way home, so we made reservations to return to Shanghai by train.

The French doctor would take a while to set the broken leg and put it in a cast, so it fell to me to hold the seats on the train, as the lieutenant was stronger and would help Arthur hop on one leg from the hospital to the station. I went with the lieutenant to the station while the work was being done on Arthur's leg, and we boarded the train. People were already crowding and taking seats they hadn't reserved, so the lieutenant showed his Colt .45 to everybody in the compartment, gave me the gun very ostentatiously, and headed back to the hospital for Arthur. People jumped out of the way when I took my seat. Then I put my hand over Arthur's spot and slipped the gun into my pocket, proud as could be. Nobody was going to boss me around, though if they knew me, they might have. Finally Arthur and the lieutenant returned. We helped Arthur settle into his seat, then I gave the lieutenant back his gun before he left to get his jeep and drive back to Shanghai.

The winter of 1945 to 1946 was to be my last in Shanghai. Things weren't improving in the city and we definitely planned to leave, though whether it was to the United States or Canada was still up in the air. You see, there was the growing threat of the communists taking over, and the ridiculous level of inflation hadn't stopped with the war. For instance, when you were going to go to the store to buy something, you called ahead to the comprador to check the price on what you wanted to buy. Whatever he told you, you took double the money as a safe margin to cover the increase in price that would occur while you were en route.

NORTH CHINA INDUSTRIES

SILKS AND
HOUSEHOLD FURNISHING
MATERIALS

LINENS IN X-STITCH
AND APPLIQUE WORK
AND PEKING ART
OBJECT

HOME OF PEKING HANDICRAFT WORK AND OBJECT D'ART
505 BUBBLING WELL ROAD
SHANGHAI   TEL. 37345

SOLD TO
M

DATE Oct. 13 193 1

NO.	QUANTITIES	ARTICLE	$	CTS.	$	CTS.
	1 13/44 ozs	white silk gauge @	5	20	6	10
	3 1/2 yds	green "	5	20	18	20
	6 pcs.	Chorge for curtain making	1	20	7	20
	6 pcs.	charge for repairing		60	3	60
	9 pcs.	Brass ring		22	19	80
					$109	90

E. & O. E.

Two purchases at North China Industries, one in 1941, just before the war, and one in 1946. Note
the jump in the price for White Silk Gauze from $5.80 to $12,500 per yard.

華 北 實 業 商 行

NORTH CHINA INDUSTRIES
505 BUBBLING WELL ROAD
SHANGHAI, TEL. 37345

MRS. Peritz

1710/22 Ave Joffre   Date Oct. 23 1946

Quantities	Description	Price	Amount
42 yd ½	silk gauze	12500 —	525,000 —
31½ "	gold tribute silk	18000 —	567,000 —
34 "	gold & green "	18000	612,000 —
35½ "	red & tan "	18000	639,000
16½ "	rose "	18000	297,000
16¼ "	green silk	19,000	308,750
4½ "	printed satin	40000	180,000
4 "	brocade	20,000	80000
5 "	black & gold silk	17,000	85000 —
			3293750 00
	Less 10%		329375 00
		$	2964375 00

Paid in full

Chuang

Then there was the incident on the streetcar, not that it drove me away, but still, indicative of how grim a place the city had become to me. It was the spring of 1946, a beautiful day, and I decided to take a trip down to the Bund, so I caught a streetcar. A Chinese kid standing next to me kept sticking his head out the window. His hair was all messy from the wind and he was just grinning. I think it was his first time in a streetcar. Well, as we accelerated between the Kiangse Road stop and the Bund he smiled at me, put his hands on the window frame, and stuck his head way out the window to get another gulp of the still-clean Shanghai air. Another streetcar passed the other way. His knees buckled, hands still gripping the window frame, and he no longer had a head. Blood was suddenly spurting everywhere, and all of us standing near to him got covered.

Shortly after that I finished the year at SAS and it was time for me to go. Arthur and mother booked me passage on a Liberty ship called the SS *Samarkand*, and took me down to the Customs Jetty with my luggage on the appointed day, just as RG had done for Godfrey. We went aboard and I settled into my cabin, which was in the fantail, just above the propeller. There were three other passengers booked to sail to Vancouver, but I didn't meet them until we were underway. Mother and I said goodbye, then Arthur and I shook hands. They would follow me when all their affairs were tied up. I was leaving Shanghai!

Arthur and I aboard the Samarkand. Taken by my mother.

The ship got underway and I stood on deck, watching the streets slip past just as my brother had, unable to believe I was actually leaving. All the docks slipped past, most blown to bits by the bombing raids and not yet repaired. We turned into the Yangtze delta, passed junks that bobbed in our wake and sailed on just as they had seven years earlier when I ran around on the decks of the *Gneisenau*; they sailed on just as they had for centuries. I stayed up on deck for a long while, until I lost sight of land, lost sight of the huge country where I had been born, then went below decks.

What a long and boring passage it promised to be. The ship was slow and shuddering, there were no movies, and there was no first class lounge, which really didn't matter because there were no girls to flirt with. In short, I felt a little gypped not getting to travel aboard something like the *Coolidge*. Oh sure, these were safer times than when my brother crossed; there was no sudden declaration of war, no threat of a submarine attack, no zipping and zapping, but there wasn't any adventure either. And I didn't have any friends with me. The other passengers were old men and absolute bores. Mr. Cunningham never stopped expressing his views on everything, and they were always negative, especially about jazz. I mainly sulked in my cabin, leaving it only to eat my meals in the mess.

Well, things were about to change. We were near Japan and having lunch forward in the ship, when, **BOOM!** Being youngest and fastest, I lead the rush of all four passengers up top. Smoke was pouring from the stern. The ship's rudder had hit a mine, and the explosion had blown off the fantail. I would have been killed if it had happened at any point after lunch.

S.S. SAMARKAND.

O THE
    NAVAL OFFICER IN CHARGE
  R., MESSRS BUTTERFIELD & SWIRE,
    YOKAHAMA. JAPAN.

MESSRS. A. HOLT & CO. LTD.
BLUE FUNNEL LINE.
29/7/46.

DEARS SIRS,
    TO CERTIFY THAT AT 0500 G.M.T. ON THE 25TH JULY,
"SAMARKAND" LOST HER PROPELLER.
TO FURTHER CERTIFY THAT MR. B.T. CUNNINGHAM, MR. T.J. GOODMAN,
MR. P. E. KELLER, AND MR. D.I. GREGG, WERE ALL PASSENGERS ABOARD
ABOVE VESSEL, HAVING EMBARKED AT SHANGHAI AND BOUND FOR VANCOUVER.
THEY HAVE BEEN TRANSFERRED AT SEA BY FAVOUR OF THE CAPTAIN OF
THE UNITED STATES DESTROYER "THOMAS".
"SAMARKAND" IS UNDER THE MANAGEMENT OF ALFRED HOLT & CO.,
                     WATER STREET, LIVERPOOL
                       ENGLAND.
YOKAHAMA AGENTS PREVIOUS TO WAR WERE MESSRS BUTTERFIELD & SWIRE
I WOULD BE OBLIGED IF YOU COULD ASSIST THE ABOVE PASSENGERS IN
ANY WAY POSSIBLE.
            YOURS FAITHFULLY,

                     MASTER.

SS Samarkand incident report.

Luckily the watertight doors in the bulkhead held and the ship stayed afloat. We drifted around for a couple of days then finally got a tow into Yokohama by a liner (I believe called *The Polaris*) aboard which Arch Carey, an old Shanghailander whose book I've cited, was a passenger. The USS *Thomas* intercepted and took us passengers from the *Samarkand* into port, but we had a problem, because non-Japanese civilians were definitely not allowed free movement in Japan at that point. Well, it wasn't a problem if we were willing to stay aboard ship until other arrangements could be made (we were allowed to make short trips to the Allied Shipping Office), but it was July and roasting-hot aboard the *Thomas*, and even if it hadn't been hot, I had to get away from Cunningham!

I set off with only the dirty clothes on my back (everything I owned was blown to bits and on the bottom of the Pacific) and my letter from the *Samarkand's* Master. Unfortunately, the shipping office was of course close to the port, and I really couldn't sneak off because the *Thomas* was within sight of the office's front door. So, I went there every day for the better part of a week, but no one would give me the time of day. Then, one day, as I trudged into the lobby ready to be ignored again, something miraculous happened: John Alexander was standing there!

"Dwight, what the devil are you doing here?" he asked me in his very upper-crust English accent, clearly shocked.

"Well, we had a bit of a mishap," I began, then explained the whole incident, including that joker Cunningham's views on jazz and therefore why I had to get going on another ship, or find a way to stay ashore. John was actually chuckling by the time I finished my harrowing tale. Then he started to make things happen in the office. Boy did they jump, because John had recently been promoted above his old position of Press Attaché to the British Embassy. He had been appointed as 1st Secretary and Consul of the UK Delegation to the United Nations following his release from internment in Shanghai. John had in fact just flown in from New York City for a meeting with the chief of the shipping administration.

At any rate, John went back upstairs and twisted the arm of the chief of the shipping administration to find me a way "home". There were no other sailings for Vancouver for quite a while, but there was a ship leaving for San Francisco in ten days. The chief booked me on that sailing, but that left the problem as to what I would do in the interim. Well, I found myself within moments being fitted for an American khaki uniform, though without

To be shown to
Canadian Authorities
concerned.
John Alexander
28/7/46.

New York City. N.Y.
c/o UK Delegation to
    the United Nations.
43, Exchange Place.

28.7.46.

Dear Mrs. Peretz,

Your letter of 20th June only reached me
just as I was leaving Ireland to take up a post in
New York and I am very disturbed by what you write.

You will however appreciate that as a
British U.K. foreign service official it would be
difficult for me to question any decision taken by
the Canadian Department of External Affairs or other
governmental agency.   Nor would such intervention
assist you in the long run.   The reasons which
may have prompted the Cnadian authorities to take
the decision they have taken may be so varied and
are indeed likely to be so little derogatory to
you or your husband that they could be of little
interest. Nor would insistance on your part on
being given a reason assist you either.

In these circumstances I would take the
occasion of this letter which you may show to
any competent or interested Canadian official
concerned who will I am sure give you every
courtesy and consideration which are within his
power, to renew your application.

I have no hesitation in stating that
you and your husband during my tour of duty in
Shanghai enjoyed a high and honourable reputation
and while I was interned, your husband at very
real danger to his life and liberty, assisted
more than one allied subject to reach safety. In
particular I might mention the case of M.J.Marcuse
who was being sought byvthe Japanese authorities.
Without Dr.Peretz intervention there is no doubt
that the Japnese Military police would have found
arrested and killed M.Marcuse.

In gratitude for the part Dr.Peretz played
and as a token of esteem I trust therefore that
any British or Dominion authorities will give your
husband application the most sympathetic consideration.

I hope therefore that you may be able
before too long to rejoin your freinds and relations
and that, if exceptional treatment can be given to
you and your husband your case may be re-opened.

Yours sincerely,

John Alexander.

J.A.C.C.Alexander.
1st Secretary and Consul
— formerly Press Attache
British Embassy.Shanghai.

John Alexander was a great man and a real help to our family.

any insignias of course. John gave me USO documentation, forced me to take some pocket money, and we shook hands. I walked out of that building as probably the first person on earth to gain freedom by *putting on* a uniform! That was the last I ever saw of John Alexander.

The next ten days were absolutely fantastic. I got into all the USO shows, dropped in to the supply shops and picked up whatever I needed, and traveled all over Japan. I must say though that people thought I was a bit sinister, a kid in a uniform without insignias. They thought I was a spy, apparently. Perhaps my work in Shanghai was finally showing through!

I'll never forget my last USO activity before boarding my ship home. They were giving tour flights in C-47s at a very high altitude over Hiroshima and I boarded one. Well, how do I describe the destruction below? I can't. All I can say is that I'll never understand the things people do to each other.

Epilogue

A couple of weeks later I arrived in San Francisco and was picked up by my aunts Phyllis and Gene. I put off going up to Vancouver, and ended up living in their house in SF for two years, attending Fremont High. My Aunt Phyllis was quite an entrepreneurial individual and was away from the house the vast majority of times. Hence I developed an excellent cooking facility. Second or third day, I went down to the grocery store and asked for some "tinned milk". She looked at me like, "what do you mean?"

"What, didn't you hear me? I said I want some *tinned milk*."

"I heard you alright, but I've never heard of it," she said.

"Of course you have, it's one of the major things you sell, milk *in a tin*."

"Ohhh, you mean a *can* of milk," she said, turning around to the shelves behind the counter, shelves that contained not one vial of opium.

Eventually my mother flew over on the China Clipper (Pan Am) and bought a big black Buick Roadmaster. When mother went back to Shanghai a couple of weeks later, she rented a garage a block from Aunt Phyll's house and locked the car in there. Little did my mother know that I not only had a copy of the key to the garage, but also a copy the key to the car.

At fifteen years old I was underage and had never driven a car in my life, but, there we were, four good friends from Fremont High, and we all wanted to travel. So, the first Saturday morning after mom left, I walked down the street to the garage, took the car out, put some gas in it (25 cents a gallon!) at the filling station adjoining the garage, then drove off down the road to pick up my buddies.

At the first traffic lights I encountered, there was a problem. In China, there was only red and green, stop and go. Suddenly, there was now red, orange, and green. And I had no idea what I should do on the orange! There was lots of horn blowing all around as I did a dance with the brake pedal and the gas before skidding to a stop just in time.

I turned right down a narrower street and at its end there was an octagonal sign that said, "STOP". So I stopped. After about a minute or two, a car pulled up behind me (this is 1946, remember). They waited a while then started to honk and I thought, "who are you honking at?" I even turned around and shot them a look. Then I realized, *minutes* later, as several cars had arrived, honked, then passed me and roared through, that this stop sign was never going to flip around to say "GO".

Appendix A

Shanghai and China, 1930-40, Pre-Pearl Harbor

by Arthur Anatole Knight

We were a middle-class English family of four. Dad was a mid-management accountant with the Shanghai Municipal Council (City Hall).

In 1940 he took early retirement at age 42 as Assistant Commissioner of Accounts, the reason being the impending explosive Pacific situation at that time. In 1938, about 70,000 foreigners and 3 million Chinese resided in Shanghai. Shanghai was part of the Yangtze delta and means in English, "above the sea".

We were fortunate in that every five years, 1930 – 1935, Dad and family were granted long leave away from Shanghai (climate) to go back to England for six months. We usually went by passenger steamer, five weeks in transit each way. One year (1935) as a family we went back via the Trans-Siberian Railway, across Russia.

The school my brother and I went to was known as the "Cathedral School for Boys". It was in downtown Shanghai. The school had its own church (cathedral) and cloisters, indoor gymnasium with a running track, and manse. Its teachers were from Britain and it occupied a city block. Scholastics were important. However, sports were encouraged, such as rugby, track, soccer, cricket, swimming, as well as other activities – scouting, riding, and walking in the countryside. We went to school by bus from our residence in the suburbs.

The family usually leased a large garden apartment each time we returned from long leave. These were about 2000 square feet, plus servants' quarters and parking at the rear. Several small parks were within walking or bicycling distance from our home. Our playmates in the area, as well as some of our school friends, consisted of a small international set of characters: English, Portuguese, German, American. The common denominator was the English language and living in the same neighborhood. This group had a sense of freedom; we could traverse the city on our own to go to movies, doctor appointments, music lessons, without fear, by bus, tram or bicycle.

My parents had a variety of friends from many countries. I can remember they went to Christmas parties, celebrated the Scottish New Year, Russian Christmas, Chinese New Year, Orthodox and Anglican Easter functions.

In 1937 heavy fighting broke out between the Japanese and Chinese armies around the perimeter of the Shanghai International Settlement, and at night from the rooftop of our apartment we saw the whole skyline of outer Shanghai in flames.

Many Caucasian women and children were evacuated by boat to Hong Kong as refugees, approximately 1200 miles to the south.

My mother, brother and I left on a British destroyer, HMS *Duncan*, conveyed 14 miles up the Whangpoo River to Woosung on the Yangtze River to meet the P & O ship, *Rajputanta*, which was to convey us to Hong Kong. As we were being transferred from destroyer to passenger ship, an artillery duel was taking place between the Japanese and Chinese armies over the top of our ship. The ship was overcrowded with refugees and we slept on mattresses on the promenade deck. Six months later, after the fighting was over, we returned to Shanghai. Things having settled down, our routines resumed.

As a family, we could on the weekends picnic, sightsee and buy fresh vegetables and eggs outside the International Settlement in an area now occupied by Japanese troops. We were allowed to drive around in our Ford Model B sedan.

In the hot, humid summers in Shanghai of 1937 and 1938 we went to Japan to the cities of Beppu or Unzun on the inland Sea of Japan's South Island. Dad commuted to Shanghai.

In June 1940 when I was 12 years old we left for Canada.

Appendix B

The Northern Port of Tsingtao

by Peter Reeves

Tsingtao, a northern port on the Yellow Sea, was occupied by German naval forces in 1897 following the murder of two German missionaries in China. By treaty in 1898 a territory was leased by China to Germany for 99 years. A German governor was installed who administered the city and territory. A modern, well-built city was developed and named Kiaochow. The German governor's palace, substantial administration buildings, roads, port facilities and residential areas were installed. Large concrete fortifications overlooking the sea approaches to Kiachow were constructed and equipped with naval guns. A well-trained police force was established, and a postal service instituted in 1900.

The area has a temperate climate, with hot summers, but without the humidity of coastal China. The winters however do have cold spells, with some snow and frozen ponds.

The city grew as Shantung Province developed and trade increased. People of many nationalities settled in the city, with schools and churches installed. A large Catholic cathedral and convent were constructed. Sea walls, parks, water, sewers and power were installed, and a telephone service was installed much later. With the outbreak of the 1914 war, the Japanese laid a three-month siege and the territory was surrendered to them, after a battle between Germany and Japan. The territory was returned to China on February 4, 1922 (we have to realize that the Japanese in the First World War were allies of England, the United States, and the Allied Forces, whereas of course Germany was belligerent to us) after a disarmament conference in Washington, D.C.

Earlier it had been proposed that the Japanese would be ceded the territory, which immediately precipitated riots and disturbances all over China, and a boycott on all foreign goods was instituted as China had entered the war on the British side.

A combination of trade, good infrastructure and climate attracted many foreign residents, investors and visitors to Tsingtao in the 1930's. It became a regular port of call for many naval ships of various nations, primarily British, U.S. and Japanese.

The city is very scenic and surrounded by forested mountains. Good steamship service from Shanghai and other ports provided access, as well as the railroad.

It became a very popular summer resort, with excellent swimming on long, clean, sandy beaches. The water was warm, and there was an abundance of excellent seafood. All types of accommodations were available from first class hotels to German boarding houses. Many visitors stayed with friends who lived in large houses and grounds. The city has well developed parks, gardens, seawalls and a good bus service was available, as were taxi and car hire.

The city was well equipped with stores, restaurants, dance palaces, beach clubs, bars and cafés, two movie houses showing up to date Hollywood and German films, a zoo, a racetrack, riding stables, an aquarium, scenic drives, a Coca Cola bottling plant, and a brewery which is today the largest brewery in Southeast Asia. The mountain waters are particularly clean and clear, and perfect for brewing.

There were several foreign schools, the British school being St. Giles School, a co-ed day and boarding school, and in the summer months several boys' camps were operated.

The Americans liberated the city at the end of World War II from the Japanese. Today Tsingtao, now called Qingdao, continues to grow and expand.

Appendix C

St. Giles School

by Peter Reeves

Looking back over these many years, St. Giles British School was a very good school. We boarders were well looked after, our minds were challenged, and we had fun. Located in Tsingtao, China, this co-ed day and boarding school was situated away from the downtown core on high ground, overlooking the racecourse.

Students ranged from kindergarten to Form 7, and all normal subjects were taught as in other British schools, including art, which was sent to England to be marked at the Royal Academy.

The school was run by B.G. Inge, an Englishman, and Miss Teeling was second in command. She was in my memory a strong lady, and taught English, History and Geography. The other teachers were all competent and of many nationalities. The French teacher, who was really Polish, was Madam de Fryde, a large lady who brooked no nonsense. She lived in the boarders' residence, and on one occasion I was summoned to her drawing room, for what purpose I do not recall.

I was much impressed by a very large crock of alcohol, with an orange suspended above, the whole covered with a piece of glass. She was no doubt making orange vodka! but at the time I had no idea of what she was doing. Mr. Milovkin, a Russian and an architect, taught Math. No doubt he was one of many Russians who escaped the Bolshevik revolution and relocated in Manchuria, China and other countries of the Orient. I can remember an old Chinese gentleman, dressed in a long scholar's dark blue gown, who taught us Chinese and very simple calligraphy, all of which I have now forgotten. He commanded attention and respect, and carried a long cane, which was used to get attention if it wandered.

Much emphasis was paid to scholarship at the school, with monthly recognition of achievements, attended by the whole school. Term report cards were issued, and form prizes given, as were subject prizes in English, French, Mathematics, History, Latin, etc., and for other subjects like Music, Drill and Scriptures.

The boarders' day started early and after washing and brush up, cleaning the dormitory, we went to breakfast and then school, until the morning break, at which we were given fresh fruit and I think I recall milk, and then school till noon. Lunch was a sit down formal lunch in the main residence, with some day pupils attending. Then more classes and a quiet period for Kindergarten, Form 1.

After the classes were completed for the day, we always had sports in the afternoon, which ranged from rounders, a British type baseball game, to runs, paper chases, grass hockey, and lots of complicated marching drills, held on the racecourse grounds. Of course in the winter, outside activities were very restricted except we could skate on a nearby lake, and in rainy weather, sports were curtailed. I can't speak for the others, but supper and bedtime came early for us young ones.

We boarders were very much controlled by the school matrons. They made sure we were clean and healthy, and attended all our bumps, bruises and cuts. It was part of the annual routine for all boarders to have a local doctor examine us, and to be given vaccinations and inoculations for a wide variety of diseases, such as smallpox, typhoid, cholera, etc. If we needed more serious treatment we were taken downtown by taxi to see the doctor. The driver of the Terraplane always shut off his motor and coasted on all downhill sections to save gas!

Tsingtao had a very good German hospital, with full surgical facilities, and an isolation building for serious communicable diseases. I spent some time there when there was an outbreak of scarlet fever, together with about five of my classmates, and later when we contracted a severe form of measles. Once we got over the acute phase we had lots of fun in the ward, in spite of the strictness of those nursing sisters. When you think there were no antibiotics in those days, we survived because of the really fine care.

Earlier I had survived a ruptured appendix, and remember to this day being held down by two large Chinese orderlies while a wad of cotton soaked in chloroform was held over my face until I passed out. I obviously survived due to the skill of those German surgeons, but it took about five months before the drain could be removed.

We boarders, while often confined indoors, due to cold or heavy weather, always were taken somewhere on the weekends. It could be a hike in the mountains, exploring the heavily damaged German fortifications, or a visit to the zoo, aquarium, or to the downtown movie theatres, the Star and Fulazoo (?spelling) or perhaps to the large Japanese market consisting of shops and stalls, and selling a huge variety of things.

Horse riding was available if your parents could pay the fee. The stable was owned by a Russian, who always told us he was a Cossack. He rode a large horse and impressed us kids with his skills. We rode rather bad tempered Mongolian ponies who had a mind of their own, and were inclined to bolt at times. We held Gymkhanas for jumping and racing, and when the weather was warmer we went onto Long Beach, which has firm packed sand, and let them run. Then we would take them into the surf to cool.

Sundays were somewhat quieter. I don't remember a Sunday service at the school, but prayers were said every school morning. The school grounds were large, with lots of areas for games and roller skating on a bowl near the racecourse.

On special occasions, such as the death of King George, the Coronation of the new King and Queen, and Armistice Day, we would mark these events at the British Consulate. The Consul was H.F. Handley-Derry, Esq, C.B.E., H.B.M., Consul General, in full regalia befitting the occasion. We always had ice cream, which was very much a treat due to the lack of refrigeration during those years.

I left China in early 1939, and went home to school in England. The Japanese had earlier occupied Tsingtao, with the occupying troops marching past our school one morning. The columns of men and equipment were led into the city by an officer in full uniform and riding a very large white horse, followed by two clanking tanks, cavalry, horse drawn field guns, and a very large contingent of troops. We kids were very impressed. The night before the skies were lit by the fires in the cotton mills, as the Chinese adopted a scorched earth policy. Three ships were sunk in the inner harbour in an effort to block it, but I can remember we took a Japanese passenger liner *(Tsingtao Maru)* to Shanghai, which was able to get around the sunken ships.

When we got to Shanghai, life was absolutely normal. However, my sister and I were sent to school in England. Our parents came with us, and we spent two months in France with one of my mother's sisters. War broke out, my parents returned (?) to Shanghai, and were interned in Shanghai. We came to Vancouver during the war.

I have been back to Tsingtao once, many years after we left. The city is much changed, - very modern, and still as beautiful as ever. I was not able to find the school in the time we had there, but did find the house where we had spent a summer holiday. That lovely house was quite run down and housed an officers' hospital.

If you have a chance to visit that lovely city, you will be impressed.

Appendix D

Chinese Architecture

The following is an essay I wrote shortly after returning from China for a Mrs. Tyson in Fremont High School in San Francisco. I received an A-.

It is often said that China has no real architecture it can call its own. It is true that there are few buildings over five hundred years old, although the gateway near Kweifu is said to be two thousand years old; the pagoda in Soochow is at least one thousand six hundred and the two repaired pagodas in Hangchow date back to the tenth century. Some think that the great brick temple over the Pusien is the oldest building in China.

Perhaps to our Western eyes there is no structure which can compare with the grandeur of the old gothic cathedrals or the traditional structures of England that date back to somewhere in the seventeenth or eighteenth century; but for the roof curve, and harmony that blends with its natural surroundings, Chinese buildings are unrivalled.

The Chinese are a queer people, or so it seems to our eyes, because they are noted for doing things in the reverse way that we do them. They write from right to left, they knit stockings from the toe upward, why should they not build a house from the roof down: why not? That is exactly what they do. Amazing as it may sound, they actually do build a house from the roof down.

First, the four stacks are driven into the ground and the roof built onto these. Walls serve the Chinese only to keep out the wind and to secure privacy. Few nails are ever used, mud taking their place to bind the various parts of the house together.

The roof is built in the following manner: tiles are laid on the roof before the walls are built up; these tiles are curved in a sort of semi-circle, alternative rows have the curves turned upward and downward; thus every row serves as a gutter for the water to flow down from the row next to it when it rains. These tiles are not fastened in any way but are held down with some heavy object; stones in the poorer homes and very decorative objects in rich homes, two dragons meeting in the middle being the favorite design. These dragons, therefore, like all objects in the East, are put to a definite purpose and are not just a decoration.

The curves in the roof are reputed survivals from the tents in which their nomadic ancestors dwelt; even the slight downward drop towards the center of the ridge. Gradually the upturned curves, at the point where the eaves of old received the support of the tent poles, have been turned higher and lengthened until they resemble the upturned boughs of a tree. These curled eaves now serve to fix the unfastened tiles in position and prevent them from slipping in rain or wind. The Chinese usually use the colors of green and imperial yellow for their decorations, both inside and outside the house.

One peculiarity with some of the Chinese buildings is that the stone work is cut to look like carved wood; some even go so far as to put in the grain of the wood. But, generally speaking, Chinese buildings from the lowest hut to the richest mansion are made to harmonize with the surroundings, thus trying to come as near to nature as is possible for humans to come.

Windows in China are made rather like our western style latticework, the crevice being covered over with paper instead of glass. This paper often has a pattern outlined in color upon it, and the light which filters through has a much more chastened effect than that which comes through glass. As a rule, a small glass pane is inserted in this window to admit a little more light that the paper would otherwise permit.

Chinese seldom, or never, put up a monotonous wooden railing such as we so often see in America and England and other European countries; they use a modification of one of their many decorative designs.

Among the oldest buildings in China are the pagodas, which seem to serve the same purpose as the spires on western churches and the bulbous domes of the Middle and Near East, rising up to Heaven. These pagodas are five, seven, nine or any other uneven number of stories, and are placed in accordance with the rules of Fung Shui, which some call the religion of China. "Fung" means wind; and "shui" (pronounced shway) means water, so this religion might be called the religion of wind and water, or the doctrine of influence, because wind and water influence our way of life. Pagodas are usually, though not always, erected to keep some mountain (that to the Chinese mind is menacing) in check, or to watch over a river which has given much floodwater to the land.

The Chinese believe that to have a happy site for a city the following must be present: the landscape must be surrounded by mountains (this representing the dragon for oriental fame) and the city must sit in the center (representing a turtle). The head of the turtle would be a temple built in the city, while the tail of the dragon would be a pagoda built on the mountaintop. Pagodas, being so novel to the western eye, are often connected with the idea of Eastern architecture, although the picturesque curves of their successive roofs will never have the graceful beauty of the long and slender roofs of the temple.

The pagoda, it must be borne in mind, is a place of Buddha worship. Pagodas are very solidly built, as they must have been to withstand all the civil strife and wars that have taken place in their long histories. The Lunghwa pagoda, just a stone's-throw outside Shanghai, is somewhere in the neighborhood of nine hundred years old.

Probably no finer specimens are to be seen than in the fine old buildings of Peking, and also in Nanking, although many still maintain that the roof of the Yuen Quan Miao at Soochow, is, taken in all, absolutely the finest in China.

Other interesting parts of Chinese architecture are the memorial arches, suspension bridges, little summer houses and the like, but as I have already run over the stipulated five hundred words by a long shot, I will close here.

Appendix E

Customs of Eating in China

by Gwendoline Peretz

(A speech given by my mother at "Gourmet Cooking", held in the Oakridge Auditorium of the Vancouver Art Gallery in May of 1969. Her comments are applicable to customs of eating in China that have been entrenched for hundreds of years.)

Having lived for thirty years in the Orient, it gives me great pleasure to speak to you briefly on the customs of eating in China. There are many aspects of China upon which westerners disagree, but as to the excellence of Chinese food there is unanimity of opinion. Its food with its subtle blendings and unusual flavors is a delightful mystery.

It would be well perhaps if we first altered some of our preconceived ideas regarding the Chinese diet. Many people believe that the Chinese live entirely on rice. Some believe that rats occupy an important place in the daily menu. Both ideas are mistaken and they should be discarded. Rice does form a staple in approximately two fifths of the Chinese people, but the majority of the 700 millions [now, in 2005: 1.36 billion] depend upon wheat and barley. As for rats, such things are never heard of, although snakes and eels are eaten in south China.

Two meals a day is the usual, with a petit dejeuner shortly after rising, if so inclined. This would consist of a cup of tea accompanied by a ring of light batter, which has been fried in deep fat and I warn you, you would not like it, although foreign children brought into China love such things. It is a sort of a prehistoric doughnut cold, limp, insipid and shining in its cooled grease, it is not at all the sort of thing that would appeal to one at seven o'clock in the morning. Therefore we can safely and speedily pass over this business of a Chinese breakfast, it leaves a lot to be desired.

At 10:00 am however, the thoughts of the nation turn to food. Much work has already been done and the appetite has become keen. With the people of the lower classes the main and most substantial part of this first meal is a basis of either rice or flour, and even in the humblest Chinese home it is cooked far better than the sticky glutinous mess, which is prepared so poorly abroad. Flour is prepared in many forms: there are neat little round cakes baked to a brown in a mud oven; and pale little doughballs which have been steamed over a huge boiling pot in a mesh basket. These little dough balls are called Jow zee, they are sometimes filled with ground pork, or chicken, or vegetables and they are very, very good.

With the better class one to four dishes are served with the staples. These are called Chow tsy, and it is here that the Chinese chef shows wonderful ability. The word Ch'ao in Chinese means either to sauté or fry. You can Ch'ao anything, if you have the proper imagination. The essentials to this feat are threefold: oil, Soya sauce and vegetables. There are myriads of combinations and the cook is governed by what he finds available in the market. To many hundreds of thousands even one Ch'ao is denied and some simple alternative is resorted to. This may be a bowl of noodles, meagerly covered with a red pepper sauce, or a bowl of rice with a few minced salt turnips. Such simple additions relieve the monotony of rice or flour eaten alone, and give a bit of zest to the simplest meal.

Let us now turn to that much-heralded event: the Chinese dinner party. The Canadian or American or European would invite his guests to dinner; in China the invitation is issued "to eat" and here lies the difference. Needless to say, there are formal and informal dinner parties. The distinction lies in certain rites and ceremonies, rather than dress, table etiquette, or food. The host may well bid by word of mouth a few friends to dine with him, and if so the informality of the affair would be understood. On the other hand, invitations written on huge oblong sheets of red paper might be circulated, and it would then be known that the affair was formal. Rare indeed is the banquet which is held within a private home, the exception occurring when no fitting restaurant is available, such as in a small village.

The evening meal is served between 4:30 P.M. and 6 P.M. and in all cases this is more elaborate than the morning meal, but this is probably governed by the state of the purse. I have been to Chinese dinners where there were as many as fifty-two courses served. Although it is undeniable true that there are certain niceties and refinements of Western table etiquette, still many of our conventions carried out in their most rigid form do not permit of a full enjoyment of food. The Chinese have developed a multitude of conventions which are concerned with the matter of eating, but few of them govern the actual consumption of food and the diner in China feels complete liberty to indulge as he thinks best. "Suit yourself," is the golden rule of eating.

In the first place the service of food involves none of the complications of Western table etiquette. What we know as chop sticks are really called in China "quick little boys" or K'Wai Tzu. This term is applied to them on account of their nimbleness and speed when once in action and it is a most appropriate name. One pair of K'Wai Tzu, a small porcelain bowl, and a spoon is the entire equipment needed per person. One teacup completes the service. We Canadian housewives might well wish that our dishwashing worries could be reduced to such a minimum.

Nearly all Chinese food when served has been previously sliced, minced, or reduced in some manner to proportions which need no further dissection, and when once placed on the table it is fair prey to all present. The table is always round (so no one sits at the head) and seats ten. Food in China is never passed, but can be spun around to different diners on a roundabout. Tea is served before and after the meal. No napkins are provided, but several times during the meal a servant will enter with an adequate number of small towels, which have been wrung out in boiling water. Each diner takes one, wipes his hands and face, and thus refreshed settles back to his task of eating with renewed vigor and enthusiasm. Of all Chinese customs I know of none is so luxurious as this.

The Chinese dinner table is also not subject to the awkward conventions of late arrivals and early departures. One does not have to get a permit from his guest to retrieve the missing handkerchief. One arises and departs with a firm step and an unblushing countenance, returning with equal confidence and continuing the noble work which he has started.

In 1936 there was a world competition in cooking, which took place in Zurich, Switzerland, in which the Austrians came first, the French second, and the Czechs third. I am sure that had the Chinese entered they would have taken first place. Let me end with this Chinese proverb:

IN ORDINARY LIFE, YOU MUST BE ECONOMICAL, BUT WHEN YOU INVITE GUESTS YOU MUST BE LAVISH IN ENTERTAINMENT.

Appendix F

Chinglish

"No drunking or grumbling", seen at a sauna in the Banghui Hotel in Fuzhou.

"Flighting information", near the immigration line at Pudong Airport, Shanghai.

"Recycle trash and wastrels", a sign over two adjacent bins in the park at Mt. E-Mei.

All three are attributed to Angie Mills, Shanghai American School, Class of 1942.

Appendix G

China Memories

John Seddon

I arrived in Shanghai on the Empress of Australia in August of 1929 at the tender age of 6 months having been born in Vancouver when my mother was away from home, her home and that of my father being Shanghai. She had wished to be with her mother in Vancouver for my birth.

Needless to say my memories of the first years have faded but I can remember some things which happened at ages 4 and up.

I went to school at The Cathedral School for Boys which was located in the Anglican Cathedral complex in downtown Shanghai but which shortly thereafter moved to the western outskirts of the city. Because in Shanghai there was precious little for a young boy to do I started school at the age of four where I remained, subject to those times, usually every four years or so, when my family went on 'leave' for six months to England.

At school there was great competition to become first academically in one's class, know under the English system as a 'Form', but the only times when I was able to achieve that aim was when another of my classmates, whose name I have forgotten, was on leave with his family.

In my school, apart from a smattering of high court judges, doctors, lawyers etc., there were at least two boys who in later life became notable. You may have seen the Steven Spielberg film called Empire of the Sun about a boy who was rounded up by the Japanese in 1942 after the attack on Pearl Harbour by the Japanese. That film was based on a book written by Jim [James Graham] Ballard who was in my school but who seems to have been absent from the school photograph which I still have. The book, and thus the film, were the imaginings of a small boy and not to be taken as accurate.

Another was Robin Bourne, now deceased, who was a son of the second in command of the pre war Shanghai Police force and who became the Chief of Police after the war. Robin came to Canada and after some time, was appointed as the head of Canadian Army intelligence which post he held for some time until he headed up C.S.I.S. and thereafter joined the office of the Attorney-General of British Columbia.

As a child I was particularly friendly with Robin and remember his house very well where we played.

My father, having spent his time in the trenches of World War I, took his degree in law in England. Rather than rely on his father for support until he could earn a living as an English barrister when he saw an advertisement on the bulletin board of his Inn of Court seeking a lawyer to practice in Shanghai he applied and was accepted. This was in the dying days of English imperialism.

Each of the nations who had entered into treaties with China had their own courts of law which operated to judge cases in which their own nationals were involved. In instances in which nationals of different countries were involved the court and the law of the accused or the defendant, as the case might have been, were used. The result was that a deal of manoeuvring. The reason for the establishment of 'foreign' law was that the Manchu emperors looked on foreigners with contempt and were told that it was up to them to settle their own petty squabbles as they were unworthy of notice by the Chinese.

Non treaty countries, for example Germany after the First World War, did not have the right to establish their own law courts, but in 1911 as a result of some dispute or other, the Chinese judges all resigned and the Municipal Council of Shanghai took over the court system for those non-treaty powers.

As a child growing up in Shanghai there wasn't a great deal to do or that I was allowed to do. We certainly were not encouraged to go out on our own as the city was not a safe place for a young child to roam around. Kidnapping was fairly common but this was only a way for kidnappers to earn ransom money. Apart from playing sports arranged by my school my activities were limited to sports, cubs, piano lessons, playing with my friends at their houses or mine and to swimming at the Country Club which despite it's name, was downtown.

Our family was not rich, father having to work hard to establish his law practice, but despite that we did have five servants and they were: the Boy [the name assigned to the person who acted more or less as a butler and general factotum to the family]; his wife, my Amah [which was the name assign to a nursemaid]; the cook; a 'coolie' who was under the jurisdiction of the 'Boy' and who performed those tasks which were below the dignity of the 'Boy'; our chauffeur who was hired because if an accident occurred when a 'foreigner' was driving that foreigner could be in considerable difficulty and in danger of being dragged out of his car and beaten up whereas a Chinese would treated rather better; and a rickshaw 'coolie' or runner. That was about the minimum number of staff that a foreigner would have. Wealthier families would likely have had a far greater number of servants. There was cooperation between the staff at various houses and it was not at all unusual to find that one's own staff were helping out a other houses when they were giving parties. The 'Boy' played a great part in running 'his' house and would usually buy all those things necessary for the operation of the house including food. He would consult with the woman of the house, know as 'Missy', about the menus for the day. For these responsibilities he took a commission, cumshaw, of about 10% of the money paid on purchases. This was known to happen but was never the subject of discussion. It was only when the amounts became excessive that words would pass. Each month, in addition to the monthly salary for each servant, they would be given a measure of rice. The total household monthly wages did not amount to much but to quantify them would be meaningless without reference to prices applicable at that time. The male household head was called 'Master' an children, 'Little Master' or 'Little Missie'

Possibly to compensate for the lack of things to do other that to try to make money, social life in Shanghai was hectic and one had to keep a sharp eye on calendar books to make sure that events did not conflict. Young children were restricted to the usual birthday parties which usually had some kind of entertainment such as a magician known as a 'gully gully man'. They were invariably Chinese and very skilled, certainly as far as a child was concerned but also to an adult.

A periodic event was the appearance of a pedlar selling curios such as ivory figurines, glass representations of animals and the like and all sorts of carved wooden 'things'. The pedlar would come into the house with a large sheet over his shoulder made into a bag, just like the mythical Santa Claus, and proceed to lay the sheet out on the living room floor and then offer all for sale. Bargaining was the rule and the purchase price would bear little resemblance to the asking price. This was expected.

From time to time there was horse racing at the race track, know as the Race Course and which is now known as the 'Peoples Park' where people gather in droves, some to practice their English and they are a menace to foreigners who chance their way as it is very difficult to get away from them. The Peoples Park is now also used as a place of public execution. None of that sort of thing happened when I was growing up. The jockeys were all amateur except for trainers and other people [known as 'mafoos'] who looked after the horses. The was a very lively betting scene at the races. School track meets were held outside the race course and all sorts of other athletic events such as rugby were also held there. Matches were held between the regiments of various nations stationed in Shanghai. Some of the matches became quite acrimonious and at one match between a Scottish regimental team and an Italian team knives were drawn by the Italians who didn't manage to do much damage to the Scots who acquitted themselves well with fists. The Shanghai police, much smaller than the players but very wiry and accomplished, restored order promptly.

Water that was piped into house was taken from the Whangpoo River which is a tributary of the Yangtze. The River was filthy and contained all manner of garbage, sewage, dead animals and human bodies were not unknown. The water was filtered through sand and filtered some more and finally chlorinated. The Water Works maintained that the water was totally pure and could be drunk but it tasted foul. Generally people made sure that water for drinking was filtered in the house and then was boiled. The resulting water was really unappetising and was often served as barley water which was made by simmering a barley and water mix. Whisky was drunk neat or with bottled soda water.

For adults the preferred drinks came from the Callbeck McGregor company who was the major supplier of liquor and it's catalogue was the spiritual bible . It was always said that in sub-tropical zones, which included Shanghai, one could drink more alcohol and get away with it than one could in more temperate areas. Businessmen were sometimes referred to as 'one bottle' or 'two bottle' men that is to say one or two bottles of liquor, often gin, per day.

Business offices usually opened at 9 a. m. and stayed open until 12:00, closed for a couple of hours in the heat of the day, then re-opened at 2:00 until about 6:00. The was no air conditioning so overhead fans were the rule. They didn't lower the temperature but made one feel cooler. Shirts with detachable collars, and sometimes cuffs were the rule so that one could put on a clean collar when the first one became too ripe! Watch straps were often linen and removable so they could be washed daily.

In the English courts gowns and wigs were worn but, unlike Hong Kong, in the heat of the summer barristers were permitted to plead cases wigless. A woolen wig is just too hot.

Except in business there was very little intermingling between foreigners and Chinese. That was the way that it was in those days. What intermingling there was involved Chinese such as the Soong sisters, one of whom married Sun Yat Sen, another Chiang Kai Shek and the third the Minister of Finance. Foreign lawyers all had a Chinese counterpart to whom they could refer matters which involved the Chinese courts and vice versa and the same applied to businesses. My father's Chinese counterpart lawyer was name Xu Xi How who was a much respected lawyer.

All businesses had a Chinese on staff who was a sort of manager, known as a 'comprador'. The job of a comprador was to act as an intermediary between European companies and Chinese companies and people. A very good explanation of this relationship can be found in Arthur Haley's book Noble House which was about Jardine Matheson, a large British trading company. There were two other large trading houses, Butterfield and Swire and MacKenzies and a number of smaller ones.

I have vivid recollections of the beggars who lined every block downtown. This was such a way of life that the beggars even had a union of a sort. If a businessman did not give sufficient gifts to beggars, especially on China New Year the union would picket their office until enough money was paid up. They would not usually be harassed by the police unless they were really too pushy. Children of beggars were, in some case, crippled by their parents so that they might be more effective beggars. But that was the way that it was. I do recall that a request for money by child beggars was often 'Got no father. Got no mother. Got no whisky soda.' Everybody wanted 'cumshaw', a donation or bribe. When I went 'on leave' with my parents I was surprised not to find beggars in Canada or in England.

Shanghai was governed by the Municipal Council which was appointed by the Treaty nations. The Municipal Council had responsibility for the water supply, sewage, policing, licencing rickshaws and cars and a whole host of usual municipal matters. The police consisted of Chinese who were extremely good policemen, and Sikhs who were tall good looking men made taller by their turbans, who were in evidence at all major road intersections to look after traffic control and who usually were able to create some semblance of order out of chaos. The Chinese made especially good detectives.

Traffic consisted of cars, busses, trams, bicycles, rickshaws, wheelbarrows, not of the type we are used to but rather a very large wheel surrounded with a seating platform so that people could ride while the wheelbarrow was pushed, Chinese with a bamboo pole from which a basket or some other thing would hang from either end, and pedestrians who paid not the slightest attention to any rules of the road. The traffic congestion was amazing. Some control could be had over rickshaw coolies who did not do what the traffic police told them. The police would confiscate the removable seat of the rickshaw for whatever period of time the policeman thought appropriate and so the rickshaw coolie lost his ability to take passengers.

Each weekday morning I would be taken to school by our rickshaw operated by our rickshaw coolie. He and I had a good deal of rapport and it was from him that I learned a goodly number of curses in Chinese. Most of these have now left me as a result of the passage of time. Some however remain. I could not speak Chinese as was the case with almost all 'foreigners'. We all could speak what was known as 'pidgin English' and it was in this was that most foreigners and Chinese spoke to each other. Pidgin English contained words from Chinese, English and Portuguese and possibly others. Some illustrations are: 'I wantee catchee....' [I want to get]; 'Maskee' [never mind], Tiffen [lunch] and a whole host of others now, thankfully gone. I could understand Shanghai dialect as spoken by one person to another but I really could never speak that or any other dialect. It simply wasn't necessary and in fact would have, to some extent, been considered demeaning by foreigners. 'Pidgin' is supposed to have come from the Chinese pronunciation of 'business' as 'pidginess' and then to 'pidgin' so it was really a business language allowing people who did not speak the other's language to communicate. Chinese from one area could not understand the dialect from other areas and resorted to speaking 'pidgin'.

The foreigners who suffered the most were the 'White' Russians who had fled the Russian revolution. They generally did not have any trade or calling on which they could rely. They had largely been of the wealthier class of Russians who knew ho to be 'gentlemen' but that alone did not allow them to earn a living. As a child I had very little knowledge of such matters but I did have a riding instructor, a certain Pieter Zarienkov, the spelling of which is uncertain. He had been in a Cossack regiment defeated by the Red Army and had made his way to Shanghai. He taught me to ride horses know as 'Shanghai ponies' which were rather smaller than the horses we see in this country. They were very tough, hardy animals with mouths of leather supposedly genetically inherited from the ponies rode by the Mongols in their conquest of a good part of the Orient and Europe. Occasionally I would be lent an Irish hunter on which I entered jumping contests.

I recall vividly our summer holidays, first as a small child to Ching Wan Tao and later to Wei Hai Wei both in the North China Sea. The British Far East squadron was stationed at Wei Hai Wei for summers and trips to visit those ships were arranged for foreign children holidaying in the area. On one occasion a submarine formed a part of the squadron and I can recall being on her and later on a county class cruiser for 'tea'.

In 1937 the Japanese, who were at war with China, surrounded Shanghai having defeated the Chinese forces in the area. I was then in Wei Hai where I had to stay until the consulate told us that it was safe to return. The coastal passenger ships which ran to and from various ports in the North China sea were all protected from pirates by barbed wire surrounding the bridge and other parts to make it more difficult for pirates to capture ships. This often worked but pirates were successful from time to time. What they wanted was ransom money which was usually paid. If not body parts would start to be received by those from who ransom was sought. I'm not aware of any foreigner who was killed by pirates although some may have been.

The International Concession, which formed most of Shanghai, was at first not directly affected by the war. Some interesting things did occur and some tragic. The Japanese air force bombed a very densely populated section of Shanghai which was not included in the Concession and which was referred to as the 'Chinese City' or Chapei. The result was a large loss of life and the burning of most of the houses in that area. Ashes from the burning rained over the City for some considerable time. I can remember watching Japanese aircraft dive bombing Chinese installations outside the Concession. One of the aircraft which was pulling out of a dive was hit head on by an aeroplane starting its dive. One parachute opened but I don't think that the pilots life would have been worth very much when captured.

The Japanese had bought a battleship from Britain after WWI. The ship had been built in 1913 and was renamed 'Idzuma' [maybe 'Idzumo'] and that ship was anchored in the Whangpoo river near downtown Shanghai. The Chinese tried many ways to sink her including drifting sampans loaded with explosives downstream and shelling her using a howitzer firing directly over Shanghai. The trajectory of the shells were very highly arched so that to the top of the arch the shell were travelling slowly, slowly enough that if the sun caught them in the right way the shells could be seen. In fact I did see one but none hit Idzuma or did any damage that I was aware of. In 1939 when we were preparing to 'go on leave' we stayed in an apartment building for a short while, our house having been leased for the time that we were to be away. While we were in the apartment building aircraft were Chinese flying over possibly trying to bomb Idzuma was fired on by the Japanese. A piece of shrapnel from an antiaircraft shell and a spent machine gun bullet flew though the window of the apartment but did no harm.

On another occasion a Chinese aircraft, preparing to bomb Idzuma, was intercepted by Japanese aircraft. To make itself lighter and to increase its chance of escape it jettisoned its bomb which landed in a very crowded intersection of Shanghai and killed a number of people. But life went on.

Shanghai was protected by foreign troops who ringed the City. There were far too few troops to do anything but put up a token show of force. At Christmas we would go to one or other of the outposts to give small presents such as candy and cigarettes. On one occasion I insisted that we visit a Japanese guard post which we did.

The Shanghai golf course, now the Shanghai zoo, was in an area outside the International concession in an area called 'Hungjao' which was occupied by the Japanese. I cannot recall anytime at which access to the course was denied except when actual fighting took place and then one would not want to be in the area. No one seemed to think that the war between the Japanese and the Chinese was anything much to worry foreigners who were quite sure that they would not be involved or injured. The war was generally referred to as 'the Troubles'. That was the way it was. A precious few saw the handwriting on the wall and left but they were a small minority and considered to be 'alarmists'.

Because my father and mother were English in 1939 I was sent 'home' to England to go to school despite the fact that I had been born in Canada. That was the way it was. After one term at school in England WWII started and people started dropping things and I left with my parents and was put to school in Vancouver to stay with grandparents with mother and father going back to Shanghai. Mother left Shanghai to look after her mother in Vancouver but father stayed in Shanghai and was there on 8 December, 1941 and was interned by the Japanese across the river from Shanghai in an area called Pootung [now Pudong] in a warehouse [referred to as a 'godown'] formerly owned by British-American Tobacco Company where he stayed until 1946 when the Japanese surrendered.

After the WWII inflation was unbelievable. If my father had owned a million Chinese dollars, then a very considerable amount of money, on the day he was interned in a week after he was released from internment camp he told me that he could have hardly bought a loaf of bread.

After a short holiday he returned to practice law but all was changed. Extraterritoriality had been surrendered and China assumed control of Shanghai with inflation at a rate equal or exceeding that in Germany after WWI. Stamps were overstruck to literally millions of Chinese dollars and mother, going grocery shopping, had to carry a basket to hold the currency to pay for purchases.

After WWII and the release by the treaty powers of extraterritorial rights Shanghai was under Chinese control and the person in charge was the son of Chiang Kai Shek, Chiang Ching Kuo. The city was captured by Mao's forces in 1949 and my father, having been diagnosed with cancer probably resulting from internment, flew out of Shanghai on the last civilian aircraft. His law partner stayed but could not practice law. However he was not allowed to close the office and was required to keep his staff at full pay for quite a long time. Eventually he too got out.

The rest is history.

Notes

1. Dong, page 8

2. ibid., page 22

3. Fortune Magazine

4. Bosse

5. White

6. Dong, page 224

7. Carney, page 21

8. *Harrison's Principals of Internal Medicine.* Page 1187.

9. These details, along with following quotes regarding incident are from pages 178-185 of Grover's *American Merchant Ships on the Yangtze, 1920-1941.*

10. ibid., page 179

11. ibid., page 184. Grover cites *Foreign Relations*, 1938, II. 207, 337, 513.

12. O'Neil

13. Dong, page 258

14. Maechling, page 44

15. Thompson, Page 33

16. H. Grover and Gretchen G. Grover, *Night Attack at Shanghai.*

17. The *Shanghai Times* of December 13, 1941.

18. Dong, 269.

19. White Wentworth, *Fair is the Name*, pg. 283

20. Wasserstein quoting the Shanghai times of December 30, 1941

21. My description is an amalgam of many accounts of what went on in Bridge House, drawing especially on Peter Clague's excellent account.

22. Carey, page 52.

23. United States Army Air Force Chronology. Accessed online at: http://paul.rutgers.edu/~mcgrew/wwii/usaf/ (Accessed December 9, 2005)

Works Cited

Bosse, Malcolm. *The Warlord*. New York: Simon and Schuster, 1983.

Carey, Arch. *The War Years at Shanghai: 1941-45-48*. New York: Vantage Press, 1967.

Carney, Dora. *Foreign Devils Had Light Eyes*. Toronto: Dorset Publishing Inc., 1980.

Clague, Peter. *Bridge House*. Hong Kong: Yee Tin Tong Printing Press Ltd., 1983.

Deacon, Richard. *Kempei Tai: A History of the Japanese Secret Service*. New York: Berkley Books, 1985.

Dong, Stella. *Shanghai: The Rise and Fall of a Decadent City*. New York: Perennial, 2001.

Editors, et al. "The Shanghai Boom", *Fortune Magazine*. 11, 1, January, 1935.

Grover, David H. *American Merchant Ships on the Yangtze, 1920-1941*. Westport, Connecticut: Praeger, 1992.

Grover, David H., and Gretchen Grover. *Captives of Shanghai: The Story of the President Harrison*. Napa, California: Western Maritime Press, 1989.

H. Grover and Gretchen G. Grover, "Night Attack at Shanghai", *Naval History*, 5, 4, Winter 1991, p. 37.

Maechling, Charles, "Pearl Harbor: The First Energy War", *History Today*, 50, 12, December 2000, pgs. 41-47.

Menzies, Gavin. *1421 – The Year China Discovered the World*. London: The Bantam Press, 2002.

O'Neil, Mark "The Angel of Austria's Jews", *South China Morning Post*. Date Unknown. Accessed online at: http://members.tripod.com/journeyeast/angel_of_austria_s_jews.html (Accessed September 3, 2005.)

Petersdorf, Robert J., et al Editors. *Harrison's Principals of Internal Medicine - 10th Edition*. New York: McGraw-Hill, 1983.

Thompson, Robert Smith. *A Time For War: Franklin D. Roosevelt and the Path to Pearl Harbor*. New York: Prentice Hall, 1991.

United States Army Air Force Chronology. Accessed at http://paul.rutgers.edu/~mcgrew/wwii/usaf/ (Accessed December 9, 2005)

Wasserstein, Bernard. *Secret War in Shanghai*. London: Profile Books Ltd., 1998.

White, Theodore. *In Search of History: A Personal Adventure*. New York: Warner Books, Inc., 1979.

White Wentworth, Phoebe, and Angie Mills. *Fair is the Name: The Story of the Shanghai American School, 19121950*. Los Angeles: Shanghai American School Association, 1997.

Image Sources

The map of Shanghai was drawn by P.Stanley King and based on a map published by the North China Daily News. The image itself was obtained from "Foreign Devils Had Light Eyes" by Dora Carney, published by Dorset, Canada.

Executions, Birds in Cages, Chinese Funeral, Typical Beggar, Wenchow Junk, Lunghwa Pagoda, Chinese Raincoat all from the personal collection of Arthur Middleship.

The Japanese "Imperial War Rescript" is from a *Special Supplement issued by the Shanghai Times in Commemoration of First Anniversary of Outbreak of Greater East Asia War. December 8, 1942.*

The Sapajou cartoon is from a collection of 12 of the illustrator's works, one copy owned by the author. This collection is a small chapbook without publishing information.

The image heading Chapter 7: Pearl Harbor: War in the Pacific, is from the SAS yearbook, *The Columbian*, reproduced with written permission from the Development and Alumni Affairs Coordinator, Shanghai American School.

ISBN 141207803-2